MCQ's on Agricultural Meteorology

NIPA® GENX ELECTRONIC RESOURCES & SOLUTIONS P. LTD.
New Delhi-110 034

**SCAN FOR
MORE BOOKS BY
THE SAME AUTHOR**

About the Author

Surender Singh has about thirty five years of experience with PhD in the field of Agrometeorology. Worked in Agrometeorology encompassing teaching, research, extension and administration at various capacities viz., Principal Scientist, Professor & Head, Senior Scientist, Assistant Scientist, Advisor (Recruitments) and Associate Director (Students' Counseling and Placement) at CCS Haryana Agricultural University, Hisar, India. Recipient of Two Gold Medals for Best Research Work during PhD Program and for Best PhD Dissertation (2001-02) awarded by then President of India Dr APJ Abdul Kalam. Offered UK Universities Vice Chancellors' Scholarship for Higher Studies twice (1991 & 1993) under Commonwealth Fellowship Program. Post Doctoral Fellow at Abdus Salam International Centre for Theoretical Physics, Trieste, Italy; IAC – Instituto Agronômico, Campinas, Brazil and BOKU (Met) - Institute of Meteorology and Climatology, Vienna, Austria.

He is life member of Association of Agrometeorologists, Indian Meteorological Society, Indian Society of Remote Sensing, International Society for Agrometeorology, Society for Sustainable Agric& Resource Management, Environment Science Published for Everybody Round the Earth (ESPERE), European Drought Centre, South Asian Forum on Agriculture Meteorology (SAFOAM) and The Geographical Society of India. Organized quite a few trainings/symposia in Agrometeorology and associated domains at National level. Published more than 250 research papers, popular articles, manuals/teaching aids and research bulletins/book chapters etc. Performed responsibilities as Managing Editor - Journal of Agrometeorology; Research Collaborator, Monsoon Asia Agro-Environmental Research Consortium (MARCO), Japan; SPARC Research Collaborator, ETH, Zurich, Switzerland; Member, Expert Team - CAgM-WMO, Geneva, Switzerland (2018-20). Core Committee Member on Agriculture – Drought at WMO, Geneva, Switzerland (2021-24 & 2024-27). External Expert for evaluation of research projects, COST-Association, European Union, Brussels, Belgium. Many students (UG, PG and PhD) have been trained under him and placed across the country and well settled in various positions in the field of Agrometeorology. He is widely travelled researcher/expert across the globe on many academic pursuits. He has been conferred upon Fellow of Association of Agrometeorologists (FAAM) for the year 2024 in recognition of his exemplary achievements and enduring impact on agrometeorological science.

MCQ's on Agricultural Meteorology

Surender Singh
MSc; PhD; FAAM
Professor/Principal Scientist (Agrometeorology)
CCS HAU, Hisar, Haryana, India

NIPA® GENX ELECTRONIC RESOURCES & SOLUTIONS P. LTD.
New Delhi-110 034

NIPA® GENX ELECTRONIC RESOURCES & SOLUTIONS P. LTD.

101,103, Vikas Surya Plaza, CU Block
L.S.C. Market, Pitam Pura, New Delhi-110 034
Ph : +91-11-43860225, Mob.: +91 9717133558, 9540816132
E-mail: newindiapublishingagency@gmail.com
Website: www.nipaersources.com

Print ISBN: 978-93-72196-45-0

ebook ISBN: 978-93-72198-93-5

Composed and Designed by NIPA®.

The Compilation of MCQ's on

Agricultural Meteorology

is dedicated to

Prof BV Ramana Rao

(b 1940)

Founder Project Coordinator

AICRP on Agrometeorology

Professor BV Ramana Rao - A visionary teacher, pioneering researcher, and inspiring mentor - whose lifelong contributions have laid a strong foundation for Agricultural Meteorology in India.

Prof Ramana Rao's profound scholarship, innovative teaching methods, and commitment to academic excellence have nurtured generations of students and professionals. His clarity of thought and ability to connect science with practical agricultural applications continue to guide and influence the discipline in meaningful ways.

Through this humble effort, we honor his legacy and seek to carry forward and support his mission of empowering learners and strengthening agrometeorological services as a critical enabler of climate-resilient and sustainable food systems.

Dr V Uma Maheswara Rao

Former Professor & Head
Dept of Agril Meteorology
CCS HAU Hisar, India

Former Project Coordinator
AICRP on Agrometeorology
ICAR-CRIDA, Hyderabad, India

Foreword

Agricultural Meteorology, or Agrometeorology, stands as a vital scientific discipline at the confluence of atmospheric sciences and agriculture. In an era of increasing climate variability, growing food demand and the need for sustainable farming practices, the role of agrometeorology has become more prominent than ever before. This compilation of Multiple Choice Questions (MCQ's) titled **"MCQ's on Agricultural Meteorology"** is a timely and significant academic contribution that aligns with the educational and research needs of students, extension professionals, and young scientists.

The strength of this compilation lies in its structured coverage of key topics—ranging from weather elements, crop-weather relationships, agrometeorological advisories, remote sensing and GIS applications, to simulation modeling and climate risk management. The MCQs not only serve as a tool for self-assessment and exam preparation but also facilitate conceptual clarity and critical thinking. The format is well-suited for aspirants of competitive examinations, including those conducted by ICAR, ASRB, SAUs, and public service commissions.

The effort to organize this subject into accessible and focused question banks reflects the author's deep understanding of both the discipline and the learner's perspective. Moreover, by aligning the content with current developments and practical challenges in climate-resilient agriculture, the book reinforces the centrality of agrometeorology in ensuring food and nutritional security.

I congratulate the author **Prof Surender Singh** for this meticulous work and recommend this MCQ compilation to students, educators, and practitioners alike. It is not just a question bank, but a learning companion that supports India's mission toward smart agriculture and resilient food systems.

(V Uma Maheswara Rao)

Preface

Agricultural Meteorology has emerged as a critical discipline in addressing the multifaceted challenges of climate variability, sustainable food production, and environmental stewardship. The growing complexity of agricultural systems in the context of global climate change has underscored the need for a deeper understanding of the interplay between weather, climate, and crop productivity. To support this objective, educational resources that are both accessible and application-oriented have become imperative.

This compilation, **"MCQ's on Agricultural Meteorology"** presents a structured collection of **Multiple Choice Questions (MCQ's)** designed to reinforce fundamental concepts, support examination preparation, and promote active learning among students, researchers, and extension professionals. The questions span a wide spectrum of agrometeorological themes including meteorological instruments, weather forecasting, crop-weather relationships, climate-smart agriculture, simulation modeling, and the use of remote sensing and GIS technologies.

The compilation work has been dedicated to **Professor BV Ramana Rao**, founder Project Coordinator, AICRP on Agrometeorology, ICAR-CRIDA, Hyderabad, India for his pioneering contributions to agrometeorology and for being a beacon of knowledge and humility. His scholarly legacy and dedication to teaching continue to influence generations of students and researchers. I am greatly indebted to **Dr V Uma Maheswara Rao**, former Professor and Head, Dept of Agril Meteorology, CCS HAU Hisar, India and Project Coordinator, AICRP on Agrometeorology, ICAR-CRIDA, Hyderabad, India for having soared his valuable time to provide a truly inspiring foreword.

The MCQs have been carefully curated to align with syllabi prescribed by national agricultural universities and competitive examinations such as those conducted by ICAR, ASRB, and state agricultural services. In addition to serving as a self-assessment tool, the compilation aims to strengthen conceptual clarity, encourage interdisciplinary thinking, and instill a systems-based understanding of agriculture under changing climatic regimes.

This volume is the outcome of sustained academic engagement and a commitment to enhancing learning outcomes in agrometeorology. It is my sincere hope that this resource will serve as a valuable companion for learners and practitioners alike, fostering a new generation of professionals equipped to contribute meaningfully to climate-resilient and sustainable agricultural development.

Suggestions for improvement and feedback from readers are warmly welcomed for future editions.

Surender Singh

Acknowledgements

Agricultural Meteorology has emerged as a critical discipline in addressing With a deep sense of gratitude, I acknowledge all those who have contributed directly or indirectly to the successful MCQ's compilation on *"Agricultural Meteorology – Essential Enabler of Food Production Systems."*

First and foremost, I express my sincere thanks to my teachers and mentors who have nurtured my understanding of agricultural meteorology and inspired me to contribute to this vital field. Their guidance, encouragement, and commitment to academic excellence have been a constant source of motivation.

I am particularly grateful to **Professor BV Ramana Rao**, to whom this work is dedicated, for his pioneering contributions to agrometeorology and for being a beacon of knowledge and humility. His scholarly legacy and dedication to teaching continue to influence generations of students and researchers. I also express my deepest gratitude to **Dr V Uma Maheswara Rao**, an astute and tireless agrometeorologist and mentor throughout for graciously accepting my request to write the Foreword to this compilation.

I extend my appreciation to colleagues, fellow scientists, and academicians in India and across the globe who provided valuable feedback and suggestions during the development of this MCQ compilation. Their insights helped refine the scope, structure, and content of the book.

I also thank students and aspirants whose enthusiasm and need for quality preparatory material served as the driving force behind this effort. Their curiosity and desire to learn reinforced my commitment to create a learner-friendly, exam-oriented resource that upholds both academic rigor and clarity.

Special thanks to the support staff involved in editing, formatting, and publishing, whose behind-the-scenes work was essential in giving this manuscript its final shape.

Finally, I thank my family for their patience, understanding, and continuous support throughout this journey. Without their encouragement, this endeavor would not have reached fruition.

This book is a collective effort, and I remain indebted to all who walked alongside me in this academic journey.

Surender Singh

Contents

A. Introductory Agricultural Meteorology

1

Agrometeorology - Aim, Components and Scope

Multiple Choice Questions (MCQs)

1. What is the primary aim of agrometeorology?
   a) Study of weather instruments
   b) Forecasting prices of crops
   c) Study of weather-climate impact on agriculture
   d) Marketing of agricultural products
2. Agricultural meteorology mainly assists in:
   a) Urban planning b) Military operations
   c) Efficient farming practices d) Transport logistics
3. One of the main objectives of agrometeorology is to:
   a) Create new crop varieties
   b) Study soil microbiology
   c) Optimize crop yield using weather data
   d) Determine market value of crops
4. Which of the following is not an aim of agricultural meteorology?
   a) Minimize weather-related crop losses
   b) Assist in sustainable agriculture
   c) Promote agricultural marketing
   d) Support weather-based farm decisions
5. Agricultural meteorology provides scientific basis for:
   a) Crop insurance b) Agro-tourism
   c) Fertilizer subsidy d) Soil taxonomy
6. Which is not a major component of agrometeorology?
   a) Radiation b) Temperature
   c) Humidity d) Soil fertility

7. The primary meteorological component influencing photosynthesis is:
   a) Soil moisture b) Rainfall
   c) Solar radiation d) Air pressure
8. The element most directly influencing transpiration rate is:
   a) Wind speed b) Rainfall
   c) Soil texture d) Leaf color
9. The component used to assess drought condition in agriculture is:
   a) Wind speed b) Rainfall
   c) Solar radiation d) Atmospheric pressure
10. Which of the following is a climatic variable?
   a) Seed density b) Air temperature
   c) Soil structure d) Fertilizer type
11. Evapotranspiration is influenced by:
   a) Relative humidity b) Crop price
   c) Soil color d) Pesticide use
12. Which of the following components is involved in frost prediction?
   a) Soil pH b) Air temperature
   c) Rainfall intensity d) Crop yield
13. Which weather element most affects seed germination?
   a) Wind b) Cloud cover
   c) Temperature d) Solar eclipse
14. The accumulation of heat over time is expressed in:
   a) Relative Humidity b) Degree Days
   c) Rainfall Index d) Radiation Load
15. Which of the following is a derived agrometeorological parameter?
   a) Temperature b) Wind speed
   c) Potential evapotranspiration d) Humidity
16. Agricultural meteorology is useful in:
   a) Determining food preferences
   b) Climate-resilient farming
   c) Increasing fertilizer production
   d) Controlling pests biologically

17. One key area where agrometeorology plays a role is:
    a) Forest law enforcement b) Crop weather modeling
    c) Engineering design d) Food processing
18. The scope of agrometeorology includes:
    a) Designing tractors
    b) Climate classification
    c) Rainwater harvesting design
    d) Crop-weather relationship studies
19. Agrometeorology helps in:
    a) Detecting soil pathogens
    b) Forecasting yield based on weather
    c) Enhancing seed viability
    d) Measuring crop protein content
20. Which of these farming practices benefits from agrometeorological input?
    a) Marketing strategy
    b) Weather-based irrigation scheduling
    c) Packaging of produce
    d) Crop branding
21. The scope of agrometeorology extends to:
    a) Cloud seeding b) Storage of grains
    c) Weed classification d) Harvesting using machines
22. Which of the following is not within the scope of agrometeorology?
    a) Disease and pest forecasting b) Design of irrigation canals
    c) Agricultural drought monitoring d) Weather-based advisories
23. Crop simulation models depend on:
    a) Genetic engineering b) Meteorological data
    c) Market surveys d) Farm labor
24. Remote sensing in agrometeorology helps in:
    a) Soil salinity mapping b) Seed rate estimation
    c) Harvest timing d) Surveying farmers
25. Agroclimatic zoning is based on:
    a) Marketing practices b) Climatic data
    c) Soil taxonomy d) Crop subsidies

26. Agrometeorology integrates:
   a) Physics, Chemistry, and Music
   b) Meteorology, Soil Science, Agronomy
   c) Geology, Political Science, Arts
   d) Philosophy, Ethics, Literature

27. The parent science of agrometeorology is:
   a) Agronomy b) Physics
   c) Meteorology d) Horticulture

28. Agrometeorology supports integrated farming by:
   a) Predicting labor requirements
   b) Forecasting fish and livestock stress due to weather
   c) Enhancing marketing skills
   d) Increasing market price

29. Agro-advisory services are based on:
   a) Random events
   b) Weather and crop stage data
   c) Historical myths
   d) Traditional beliefs only

30. Which discipline benefits most from agrometeorological data?
   a) Food processing b) Market economics
   c) Precision agriculture d) Social sciences

31. Weather forecasting in agriculture is essential for:
   a) Determining land rights
   b) Pesticide application timing
   c) Generating bank loans
   d) Promoting agritourism

32. An example of a short-term agromet forecast is:
   a) 10-year rainfall trend b) Weekly weather outlook
   c) Annual crop yield forecast d) Soil classification maps

33. Medium-range weather forecasts help in:
    a) Designing storage bins
    b) Irrigation planning for the next 5–10 days
    c) Genetic crop improvement
    d) Estimating fertilizer cost
34. Long-range forecasts are useful for:
    a) Selecting market agents
    b) Planning seasonal cropping patterns
    c) Weed control during germination
    d) Monitoring daily soil temperature
35. Which application is related to weather-based crop insurance?
    a) Soil mineral testing
    b) Evapotranspiration calculation
    c) Weather-indexed insurance
    d) Crop marketing campaign
36. Agrometeorology helps reduce:
    a) Political risks
    b) Weather-induced crop failure
    c) Labor wage inflation
    d) Land fragmentation
37. Use of agrometeorological data can enhance:
    a) Fertilizer production b) Water use efficiency
    c) Land mutation d) Storage life
38. Accurate sowing date recommendations are based on:
    a) Market prices b) Monsoon onset prediction
    c) Farmer preference d) Fertilizer application
39. In agrometeorology, wind direction is measured to:
    a) Choose planting depth b) Forecast pesticide drift
    c) Estimate rainfall d) Calculate slope
40. Crop calendars are designed using:
    a) Historical market prices b) Weather and crop phenology
    c) Soil organic carbon d) Seed certification data

41. Which is a modern tool used in agrometeorology?
   a) Drone-based yield monitoring
   b) Typewriter-based record keeping
   c) Manual weeding
   d) Flashcards

42. Real-time weather data for farmers is now provided by:
   a) Museums
   b) Mobile apps and SMS
   c) Libraries
   d) Government subsidies

43. Which system supports agro-advisories in India?
   a) IMD AgroMet Advisory Service (AAS)
   b) WHO Advisory
   c) ICAR Export Council
   d) CSIR Meteoric Project

44. Which of the following is used in agrometeorological modeling?
   a) WOFOST
   b) ICARDA
   c) IFPRI
   d) UNO

45. Which of the following helps in localized weather forecasts?
   a) AI models + AWS data
   b) International treaties
   c) Farm size statistics
   d) Soil classification

46. A key climatic factor in choosing a crop for an area is:
   a) Cultural practices
   b) Weather norms and variability
   c) Fertilizer subsidy
   d) Water rights

47. Which Indian institution plays a central role in agrometeorology?
   a) NASA
   b) ICAR-CRIDA
   c) IIT Delhi
   d) NDMA

48. Climate-smart agriculture depends heavily on:
   a) Daily newspapers
   b) Meteorological and climate data
   c) Crop loans
   d) Insurance agencies

49. Agroclimatic planning helps to:
   a) Optimize farm labor
   b) Match crops to weather zones
   c) Increase political representation
   d) Improve TV coverage

50. A major challenge in agrometeorology is:
   a) Lack of tractors
   b) Timely availability of quality weather data
   c) Fertilizer shortage
   d) Excessive landholding

Answer Key

1	c	2	c	3	c	4	c	5	a	6	d	7	c
8	a	9	b	10	b	11	a	12	b	13	c	14	b
15	c	16	b	17	b	18	d	19	b	20	b	21	a
22	b	23	b	24	a	25	b	26	b	27	c	28	b
29	b	30	c	31	b	32	b	33	b	34	b	35	c
36	b	37	b	38	b	39	b	40	b	41	a	42	b
43	a	44	a	45	a	46	b	47	b	48	b	49	b
50	b												

2

The Atmosphere and Solar Radiation

1. The most abundant gas in the Earth's atmosphere is:
   a) Oxygen b) Nitrogen
   c) Carbon dioxide d) Argon
2. The percentage of nitrogen in the dry atmosphere is approximately:
   a) 20.9% b) 78.1%
   c) 0.03% d) 0.93%
3. The atmosphere is held around the Earth due to:
   a) Magnetic field b) Gravity
   c) Wind d) Solar radiation
4. Which gas in the atmosphere is essential for respiration?
   a) Carbon dioxide b) Oxygen
   c) Nitrogen d) Helium
5. Which layer of the atmosphere contains the ozone layer?
   a) Troposphere b) Stratosphere
   c) Mesosphere d) Thermosphere
6. Weather phenomena mostly occur in which layer?
   a) Exosphere b) Mesosphere
   c) Stratosphere d) Troposphere
7. The boundary between troposphere and stratosphere is known as:
   a) Tropopause b) Stratopause
   c) Mesopause d) Thermopause
8. The height of the troposphere at the equator is about:
   a) 5 km b) 10 km
   c) 17 km d) 25 km

9. Which atmospheric layer reflects radio waves?
   a) Troposphere b) Stratosphere
   c) Ionosphere d) Ozonosphere
10. Which component of the atmosphere absorbs harmful ultraviolet rays?
    a) Nitrogen b) Oxygen
    c) Ozone d) Carbon monoxide
11. The primary source of energy for Earth's atmosphere is:
    a) Geothermal heat b) Solar radiation
    c) Moonlight d) Ocean currents
12. Solar radiation reaching the Earth's surface is called:
    a) Reflected radiation b) Insolation
    c) Terrestrial radiation d) Albedo
13. The solar constant is approximately:
    a) 1361 W/m² b) 1000 W/m²
    c) 850 W/m² d) 400 W/m²
14. The solar constant is measured at:
    a) Sea level b) Earth's surface
    c) Top of the atmosphere d) Ozone layer
15. Most of the solar radiation reaching Earth is in which part of the spectrum?
    a) Ultraviolet b) Infrared
    c) Microwave d) Visible light
16. The Earth receives solar energy in the form of:
    a) Conduction b) Convection
    c) Radiation d) Reflection
17. What percent of the Sun's radiation is in the visible range?
    a) 10% b) 25%
    c) 42% d) 75%
18. Which form of radiation is responsible for heating the Earth's surface?
    a) Infrared radiation b) UV radiation
    c) X-rays d) Microwaves

19. The process by which Earth emits energy back to space is called:
    a) Absorption b) Reflection
    c) Terrestrial radiation d) Transmission
20. The incoming shortwave radiation from the sun is known as:
    a) Terrestrial radiation b) Albedo
    c) Solar insolation d) Blackbody emission
21. The Earth's radiation budget involves a balance between:
    a) Oxygen and CO_2
    b) Solar input and terrestrial output
    c) Winds and currents
    d) Pressure and temperature
22. Albedo is the measure of:
    a) Absorbed radiation b) Transmitted radiation
    c) Reflected radiation d) Emitted radiation
23. Fresh snow has an albedo value of about:
    a) 10% b) 30%
    c) 50% d) 80%–90%
24. The Earth's average albedo is approximately:
    a) 0.15 b) 0.25
    c) 0.30 d) 0.45
25. Terrestrial radiation is mainly in the:
    a) UV range b) Visible range
    c) Infrared range d) Microwave range
26. Net radiation is the difference between:
    a) Rainfall and runoff
    b) Incoming and outgoing radiation
    c) Temperature and pressure
    d) Solar and lunar radiation
27. A surface that reflects all incoming solar radiation is termed:
    a) Transparent b) Black body
    c) White body d) Grey body

28. Which gas contributes the most to the greenhouse effect?
a) Oxygen b) Carbon dioxide
c) Methane d) Nitrous oxide

29. The greenhouse effect is due to:
a) Depletion of ozone
b) Reflection of sunlight
c) Trapping of infrared radiation
d) Increase in solar flares

30. Which of the following is a greenhouse gas?
a) Nitrogen b) Hydrogen
c) Methane d) Argon

31. The angle at which solar rays strike the Earth is known as:
a) Solar angle b) Zenith angle
c) Incidence angle d) Both b and c

32. Solar radiation is maximum when the sun is:
a) At the horizon b) Overhead
c) Obscured by clouds d) In the east

33. The length of day and night is equal during:
a) Summer solstice b) Winter solstice
c) Equinox d) Lunar eclipse

34. Which season receives the most solar radiation in India?
a) Summer b) Winter
c) Monsoon d) Post-monsoon

35. Seasonal variation in solar radiation is caused by:
a) Lunar cycle b) Earth's axial tilt
c) Wind direction d) Ocean currents

36. The Earth is closest to the Sun during:
a) Perihelion (January) b) Aphelion (July)
c) Equinox (March) d) Solstice (June)

37. The tilt of Earth's axis is approximately:
a) 15° b) 23.5°
c) 30° d) 45°

38. The major reason for different climates on Earth is:
   a) Ocean salinity   b) Solar flares
   c) Uneven solar heating   d) Continental drift
39. The solar zenith angle is 0° when the sun is:
   a) At sunrise   b) At sunset
   c) Directly overhead   d) At the horizon
40. A location near the equator receives:
   a) Low solar radiation
   b) Uniform solar radiation year-round
   c) No solar radiation
   d) High seasonal variation
41. Solar radiation affects:
   a) Photosynthesis   b) Seed dormancy
   c) Soil acidity   d) Fertilizer absorption
42. The efficiency of photosynthesis is highest in:
   a) Red and blue wavelengths   b) Green wavelengths
   c) UV rays   d) Infrared rays
43. Solar radiation interception is important for:
   a) Root growth   b) Flowering
   c) Canopy development   d) Leaf senescence
44. Which agricultural practice is influenced by sunlight duration?
   a) Harvesting
   b) Planting depth
   c) Photoperiod-sensitive crop flowering
   d) Fertilizer mixing
45. Radiation use efficiency (RUE) refers to:
   a) Conversion of sunlight to leaf color
   b) Conversion of solar energy to biomass
   c) Photosynthetic water loss
   d) Soil temperature variation
46. Crop yield is often proportional to:
   a) Fertilizer rate   b) Solar radiation intercepted
   c) Number of leaves   d) Soil salinity

47. Greenhouse farming depends on:
    a) Wind speed
    b) Artificial rainfall
    c) Controlled solar radiation
    d) Deep soil layers
48. A sunshine recorder measures:
    a) Solar constant
    b) Solar duration
    c) Infrared energy
    d) Ozone levels
49. Pyranometer is used to measure:
    a) Wind speed
    b) Soil heat flux
    c) Total solar radiation
    d) Relative humidity
50. Which factor most affects the rate of evapotranspiration?
    a) Solar radiation
    b) Soil pH
    c) Root length
    d) Soil type

Answer Key

1	b	2	b	3	b	4	b	5	b	6	d	7	a
8	c	9	c	10	c	11	b	12	b	13	a	14	c
15	d	16	c	17	c	18	a	19	c	20	c	21	b
22	c	23	d	24	c	25	c	26	b	27	c	28	b
29	c	30	c	31	d	32	b	33	c	34	a	35	b
36	a	37	b	38	c	39	c	40	b	41	a	42	a
43	c	44	c	45	b	46	b	47	c	48	b	49	c
50	a												

3

Air Temperature

1. The degree of hotness or coldness of air is termed as:
   a) Pressure b) Humidity
   c) Temperature d) Wind chill
2. Air temperature is usually measured at a height of:
   a) Ground level b) 0.5 m
   c) 1.25 to 2.0 m d) 3.0 m
3. The unit of air temperature in SI system is:
   a) Fahrenheit b) Kelvin
   c) Celsius d) Centigrade
4. The most commonly used temperature scale in meteorology is:
   a) Kelvin b) Rankine
   c) Celsius d) Fahrenheit
5. 0°C is equal to how many Kelvin?
   a) 100 K b) 0 K
   c) 273.15 K d) 32 K
6. Maximum temperature of the day usually occurs at:
   a) Sunrise b) Noon
   c) 2–3 PM d) Sunset
7. Minimum temperature of the day is usually recorded at:
   a) Midnight b) Sunset
   c) Early morning (just before sunrise)
   d) Noon
8. Diurnal variation in temperature refers to:
   a) Monthly variation b) Yearly change
   c) Day and night variation d) Seasonal fluctuation

9. Seasonal variation in temperature is mainly due to:
   a) Cloud movement b) Sun-Earth distance
   c) Solar angle and day length d) Rainfall pattern

10. Which season records the highest mean air temperature in India?
   a) Winter b) Summer
   c) Monsoon d) Autumn

11. Which instrument is used to measure air temperature?
   a) Hygrometer b) Anemometer
   c) Thermometer d) Barometer

12. A thermometer used to record maximum temperature is:
   a) Mercury thermometer b) Alcohol thermometer
   c) Resistance thermometer d) Six's thermometer

13. Minimum temperature is measured using:
   a) Alcohol thermometer b) Mercury thermometer
   c) Barograph d) Manometer

14. The ideal time for observing maximum and minimum temperatures is:
   a) 8 AM and 2 PM b) 7 AM and 5 PM
   c) 6 AM and 12 noon d) 7 AM and 7 PM

15. The standard screen used to house thermometers is called:
   a) Stevenson screen b) Solar box
   c) Hygro shelter d) Thermal shed

16. The difference between maximum and minimum temperature in 24 hours is:
   a) Annual range b) Diurnal range
   c) Thermal lag d) Mean temperature

17. Mean daily temperature is calculated as:
   a) (Max + Min)/2 b) (Max – Min)/2
   c) Max × Min d) Max – Min

18. A temperature inversion occurs when:
   a) Temperature increases with altitude
   b) Temperature decreases with altitude
   c) Wind speed increases
   d) Sun shines brightly

19. The lapse rate refers to the:
    a) Rate of pressure decrease
    b) Rate of wind increase
    c) Rate of temperature decrease with height
    d) Rate of rainfall increase
20. The normal lapse rate in the troposphere is:
    a) 3.5°C per 1000 m b) 6.5°C per 1000 m
    c) 9.8°C per 1000 m d) 1.0°C per 100 m
21. Temperature decreases with:
    a) Increasing pressure b) Increasing altitude
    c) Increasing wind speed d) Increasing humidity
22. Coastal areas have moderate temperatures due to:
    a) Cloud cover b) Sea breeze
    c) High pressure d) Wind turbulence
23. Land heats up and cools down __ than water.
    a) Slower b) Faster
    c) Same d) More evenly
24. Cloud cover at night leads to:
    a) Lower night temperatures b) Higher night temperatures
    c) No change d) Extreme inversion
25. Air temperature is generally highest over:
    a) Forests b) Water bodies
    c) Deserts d) Mountains
26. Air temperature affects:
    a) Crop flowering b) Soil formation
    c) Rainfall pattern d) Soil pH
27. Base temperature is defined as:
    a) Max temperature for growth
    b) Threshold temperature below which crop growth stops
    c) Average of daily temps
    d) Temp for irrigation

28. Growing Degree Days (GDD) are calculated using:
    a) Wind speed
    b) Pressure difference
    c) Temperature above base temperature
    d) Humidity difference
29. If the maximum temperature is 30°C and minimum is 20°C, GDD with base 10°C is:
    a) 15 b) 20
    c) 25 d) 40
30. Chilling requirement of temperate fruit crops is fulfilled by:
    a) High solar radiation b) Minimum humidity
    c) Low temperatures (0–7°C) d) High rainfall
31. Frost injury occurs when temperature falls below:
    a) 0°C b) 5°C
    c) 10°C d) –2°C
32. Heat stress in crops occurs when temperature is:
    a) <10°C b) >25°C
    c) >35°C d) <0°C
33. The cardinal temperatures refer to:
    a) Seasonal temperatures
    b) Leaf temperatures
    c) Minimum, optimum and maximum for crop growth
    d) Average monthly temperature
34. Crops like wheat experience terminal heat stress during:
    a) Sowing b) Germination
    c) Grain filling d) Flowering
35. Temperature extremes influence:
    a) Germination rate b) Soil color
    c) Wind erosion d) Leaf size only
36. The equator experiences relatively constant temperatures due to:
    a) Tilt of Earth b) Uniform solar radiation
    c) High rainfall d) Trade winds

37. Urban areas are warmer than rural due to:
a) Wind currents
b) Albedo effect
c) Urban heat island effect
d) Sea breeze

38. Global warming leads to:
a) Decrease in air temperature
b) More stable weather
c) Rise in average global temperature
d) Lesser GDDs

39. Which greenhouse gas has the greatest long-term impact on temperature rise?
a) CO_2
b) O_2
c) N_2
d) Neon

40. Increasing temperature accelerates:
a) Photosynthesis always
b) Crop maturity
c) Soil water availability
d) Pest death

41. Temperature forecast is crucial for:
a) Soil testing
b) Crop harvest planning
c) Rain gauge setup
d) Rock weathering

42. Which method is used for temperature interpolation in agrometeorology?
a) Thiessen polygon
b) IDW (Inverse Distance Weighting)
c) Rainfall-runoff model
d) Spectral index

43. Remote sensing estimates surface temperature using:
a) UV bands
b) Microwave radiation
c) Thermal infrared bands
d) Visible bands only

44. Satellite-derived LST stands for:
a) Local Soil Temperature
b) Land Surface Temperature
c) Low Solar Temperature
d) Land Speed Tracking

45. A sudden drop in temperature during flowering can lead to:
a) Increased yield
b) Frost escape
c) Flower drop and sterility
d) Leaf expansion

46. Which crop is highly sensitive to temperature during pollination?
 a) Cotton b) Wheat
 c) Rice d) Sugarcane

47. Evapotranspiration increases with:
 a) Low temperature b) High temperature
 c) Cloudy days d) Low radiation

48. Thermal time is another term for:
 a) Soil temperature b) Diurnal cycle
 c) Growing Degree Days d) Air humidity

49. At the same latitude, inland areas are ___ than coastal areas.
 a) Cooler b) Warmer
 c) More humid d) Wetter

50. Night temperatures below optimum reduce:
 a) Root absorption b) Leaf turgor
 c) Photosynthesis and yield d) Solar radiation

Answer Key

1	c	2	c	3	b	4	c	5	c	6	c	7	c
8	c	9	c	10	b	11	c	12	a	13	a	14	d
15	a	16	b	17	a	18	a	19	c	20	b	21	b
22	b	23	b	24	b	25	c	26	a	27	b	28	c
29	a	30	c	31	a	32	c	33	c	34	c	35	a
36	b	37	c	38	c	39	a	40	b	41	b	42	b
43	c	44	b	45	c	46	c	47	b	48	c	49	b
50	c												

4

Atmospheric Pressure

1. Atmospheric pressure is defined as:
   a) Force exerted by rain
   b) Force exerted by wind
   c) Weight of the air column per unit area
   d) Force of gravity on clouds
2. The SI unit of atmospheric pressure is:
   a) mmHg b) Pascal (Pa)
   c) Bar d) Torr
3. Standard atmospheric pressure at sea level is:
   a) 760 mm Hg b) 1013.25 hPa
   c) 101325 Pa d) All of the above
4. 1 atmosphere (atm) is equal to:
   a) 1000 Pa b) 101.325 kPa
   c) 750 mm Hg d) 10.13 hPa
5. Atmospheric pressure decreases with:
   a) Decreasing altitude b) Increasing altitude
   c) Increasing temperature d) Increasing humidity
6. Atmospheric pressure is measured by a:
   a) Thermometer b) Anemometer
   c) Barometer d) Hygrometer
7. The most commonly used barometer is:
   a) Mercury barometer b) Aneroid barometer
   c) Digital barometer d) Electric barometer
8. An aneroid barometer does not use:
   a) Mercury b) Vacuum chamber
   c) Spring mechanism d) Needle indicator

9. A barograph is used to:
   a) Measure pressure visually b) Record pressure continuously
   c) Measure wind pressure d) Forecast temperature
10. The unit millibar (mb) is equivalent to:
   a) 1 Pascal b) 100 Pascal
   c) 10 Pascal d) 0.1 Pascal
11. Pressure is highest at:
   a) Sea level b) Mountain top
   c) Airplane cruising altitude d) Troposphere
12. Atmospheric pressure decreases approximately:
   a) 10 mb every 1 km b) 100 mb every 1 km
   c) 1 mb every 1 km d) 50 mb every 1 km
13. The rate of pressure decrease is called:
   a) Lapse rate b) Pressure gradient
   c) Isobar d) Barometric depression
14. Areas with equal pressure are connected by:
   a) Isobars b) Isotherms
   c) Isohyets d) Contours
15. Atmospheric pressure decreases exponentially with:
   a) Latitude b) Longitude
   c) Altitude d) Temperature
16. A region of low atmospheric pressure is known as a:
   a) Ridge b) Trough
   c) Cyclone d) Anticyclone
17. A region of high atmospheric pressure is called:
   a) Cyclone b) Depression
   c) Anticyclone d) Trough
18. Cyclones are associated with:
   a) Outward air movement
   b) Clockwise rotation in Northern Hemisphere
   c) Inward spiral of air
   d) High pressure

19. Anticyclones bring generally:
a) Rainy weather b) Cloud formation
c) Dry and clear weather d) Windstorm

20. Wind blows from:
a) Cold to warm areas
b) Low pressure to high pressure
c) High pressure to low pressure
d) South to North

21. Temperature increases lead to:
a) Pressure increase b) Pressure decrease
c) No effect d) Erratic change

22. Warm air is:
a) Denser and heavier b) Less dense and rises
c) Heavier and settles d) Not affected by pressure

23. Humidity increases cause pressure to:
a) Decrease b) Increase
c) Remain constant d) Alternate

24. Cold, dry air exerts:
a) Low pressure b) High pressure
c) Moderate pressure d) Equal pressure

25. Vertical pressure gradient is steeper in:
a) Equator b) Upper troposphere
c) Lower atmosphere d) Stratosphere

26. In which layer is atmospheric pressure highest?
a) Stratosphere b) Troposphere
c) Mesosphere d) Thermosphere

27. Atmospheric pressure is nearly zero at:
a) 5 km b) 20 km
c) 50 km d) 100 km

28. Most weather changes occur in:
a) Stratosphere b) Mesosphere
c) Troposphere d) Exosphere

29. The weight of the air column is maximum at:
a) Mount Everest b) Sea level
c) 10,000 m d) Outer atmosphere

30. Tropospheric pressure decreases rapidly because of:
a) Wind b) Clouds
c) Air thinning d) Ozone

31. Atmospheric pressure affects:
a) Crop variety b) Rainwater harvesting
c) Wind and rainfall patterns d) Irrigation type

32. Low pressure during monsoon results in:
a) Cloud dissipation b) Heavy rainfall
c) Dust storms d) Soil erosion

33. High pressure systems in winter bring:
a) Cyclones b) Rainfall
c) Clear, cold weather d) Fog

34. Barometric pressure forecasting helps predict:
a) Soil temperature b) Irrigation need
c) Rain or storm d) Solar radiation

35. Decreasing barometric pressure often indicates:
a) Improving weather b) Stable atmosphere
c) Approaching storm d) Less humidity

36. Closely spaced isobars indicate:
a) High temperature b) Strong winds
c) Calm weather d) Humid conditions

37. Widely spaced isobars suggest:
a) Strong wind b) Gentle wind
c) Cyclone d) Thunderstorm

38. Isobars are plotted at intervals of:
a) 10 mb b) 2 mb
c) 4 mb d) 1 mb

39. On a weather map, 'L' denotes:
a) Lightning b) Low pressure
c) Latitude d) Layer cloud

40. Weather maps with low-pressure centers are used to identify:
a) Calm zones
b) Stable air
c) Cyclonic activity
d) Ozone zones

41. Pressure gradient force is directed:
a) Parallel to isobars
b) From low to high pressure
c) Perpendicular to isobars, high to low
d) North to South

42. Coriolis force deflects wind to the ____ in the Northern Hemisphere.
a) Left
b) Right
c) Equator
d) Pole

43. Hydrostatic equilibrium exists when:
a) Gravity equals pressure gradient force
b) Cyclone is forming
c) Solar radiation is high
d) Temperature is constant

44. Atmospheric pressure contributes to:
a) Cloud color
b) Dew point
c) Air mass formation
d) Soil nutrient movement

45. Jet streams form in areas of strong:
a) Pressure gradient
b) Rain
c) Sunlight
d) Ozone concentration

46. Which gas contributes most to atmospheric pressure?
a) Oxygen
b) Nitrogen
c) CO_2
d) Hydrogen

47. Weather balloons measure:
a) Soil moisture
b) Air pressure and temperature
c) Humus content
d) Solar radiation

48. Rising air pressure usually indicates:
a) Storm
b) Rainfall
c) Clear weather
d) Earthquake

49. Pressure belts are caused by:

a) Ocean currents b) Uneven heating of Earth

c) Cloud movement d) Plate tectonics

50. Atmospheric pressure influences:

a) Crop rooting depth b) Wind direction and speed

c) Soil texture d) Earth's rotation

Answer Key

1	c	2	b	3	d	4	b	5	b	6	c	7	a
8	a	9	b	10	b	11	a	12	b	13	b	14	a
15	c	16	c	17	c	18	c	19	c	20	c	21	b
22	b	23	a	24	b	25	c	26	b	27	d	28	c
29	b	30	c	31	c	32	b	33	c	34	c	35	c
36	b	37	b	38	c	39	b	40	c	41	c	42	b
43	a	44	c	45	a	46	b	47	b	48	c	49	b
50	b												

5

Wind

1. Wind is the:
   a) Horizontal movement of water
   b) Vertical movement of air
   c) Horizontal movement of air
   d) Rotation of Earth
2. Wind is caused primarily due to:
   a) Moon's gravity
   b) Temperature difference
   c) Earth's tilt
   d) Ocean currents
3. The instrument used to measure wind speed is:
   a) Hygrometer
   b) Barometer
   c) Anemometer
   d) Thermometer
4. Wind direction is measured by:
   a) Rain gauge
   b) Wind vane
   c) Barograph
   d) Altimeter
5. Wind is named based on:
   a) Direction it is blowing to
   b) Time of day
   c) Direction it is coming from
   d) Speed
6. Permanent winds are also known as:
   a) Local winds
   b) Planetary winds
   c) Cyclones
   d) Sea breezes
7. Trade winds blow from:
   a) Poles to equator
   b) Equator to poles
   c) Subtropical high to equator
   d) Equator to subtropical high
8. Westerlies blow from:
   a) East to west
   b) West to east
   c) North to south
   d) South to north

9. Polar easterlies originate from:
   a) Equator b) Subtropical region
   c) Poles d) Tropics
10. Monsoon winds are:
   a) Periodic winds b) Permanent winds
   c) Local winds d) Upper-level winds
11. Sea breeze occurs during:
   a) Night b) Day
   c) Winter d) Monsoon
12. Land breeze occurs during:
   a) Day b) Night
   c) Rainfall d) Spring
13. Loo is a:
   a) Cold wind in Himalayas
   b) Hot and dry wind in northern India
   c) Rain-bearing wind
   d) Coastal wind
14. Chinook winds are experienced in:
   a) India b) Canada and USA
   c) Russia d) Brazil
15. Mistral is a:
   a) Hot wind in Africa b) Cold wind in France
   c) Tropical wind d) Monsoon wind
16. The global wind circulation is influenced by:
   a) Ocean currents b) Moon's pull
   c) Unequal heating of the Earth d) Forest cover
17. The Coriolis force causes wind to deflect to the ___ in the Northern Hemisphere.
   a) Left b) Right
   c) North d) Equator
18. Pressure gradient force causes wind to move:
   a) From low to high pressure b) Along isobars
   c) From high to low pressure d) Circularly

19. Geostrophic wind flows:
a) Straight toward low pressure b) Perpendicular to isobars
c) Parallel to isobars d) Vertically upward

20. Wind patterns are modified by:
a) Clouds b) Sunspots
c) Friction and Earth's rotation d) Rainfall

21. Wind speed is generally measured in:
a) hPa b) Joules
c) m/s or km/h d) Degrees

22. Beaufort scale is used to classify:
a) Cloud height b) Earthquake intensity
c) Wind speed d) Temperature levels

23. Strong winds caused by differences in pressure are:
a) Monsoons b) Gusts
c) Gales d) Cyclones

24. Wind power is used in agriculture for:
a) Soil testing
b) Grain drying and water pumping
c) Pesticide spraying
d) Weed control

25. Maximum wind energy potential exists in:
a) Valleys b) Coastal and open areas
c) Forests d) Urban centers

26. A sudden increase in wind speed is called:
a) Gust b) Gale
c) Calm d) Squall

27. Wind convergence leads to:
a) Cloud clearing b) Uplift and possible rainfall
c) Temperature rise d) Dry air formation

28. Wind divergence causes:
a) Cloud formation b) Air sinking and clear skies
c) Cyclone d) Earthquake

29. High-speed upper air winds are called:
a) Cyclones b) Trade winds
c) Jet streams d) Westerlies

30. Cyclones are associated with:
a) Divergence of air b) Anticyclonic winds
c) Convergence and uplift d) Calm and stable air

31. Wind erosion is common in:
a) Flooded areas b) Humid regions
c) Dry and sandy soils d) Waterlogged fields

32. Shelterbelts and windbreaks are used to:
a) Attract wind b) Reduce wind speed
c) Increase evaporation d) Stop rainfall

33. High wind speed affects crops by:
a) Increasing yield b) Lodging and breakage
c) Enhancing pollination d) Promoting growth

34. Pollination in crops like maize is aided by:
a) Water b) Insects
c) Wind d) Birds

35. Wind helps in the dispersal of:
a) Roots b) Flowers
c) Seeds and pollen d) Fertilizer

36. Doldrums are:
a) Calm equatorial regions b) High-pressure zones
c) Stormy zones d) Polar winds

37. Horse latitudes are found near:
a) Equator b) 30° latitude
c) 60° latitude d) Poles

38. Winds deflect due to:
a) Temperature b) Clouds
c) Coriolis effect d) Precipitation

39. Windward side of a mountain receives:
a) Less rain b) Heavy rainfall
c) Snow only d) No wind

40. The leeward side of mountains is:
a) Wet b) Cool
c) Dry and warm d) Humid

41. A sudden blast of wind that lasts for a short duration is a:
a) Gale b) Gust
c) Thunderstorm d) Jet

42. The direction of surface winds in a cyclone in the Northern Hemisphere is:
a) Clockwise b) Anticlockwise
c) Radial d) Vertical

43. Anticyclones are associated with:
a) Storms b) Rainfall
c) Clear and dry weather d) Earthquakes

44. Jet streams are found in the:
a) Troposphere b) Stratosphere
c) Ionosphere d) Thermosphere

45. Jet streams are important because they:
a) Cause earthquakes b) Guide weather systems
c) Warm the Earth d) Create clouds

46. Climate change affects wind patterns by:
a) Increasing wind speed globally
b) Making wind directions unpredictable
c) Weakening monsoon winds
d) None of the above

47. Global warming may lead to:
a) Strengthened polar winds b) Stronger jet streams
c) Weaker trade winds d) Faster sea breezes

48. Wind is a form of:
a) Kinetic energy b) Potential energy
c) Chemical energy d) Thermal energy

49. The irregular variations in global wind patterns are associated with:
a) La Niña b) El Niño
c) Both d) Neither

50. Wind chill factor refers to:
 a) Wind making air feel colder b) Hot winds
 c) Effect of wind on clouds d) Speed of air conditioning

Answer Key

1	c	2	b	3	c	4	b	5	c	6	b	7	c
8	b	9	c	10	a	11	b	12	b	13	b	14	b
15	b	16	c	17	b	18	c	19	c	20	c	21	c
22	c	23	c	24	b	25	b	26	a	27	b	28	b
29	c	30	c	31	c	32	b	33	b	34	c	35	c
36	a	37	b	38	c	39	b	40	c	41	b	42	b
43	c	44	a	45	b	46	c	47	c	48	a	49	c
50	a												

6

Humidity and Evaporation

1. Humidity refers to the amount of ____ in the air.
   a) Oxygen
   b) Nitrogen
   c) Water vapor
   d) Carbon dioxide
2. The instrument used to measure relative humidity is called:
   a) Barometer
   b) Hygrometer
   c) Thermometer
   d) Anemometer
3. Relative humidity is expressed as:
   a) g/m^3
   b) %
   c) mm
   d) °C
4. Absolute humidity is the:
   a) Ratio of actual to maximum vapor
   b) Weight of water vapor in a unit volume of air
   c) % saturation
   d) Temperature difference
5. The maximum amount of moisture air can hold depends on:
   a) Wind speed
   b) Temperature
   c) Altitude
   d) Pressure
6. Relative humidity is defined as:
   a) Actual vapor pressure
   b) Saturation vapor pressure
   c) Ratio of actual to saturation vapor pressure
   d) Specific humidity
7. Dew point is the temperature at which:
   a) Evaporation stops
   b) Air gets saturated
   c) Water starts boiling
   d) Wind speed becomes zero

8. Specific humidity is:
   a) Mass of water vapor per unit mass of dry air
   b) Temperature at saturation
   c) Rainfall amount
   d) Wind effect on humidity
9. When air holds all the moisture it can at a given temperature, it is said to be:
   a) Condensed b) Dry
   c) Saturated d) Supercooled
10. Saturation vapor pressure increases with:
   a) Decreasing temperature b) Increasing altitude
   c) Increasing temperature d) Increasing pressure
11. Evaporation is the process of changing:
   a) Water to ice b) Vapor to water
   c) Water to vapor d) Ice to water
12. The rate of evaporation increases with:
   a) High humidity b) Low wind speed
   c) High temperature d) Cloudy sky
13. Which instrument is used to measure evaporation?
   a) Pyranometer b) Lysimeter
   c) Atmometer d) Class A Pan
14. Evaporation is highest during:
   a) Night b) Morning
   c) Afternoon d) Winter
15. One major factor reducing evaporation is:
   a) High temperature b) Strong winds
   c) High relative humidity d) Clear sky
16. Condensation takes place when:
   a) Air expands
   b) Air cools to below its dew point
   c) Air is heated
   d) Rain evaporates

17. Dew is formed on surfaces when:
a) Surface temperature is below dew point
b) Wind is strong
c) Air is dry
d) Humidity is low

18. When dew point and air temperature are equal, the air is:
a) Dry b) Saturated
c) Stable d) Windy

19. Fog forms due to:
a) High winds b) High pressure
c) Ground cooling air to dew point d) Solar radiation

20. Cloud formation is a result of:
a) Precipitation b) Condensation of water vapor
c) Radiation d) Evaporation from soil

21. Wet and dry bulb thermometers are used in:
a) Barometer b) Hygrometer
c) Psychrometer d) Thermograph

22. If the dry bulb and wet bulb temperatures are equal, the relative humidity is:
a) 0% b) 50%
c) 100% d) 25%

23. Larger difference between dry and wet bulb readings indicates:
a) High humidity b) Low humidity
c) Saturation d) Dew formation

24. Sling psychrometer is operated by:
a) Digital display b) Electrical charge
c) Manual rotation d) Satellite

25. The temperature recorded by a wet bulb thermometer is always:
a) Lower than dry bulb b) Higher than dry bulb
c) Equal to atmospheric pressure d) Same as dew point

26. High humidity favors:
a) Rapid transpiration b) Reduced disease
c) Increased fungal attack d) Reduced plant growth

27. Evapotranspiration is the combined loss of water from:
    a) Soil and rainfall
    b) Plant and sun
    c) Evaporation and transpiration
    d) Clouds and sky
28. Evapotranspiration is maximum in:
    a) Winter
    b) Night
    c) Summer midday
    d) Rainy days
29. Crop water requirement increases with:
    a) High humidity
    b) Low evaporation
    c) High evaporation
    d) Cloudy sky
30. Humidity affects the drying rate of grains by:
    a) Speeding it up
    b) Reducing it
    c) Stopping it
    d) Freezing it
31. Relative humidity is generally highest during:
    a) Noon
    b) Sunrise
    c) Afternoon
    d) Sunset
32. Relative humidity decreases as:
    a) Temperature falls
    b) Dew forms
    c) Temperature rises
    d) Clouds appear
33. Maximum evaporation occurs in which season?
    a) Winter
    b) Monsoon
    c) Summer
    d) Autumn
34. Evaporation from open water is less during:
    a) Windy days
    b) Cloudy days
    c) Hot days
    d) Dry days
35. Relative humidity increases with:
    a) Rising temperature
    b) Falling temperature
    c) More sunshine
    d) More wind
36. Fog is more likely to form when:
    a) Dew point is far below air temperature
    b) Dew point and temperature are close
    c) No clouds are present
    d) Wind speed is high

37. Transpiration is maximum when:
   a) Humidity is high b) Soil is dry
   c) Temperature and wind are high d) It is raining
38. Evaporation from soil surface reduces when:
   a) Soil is bare b) Soil is mulched
   c) Wind is high d) Sunshine is high
39. The unit of actual vapor pressure is:
   a) mm b) °C
   c) hPa or mb d) %
40. Water vapor constitutes about what percent of the atmosphere by volume?
   a) 0–4% b) 10–15%
   c) 20–30% d) 50%
41. High vapor pressure deficit indicates:
   a) High humidity b) Low humidity
   c) Fog formation d) Dew point
42. Cloudiness reduces evaporation due to:
   a) Solar radiation blockage b) Increased wind
   c) High temperature d) Low pressure
43. As temperature increases, the capacity of air to hold water vapor:
   a) Decreases b) Remains same
   c) Increases d) Vanishes
44. The latent heat of vaporization of water is:
   a) 100 cal/g b) 540 cal/g
   c) 1,000 cal/g d) 10 cal/g
45. Vapor pressure deficit is:
   a) Difference between saturation and actual vapor pressure
   b) Difference between dry and wet bulb temperature
   c) Relative humidity
   d) Saturation vapor pressure
46. Lysimeter is used to measure:
   a) Rainfall b) Soil moisture
   c) Evapotranspiration d) Temperature

47. High relative humidity is generally favorable for:
a) Cotton b) Wheat
c) Tea and rice d) Pearl millet

48. In the early morning, evaporation is:
a) Maximum b) Moderate
c) Minimum d) Unaffected

49. Fog is a form of:
a) Evaporation b) Condensation
c) Precipitation d) Insolation

50. During high humidity, perspiration becomes:
a) Easier b) Rapid
c) Less effective d) Unaffected

Answer Key

1	c	2	b	3	b	4	b	5	b	6	c	7	b
8	a	9	c	10	c	11	c	12	c	13	d	14	c
15	c	16	b	17	a	18	b	19	c	20	a	21	c
22	c	23	b	24	c	25	a	26	c	27	c	28	c
29	c	30	b	31	b	32	c	33	c	34	b	35	b
36	b	37	c	38	b	39	c	40	a	41	a	42	a
43	c	44	b	45	a	46	c	47	c	48	c	49	b
50	c												

7

Spatial Technologies for Agromet Applications

1. What does GIS stand for?
   a) Global Imaging System
   b) Geographic Information System
   c) General Information Software
   d) Geographic Imaging Sector
2. Remote sensing is the science of:
   a) Manual surveying
   b) Observing objects from a distance
   c) GPS navigation
   d) Underground sensing
3. Satellite data is mainly used in agrometeorology for:
   a) Soil compaction b) Weather analysis
   c) Water filtration d) Manure testing
4. GPS stands for:
   a) General Positioning System b) Global Precision Survey
   c) Global Positioning System d) Ground Point Sensor
5. Which satellite sensor provides high-resolution weather data?
   a) MODIS b) AVHRR
   c) Landsat d) INSAT-3D
6. Remote sensing data are primarily collected via:
   a) Ground stations b) Satellites and drones
   c) Weather balloons only d) Soil probes

7. NDVI stands for:
   a) Normalized Differential Vegetative Index
   b) Normalized Difference Vegetation Index
   c) Nominal Density of Vegetative Information
   d) None of the above
8. NDVI is used to assess:
   a) Soil fertility b) Crop health and biomass
   c) Water quality d) Soil erosion
9. What is the spatial resolution of MODIS sensor?
   a) 30 m b) 250 m – 1 km
   c) 5 m d) 1.5 m
10. Drones are increasingly used in agriculture to:
   a) Replace farmers b) Spray pesticides only
   c) Capture real-time spatial data d) Repair irrigation systems
11. GIS can help in creating:
   a) Crop genome maps b) Weather alert systems
   c) Spatial crop weather calendars d) Fertilizer compositions
12. In agrometeorology, spatial interpolation in GIS helps in:
   a) Randomizing rainfall
   b) Filling data gaps in observations
   c) Groundwater depletion
   d) Temperature correction
13. GIS integrates:
   a) Only maps b) Maps and databases
   c) Only statistics d) Weather codes only
14. One common spatial analysis technique used in agromet is:
   a) Geocoding b) Kriging
   c) Image stitching d) Transcription
15. Raster data in GIS refers to:
   a) Tabular data b) Vector shapes
   c) Pixel-based grid data d) Narrative maps

16. INSAT-3D provides information on:
    a) Soil pH
    b) Solar radiation and rainfall
    c) Underground minerals
    d) Crop residue
17. What is the main advantage of using satellite weather data in agriculture?
    a) Low accuracy
    b) Real-time, large-area coverage
    c) Only usable in cities
    d) Too expensive for farming
18. Sentinel-2 satellites are used for:
    a) Ocean tide modeling
    b) Land and vegetation monitoring
    c) GPS navigation
    d) Mobile communication
19. Microwave remote sensing is useful in:
    a) Cloud classification
    b) Soil moisture estimation
    c) Wind speed forecasting
    d) Water salinity detection
20. Vegetation indices from satellites are widely used for:
    a) Yield estimation
    b) Crop insurance
    c) Pest prediction
    d) All of the above
21. Weather forecasting models often use spatial inputs from:
    a) Soil probes only
    b) Farmer reports
    c) Satellite and radar data
    d) Manual surveys
22. Crop yield prediction using spatial data is most effective when integrated with:
    a) Rain gauges only
    b) Soil chemistry
    c) Weather and crop models
    d) Fertilizer trials
23. Evapotranspiration mapping can be done using:
    a) GIS alone
    b) MODIS or Landsat imagery
    c) Radar plots
    d) Rainfall-only stations

24. Real-time drought monitoring in India is supported by:
    a) IMD only b) NRSC Bhuvan
    c) FAO satellites d) Mobile weather apps
25. Early warning systems using spatial tech can help in:
    a) Reducing pesticide use
    b) Flood and drought preparedness
    c) Improving tractor mileage
    d) Grain polishing
26. BHUVAN is an Indian platform developed by:
    a) ICAR b) ISRO
    c) IARI d) FAO
27. Which organization operates Agri-DSS (Decision Support Systems) in India?
    a) IMD b) ISRO
    c) ICAR d) Ministry of Railways
28. The "FASAL" project uses remote sensing for:
    a) River monitoring b) Forest mapping
    c) Crop forecasting d) Fertilizer import
29. Which software is widely used for GIS-based agromet analysis?
    a) MS Paint b) Google Chrome
    c) ArcGIS/QGIS d) VLC Player
30. The Indian satellite RISAT is used mainly for:
    a) Thermal imaging b) Rainfall collection
    c) Radar imaging d) UV detection
31. Spatial technologies help precision agriculture by:
    a) Making farming complex
    b) Applying uniform inputs
    c) Managing variability within fields
    d) Standardizing all crops
32. Variable Rate Technology (VRT) relies on:
    a) Same input rates b) Manual timing
    c) Spatial data layers d) Labor-intensive work

33. Drones assist in precision irrigation by:
a) Carrying water
b) Measuring soil salinity
c) Mapping moisture variation
d) Increasing evaporation

34. Geo-tagged advisories to farmers are possible through:
a) SMS only
b) GIS-integrated DSS
c) Manual forecasting
d) Soil testing kits

35. Farm-level weather alert systems are now enabled by:
a) Weather balloons
b) Local newspapers
c) Hyperlocal weather forecasts with GPS
d) Static forecasts

36. A major challenge in spatial technologies in agrometeorology is:
a) Lack of software
b) Lack of data
c) Lack of trained manpower and infrastructure
d) Lack of fertilizer

37. Accuracy of satellite data improves with:
a) Cloud cover
b) Ground-truthing
c) Noise signals
d) Manual drawing

38. UAVs are increasingly popular because:
a) They require no skill
b) They are government-mandated
c) They are low-cost and effective for small areas
d) They replace rainfall

39. Use of machine learning with spatial weather data helps in:
a) Harvesting
b) Irrigation only
c) Pest and disease forecasting
d) Removing weeds

40. Open-access data for agrometeorological use is available from:
a) NASA, NOAA, ISRO
b) FAO, WTO, WHO
c) WHO, IMF, RBI
d) ICAR only

41. India's Gramin Krishi Mausam Sewa (GKMS) integrates:
 a) TV shows
 b) Farmers' apps and weather forecasts
 c) River mapping
 d) None of these

42. The Mahalanobis National Crop Forecast Centre (MNCFC) supports:
 a) Water testing
 b) Crop area and production forecasting
 c) Bee pollination
 d) Soil sterilization

43. The Indian satellite INSAT-3DR provides:
 a) Long-range radar
 b) Oceanography data
 c) Weather and environment monitoring
 d) Cellular services

44. "Kisan" drone initiative aims to:
 a) Replace tractors
 b) Empower rural youth in drone-based farming
 c) Import weather data
 d) Supply fertilizer

45. AMFU stands for:
 a) Agricultural Meteorological Forecasting Unit
 b) Automatic Mapping Facility Unit
 c) Agro-Met Functional Unit
 d) Agriculture Machinery and Fertilizer Unit

46. Hyperlocal weather forecasts benefit:
 a) Space missions b) Individual farmers
 c) Policymakers d) National transport

47. GIS layering can help visualize:
 a) Rain only
 b) Soil, crop, and weather zones together
 c) Pesticide brands
 d) Irrigation pipes

48. Real-time decision support systems use:
 a) Past weather data
 b) Satellite + in-situ + model data
 c) Manual records only
 d) SMS alone

49. The temporal resolution of a satellite refers to:
 a) Number of bands
 b) How often it revisits an area
 c) The height of satellite
 d) Length of data files

50. Use of spatial technology in agromet enhances:
 a) Agricultural marketing
 b) Irrigation design
 c) Climate-smart agriculture
 d) Seed breeding

Answer Key

1	b	2	b	3	b	4	c	5	d	6	b	7	b
8	b	9	b	10	c	11	c	12	b	13	b	14	b
15	c	16	b	17	b	18	b	19	b	20	d	21	c
22	c	23	b	24	b	25	b	26	b	27	c	28	c
29	c	30	c	31	c	32	c	33	c	34	b	35	c
36	c	37	b	38	c	39	c	40	a	41	b	42	b
43	c	44	b	45	a	46	b	47	b	48	b	49	b
50	c												

8

Condensation and Precipitation

1. What is condensation?
   a) Change of solid into gas
   b) Change of gas into liquid
   c) Change of liquid into gas
   d) Change of solid into liquid
2. Condensation occurs when air is:
   a) Heated
   b) Saturated and cooled
   c) Pressurized
   d) Dry
3. The temperature at which condensation begins is called:
   a) Boiling point
   b) Saturation point
   c) Dew point
   d) Melting point
4. Which of the following is not a form of condensation?
   a) Dew
   b) Frost
   c) Fog
   d) Hail
5. Fog is an example of:
   a) Precipitation
   b) Sublimation
   c) Surface runoff
   d) Condensation near ground
6. Dew forms when:
   a) Air temperature falls below 0°C
   b) Soil evaporates
   c) Moist air touches cool surfaces
   d) Rainfall increases
7. When dew point is below freezing, we get:
   a) Mist
   b) Hail
   c) Frost
   d) Drizzle
8. Clouds are formed due to:
   a) Evaporation
   b) Condensation of water vapor in air
   c) Rainfall accumulation
   d) None of the above

9. Which is not a high-level cloud?
a) Cirrus b) Cirrostratus
c) Cirrocumulus d) Nimbostratus

10. The cloud type associated with thunder and lightning is:
a) Cirrus b) Cumulonimbus
c) Stratus d) Altostratus

11. Clouds are classified based on:
a) Altitude and appearance b) Temperature only
c) Humidity levels d) Rainfall types

12. Which cloud type resembles cotton balls?
a) Cirrus b) Stratus
c) Cumulus d) Fog

13. Stratus clouds are typically found:
a) At high altitudes
b) At the ground level
c) At low levels
d) In the upper atmosphere only

14. Which cloud type often leads to continuous rain?
a) Nimbostratus b) Cumulus
c) Cirrus d) Cirrocumulus

15. Altostratus clouds occur at:
a) Surface level b) Mid-level altitude
c) High-level d) Near the poles only

16. What is precipitation?
a) Evaporation from oceans
b) Condensation on cold surfaces
c) Any form of water falling from atmosphere
d) Collection of pollutants

17. Which of the following is not a form of precipitation?
a) Rain b) Fog
c) Snow d) Hail

18. Rainfall occurs when:
    a) The sun sets
    b) Air pressure increases
    c) Cloud droplets coalesce and become heavy
    d) Air becomes static
19. Precipitation in the form of ice pellets is called:
    a) Sleet b) Hail
    c) Snow d) Frost
20. When precipitation falls in crystalline form, it is called:
    a) Rain b) Fog
    c) Snow d) Drizzle
21. Which is not a major type of rainfall?
    a) Convectional b) Orographic
    c) Cyclonic d) Tectonic
22. Orographic rainfall occurs due to:
    a) Air rising over mountains b) Heating of land
    c) Rotation of the earth d) Air descending from hills
23. Convectional rainfall is common in:
    a) Polar areas b) Deserts
    c) Equatorial regions d) Mountain peaks
24. Cyclonic rainfall is associated with:
    a) Volcanoes b) Low-pressure systems
    c) High-pressure zones d) Earthquakes
25. The rain shadow area receives:
    a) Heavy rainfall b) No rainfall
    c) Moderate rainfall d) Less rainfall
26. Rainfall is measured using:
    a) Hygrometer b) Thermometer
    c) Barometer d) Rain gauge
27. The unit of rainfall is:
    a) °C b) mm
    c) kg d) bar

28. Snowfall is commonly measured using:
a) Radar b) Rain gauge
c) Snow gauge d) Wind vane

29. Which instrument helps in measuring cloud height?
a) Ceilometer b) Barometer
c) Wind vane d) Hygrometer

30. Doppler radar helps in detecting:
a) Soil moisture
b) Lightning
c) Precipitation and wind movement
d) Solar radiation

31. Maximum rainfall in India is received during:
a) Winter b) Summer monsoon
c) Post-monsoon d) Pre-monsoon

32. Western disturbances cause rainfall in:
a) Kerala b) Rajasthan
c) Punjab and North India d) Tamil Nadu

33. Precipitation in Tamil Nadu during Northeast monsoon is mainly due to:
a) Cyclonic storms b) Snowfall
c) Fog d) Radiation cooling

34. The average annual rainfall in India is around:
a) 100 mm b) 500 mm
c) 1000 mm d) 4000 mm

35. Which Indian region receives the highest rainfall?
a) Rajasthan b) Punjab
c) Meghalaya (Mawsynram) d) Gujarat

36. Precipitation formation requires:
a) Clear skies
b) Cooling, condensation, and uplift of air
c) Warm surface
d) Strong sunlight

37. Cloud seeding is done to:
a) Dissipate clouds b) Prevent rainfall
c) Enhance rainfall d) Reduce humidity

38. Supercooled water exists at:
a) Above 100°C
b) Below 0°C but in liquid form
c) Room temperature
d) -50°C

39. What is virga?
a) Rain that evaporates before reaching the ground
b) High-level frost
c) Drizzle in deserts
d) Dew during fog

40. Hail forms in:
a) Nimbostratus clouds b) Cirrostratus clouds
c) Cumulonimbus clouds d) Fog

41. What is drizzle?
a) Heavy rainfall b) Light, fine rain
c) Freezing rain d) None of the above

42. Cloud droplets typically have a diameter of:
a) 0.2 mm b) 0.02 mm
c) 2 mm d) 20 mm

43. Which factor influences the type of precipitation?
a) Wind speed b) Atmospheric pressure
c) Vertical temperature profile d) Cloud color

44. Acid rain contains:
a) HCl b) Sulfuric and nitric acid
c) Oxalic acid d) None of the above

45. Graupel refers to:
a) Small soft hail or snow pellets b) Ice needles
c) Dense fog d) Fine mist

46. Reduced precipitation over time causes:
a) Flood
b) Humidity
c) Drought
d) Cyclones

47. Global warming can alter:
a) Only temperature
b) Evaporation and precipitation patterns
c) Earth's rotation
d) Tectonic plates

48. Monsoon failure results in:
a) Excess rainfall
b) Flood
c) Agricultural drought
d) Hailstorms

49. Which gas plays a major role in cloud formation?
a) Oxygen
b) Nitrogen
c) Water vapor
d) Carbon monoxide

50. Condensation is a process that:
a) Warms the atmosphere
b) Releases latent heat
c) Absorbs solar radiation
d) Prevents rain

Answer Key

1	b	2	b	3	c	4	d	5	d	6	c	7	c
8	b	9	d	10	b	11	a	12	c	13	c	14	a
15	b	16	c	17	b	18	c	19	a	20	c	21	d
22	a	23	c	24	b	25	d	26	d	27	b	28	c
29	a	30	c	31	b	32	c	33	a	34	c	35	c
36	b	37	c	38	b	39	a	40	c	41	b	42	b
43	c	44	b	45	a	46	c	47	b	48	c	49	c
50	b												

9

General Concepts of Crop Climate

1. The term climatic requirement of a crop refers to:
   a) Soil pH required
   b) Temperature, rainfall, and humidity needed
   c) Fertilizer needed
   d) Pesticide needed
2. The key climatic factor determining crop growth is:
   a) Wind speed   b) Soil color
   c) Temperature   d) Tillage
3. A crop that completes its lifecycle within one growing season is called:
   a) Perennial   b) Annual
   c) Biennial   d) Deciduous
4. Which of the following crops requires the lowest temperature for germination?
   a) Wheat   b) Cotton
   c) Rice   d) Maize
5. The critical temperature range for photosynthesis in most crops is:
   a) 5–10°C   b) 15–35°C
   c) 40–50°C   d) >60°C
6. Rabi crops are mainly sown in:
   a) July-August   b) October-November
   c) April-May   d) January-February
7. Kharif crops are mainly dependent on:
   a) Winter rain   b) Irrigation
   c) Monsoon rainfall   d) Hailstorm

8. Wheat requires a temperature of:
   a) 35–40°C
   b) 10–15°C (germination), 21–26°C (growth)
   c) 5°C throughout
   d) >30°C
9. Paddy (rice) grows best under:
   a) Cool and dry weather
   b) Hot and humid weather
   c) Cold and dry climate
   d) Freezing temperatures
10. Maize requires:
   a) Warm weather and moderate rainfall
   b) Frosty winter
   c) Heavy continuous rainfall
   d) Low humidity
11. Ideal temperature for germination of rice is:
   a) 10°C
   b) 18–32°C
   c) 40°C
   d) <10°C
12. Ideal temperature for wheat grain filling is:
   a) >35°C
   b) 10°C
   c) 15–20°C
   d) 25–30°C
13. Pulses like chickpea (gram) prefer:
   a) Very humid climate
   b) Dry and cool climate
   c) Waterlogged fields
   d) Frost
14. Lentils are typically grown in:
   a) Hot summers
   b) Rabi season with mild cold
   c) Flooded conditions
   d) Desert zones
15. Which crop is highly sensitive to waterlogging?
   a) Rice
   b) Lentil
   c) Sugarcane
   d) Banana
16. Groundnut prefers:
   a) Cool wet conditions
   b) High altitude
   c) Well-distributed rainfall and warm temperatures
   d) Sandy deserts

17. Mustard is primarily grown in:
    a) Kharif season
    b) Rabi season
    c) Zaid season
    d) Monsoon end
18. Sunflower can be grown in:
    a) Only cold season
    b) All seasons
    c) Only during floods
    d) Snowfall zones
19. Cotton requires how many frost-free days for good yield?
    a) 50–60
    b) 75–100
    c) 150–200
    d) 365
20. Jute is best suited to:
    a) Cold desert
    b) Dry uplands
    c) Warm and humid climate
    d) Alpine zones
21. Banana grows best in:
    a) Cold hilly regions
    b) Tropical humid climate
    c) Dry desert
    d) Freezing plains
22. Apple requires a chilling period of:
    a) 0–50 hours
    b) 400–1,000 chilling hours
    c) No chilling required
    d) 2 hours/day
23. Grapes thrive in:
    a) Tropical wet zones
    b) Cool and humid regions
    c) Dry and warm regions
    d) Snow-covered lands
24. Tea grows well in:
    a) Hot dry plains
    b) Cool and humid climate with well-distributed rainfall
    c) Freezing zones
    d) Saline areas
25. Coffee is best suited to:
    a) Temperate zones
    b) Dry grasslands
    c) Tropical highlands with shade and moderate rainfall
    d) Saline coastal belts

26. Sugarcane grows best in:
    a) Desert climate
    b) Cold highlands
    c) Tropical and sub-tropical with long frost-free period
    d) Wetlands

27. Potato requires a temperature range of:
    a) 10–25°C b) >35°C
    c) 0–10°C d) Constant rainfall

28. Tomato grows well in:
    a) Below 5°C b) 20–27°C
    c) >40°C d) Wetland

29. Onion prefers which climate for bulb formation?
    a) Cloudy and rainy b) Cold desert
    c) Dry and moderately warm d) Frost

30. Cauliflower is grown successfully in:
    a) Tropical lowlands b) High temperatures
    c) Cool and dry season d) Floods

31. Saffron needs which kind of climate?
    a) Humid and hot b) Cold and dry
    c) Tropical wet d) Marshy

32. Rubber plantations thrive in:
    a) Cold dry climate
    b) Equatorial hot and moist climate
    c) Sandy desert
    d) Alpine region

33. Black pepper requires:
    a) Cool, dry weather b) Moist, warm tropical forests
    c) Arid lands d) Saline soil

34. Cocoa is grown in:
    a) Dry plains
    b) High rainfall and shade regions
    c) Snowfields
    d) Cool desert

35. Arecanut grows well in:
   a) Temperate regions
   b) Cold dry lands
   c) Moist tropical areas with filtered sunlight
   d) Dry riverbeds
36. Rice is dominantly grown in:
   a) Rajasthan
   b) Kerala and West Bengal
   c) Jammu & Kashmir
   d) Punjab only
37. Wheat grows best in:
   a) Northeast India
   b) Central India
   c) Northern plains (Punjab, Haryana, UP)
   d) Coastal areas
38. Bajra (Pearl millet) is suited for:
   a) Humid climate
   b) Cold hills
   c) Dry semi-arid regions like Rajasthan
   d) Waterlogged fields
39. Which state is ideal for tea cultivation?
   a) Gujarat
   b) Assam
   c) Rajasthan
   d) Bihar
40. Grapes are predominantly grown in:
   a) Kerala
   b) Maharashtra and Karnataka
   c) Punjab
   d) Assam
41. Frost damages:
   a) Rice
   b) Cotton
   c) Wheat during germination
   d) Banana
42. Hailstorms are most damaging to:
   a) Sugarcane
   b) Maize
   c) Fruit crops at flowering stage
   d) Pulses

43. Delayed monsoon affects:
a) Rabi crops
b) Kharif sowing
c) Irrigated areas
d) None

44. Flooding affects which crop most adversely?
a) Jute
b) Rice
c) Groundnut
d) Banana

45. Drought during flowering stage causes:
a) Increased yield
b) No effect
c) Yield reduction and grain sterility
d) Better flowering

46. Ideal temperature for sugarcane growth:
a) 15–20°C
b) 32–38°C
c) 5–10°C
d) 45–50°C

47. Ideal climate for pearl millet:
a) Cool and wet
b) Hot and dry
c) Cold with snow
d) Waterlogged

48. Barley is best suited for:
a) Cold arid zones
b) Tropical zones
c) Desert zones
d) Only lowlands

49. Sorghum (Jowar) tolerates:
a) Frost
b) Heavy rain
c) Drought and heat
d) Waterlogging

50. Castor is grown in:
a) Frost-prone areas
b) Tropical and sub-tropical areas
c) Only irrigated lands
d) Cold deserts

Answer Key

1	b	2	c	3	b	4	a	5	b	6	b	7	c
8	b	9	b	10	a	11	b	12	c	13	b	14	b
15	b	16	c	17	b	18	b	19	c	20	c	21	b
22	b	23	c	24	b	25	c	26	c	27	c	28	b
29	b	30	c	31	b	32	b	33	b	34	b	35	c
36	b	37	c	38	c	39	b	40	b	41	d	42	c
43	b	44	c	45	c	46	b	47	b	48	a	49	c
50	b												

10

Climate Change

1. What is the main cause of climate change?
   a) Volcanoes
   b) Plate tectonics
   c) Greenhouse gas emissions
   d) Ocean currents
2. Which gas is primarily responsible for global warming?
   a) Nitrogen
   b) Oxygen
   c) Carbon dioxide (CO_2)
   d) Hydrogen
3. The greenhouse effect refers to:
   a) Cooling of the Earth
   b) Trapping of heat by gases in the atmosphere
   c) Plant growth in greenhouses
   d) Increased rainfall
4. Which of the following is not a greenhouse gas?
   a) Methane
   b) Carbon dioxide
   c) Oxygen
   d) Nitrous oxide
5. The IPCC stands for:
   a) International Panel for Climate Control
   b) Intergovernmental Panel on Climate Change
   c) Indian Panel for Climate Change
   d) International Program for Climate Control
6. Which greenhouse gas has the highest global warming potential (GWP)?
   a) CO_2
   b) CH_4
   c) N_2O
   d) CFCs
7. The largest contributor to greenhouse gas emissions globally is:
   a) Agriculture
   b) Industrial processes
   c) Energy sector (fossil fuels)
   d) Transportation

8. Which human activity emits the most carbon dioxide?
   a) Deforestation b) Burning fossil fuels
   c) Agriculture d) Land use change
9. Methane emissions are mainly from:
   a) Automobiles b) Wetlands and livestock
   c) Volcanoes d) Jet fuel
10. Nitrous oxide emissions are mostly from:
   a) Burning wood b) Fertilizer use in agriculture
   c) Air conditioners d) Plastic waste
11. Which of the following is clear evidence of climate change?
   a) Seasonal rainfall b) Sea level rise
   c) Static glacier size d) Constant temperatures
12. Global warming has caused glaciers to:
   a) Expand b) Melt and retreat
   c) Remain unchanged d) Solidify
13. Which satellite mission monitors climate-related data?
   a) INSAT b) Aqua/Terra (NASA)
   c) IRNSS d) Chandrayaan
14. Which decade was the warmest on record (as of 2020)?
   a) 1970s b) 1980s
   c) 2000s d) 2010s
15. Which region is most affected by melting ice due to climate change?
   a) Amazon b) Himalayas
   c) Antarctica and Arctic d) Sahara
16. Which sector is highly vulnerable to climate change in India?
   a) IT b) Education
   c) Agriculture d) Mining
17. Climate change leads to:
   a) Decrease in sea levels b) More extreme weather events
   c) Fewer droughts d) Lower global temperatures

18. Ocean acidification is caused by:
   a) Increased pH
   b) Decreased CO_2
   c) Increased CO_2 absorption by oceans
   d) Methane emissions
19. Which crop is most sensitive to rising night temperatures?
   a) Cotton b) Rice
   c) Maize d) Sugarcane
20. Climate change can increase pest and disease incidence because:
   a) Colder nights b) Disrupted life cycles
   c) Warmer and humid conditions d) Less rainfall
21. The Paris Agreement was signed in:
   a) 1992 b) 1997
   c) 2015 d) 2021
22. The main goal of the Paris Agreement is to limit global temperature rise below:
   a) 3°C b) 2°C
   c) 5°C d) 4°C
23. The Kyoto Protocol deals with:
   a) Air pollution b) Greenhouse gas reduction
   c) Noise pollution d) Recycling
24. COP in climate negotiations stands for:
   a) Council of Parliament b) Conference of the Parties
   c) Coalition of Parties d) Climate Operational Plan
25. India's commitment under Paris Agreement is called:
   a) NGT
   b) SAP
   c) NDC (Nationally Determined Contribution)
   d) SDG
26. NAPCC stands for:
   a) National Action Plan on Climate Change
   b) National Agriculture Policy on Climate Change
   c) New Agricultural Plan for Climate Change
   d) None

27. How many missions are under NAPCC?
    a) 4 b) 6
    c) 8 d) 10
28. Which is not a mission under NAPCC?
    a) National Solar Mission
    b) National Mission on Sustainable Agriculture
    c) National Mission on Space Research
    d) National Water Mission
29. The Indian state with the first climate change department is:
    a) Rajasthan b) Gujarat
    c) Kerala d) Punjab
30. "State Action Plans on Climate Change" (SAPCCs) are meant to:
    a) Replace NAPCC
    b) Decentralize climate adaptation
    c) Create central policy
    d) Avoid Paris commitments
31. Climate mitigation means:
    a) Adjusting to effects b) Reducing greenhouse gases
    c) Raising temperatures d) Monitoring rainfall
32. Climate adaptation involves:
    a) Cutting trees
    b) Adjusting to changing climate
    c) Increasing carbon emissions
    d) Banning agriculture
33. Which is an example of mitigation?
    a) Growing drought-resistant crops b) Switching to solar energy
    c) Building flood shelters d) Crop insurance
34. Afforestation helps in:
    a) Emitting CO_2 b) Increasing land erosion
    c) Absorbing atmospheric CO_2 d) Melting glaciers
35. Use of energy-efficient appliances is a:
    a) Cause of warming b) Adaptation strategy
    c) Mitigation strategy d) None

36. Climate models are used to:
   a) Predict stock market trends
   b) Forecast future climate scenarios
   c) Study pollution
   d) None
37. RCPs in climate modeling refer to:
   a) Radio Controlled Points
   b) Representative Concentration Pathways
   c) Regional Climate Protocols
   d) Rainfall Classification Points
38. RCP 8.5 represents:
   a) No change scenario b) Low emission scenario
   c) High emission scenario d) Cooling trend
39. Which organization develops global climate projections?
   a) FAO b) IPCC
   c) IMF d) UNESCO
40. India's climate projections are handled by:
   a) IITs only b) IMD and MoEFCC
   c) NITI Aayog d) CSIR alone
41. Climate change affects crop yields through:
   a) Reduced sunlight
   b) Heat stress and rainfall variability
   c) Machine use
   d) Irrigation
42. Which technique helps adapt to changing climate in agriculture?
   a) Monoculture b) High-input farming
   c) Climate-smart agriculture d) Slash and burn
43. Carbon farming aims to:
   a) Emit carbon b) Burn carbon
   c) Sequester carbon in soil d) Increase fertilizers
44. Heat waves most affect which crop stage?
   a) Germination b) Vegetative
   c) Flowering and grain filling d) Dormant

45. Climate-resilient agriculture promotes:
   a) High chemical use
   b) Dependence on rainfall
   c) Reduced vulnerability to weather extremes
   d) Plantation forestry

46. SDG Goal 13 deals with:
   a) Gender equality b) Industry
   c) Climate action d) Education

47. Which year is targeted for net zero emissions by India?
   a) 2025 b) 2030
   c) 2047 d) 2070

48. Climate literacy aims at:
   a) Teaching geography
   b) Raising awareness of climate issues
   c) Promoting pollution
   d) Reducing CO_2 production

49. Climate change awareness is important for:
   a) Policy only b) Scientists only
   c) All citizens d) Only farmers

50. Which method is best for educating farmers about climate change?
   a) Social media
   b) SMS alerts and agro-advisories
   c) Satellite TV
   d) Newspapers

Answer Key

1	c	2	c	3	b	4	c	5	b	6	d	7	c
8	b	9	b	10	b	11	b	12	b	13	b	14	d
15	c	16	c	17	b	18	c	19	b	20	c	21	c
22	b	23	b	24	b	25	c	26	a	27	c	28	c
29	b	30	b	31	b	32	b	33	b	34	c	35	c
36	b	37	b	38	c	39	b	40	b	41	b	42	c
43	c	44	c	45	c	46	c	47	d	48	b	49	c
50	b												

11

Agroecological Classification

1. Agroecological classification is primarily based on:
   a) Soil color
   b) Weather only
   c) Integration of climate, soil, and physiography
   d) Irrigation system
2. The term "agroecological zone" refers to:
   a) Soil erosion area
   b) A climatic belt only
   c) Homogeneous land units with similar agroclimatic and soil characteristics
   d) Irrigated zones only
3. Which organization introduced the concept of Agro-Ecological Zones (AEZs) globally?
   a) FAO b) ICAR
   c) NASA d) IMD
4. The primary determinant for classifying agroecological regions is:
   a) Human population b) Temperature alone
   c) Length of growing period d) River proximity
5. Which of the following is not an agroecological factor?
   a) Soil b) Rainfall
   c) Social customs d) Temperature
6. Who classified India into 20 agroecological regions?
   a) Indian Meteorological Department
   b) Planning Commission
   c) National Bureau of Soil Survey and Land Use Planning (NBSS&LUP)
   d) ICAR-CSSRI

7. How many Agro-Ecological Regions (AERs) are identified in India by NBSS&LUP?
   a) 10 b) 15
   c) 20 d) 25
8. Agroecological regions in India are classified based on:
   a) Cropping patterns
   b) Soil-climate-physiography and length of growing period
   c) Market access
   d) Irrigation type
9. Agroecological sub-regions (AESRs) in India are:
   a) 50 b) 60
   c) 120 d) 200
10. Length of growing period (LGP) in agroecological classification refers to:
    a) Time required for seed germination
    b) Number of crop days in a year
    c) Period suitable for crop growth with sufficient moisture
    d) Rainy days
11. Which parameter is not used in agroecological zoning?
    a) Physiography b) Soil taxonomy
    c) Political boundaries d) Climatic conditions
12. In AEZ, climate includes:
    a) Only wind
    b) Only temperature
    c) Temperature, rainfall, humidity
    d) Soil pH
13. The LGP < 90 days represents which agroecological condition?
    a) Humid b) Semi-humid
    c) Arid d) Perhumid
14. The temperature regime for tropical AEZs is:
    a) < 5°C b) > 5°C throughout the year
    c) Always below freezing d) Less than 10°C

15. Physiography refers to:
    a) Vegetation
    b) Physical features like hills, plains, and plateaus
    c) Fertilizers used
    d) Crop rotation
16. Western Himalayan region is characterized by:
    a) Arid and dry
    b) High elevation and cool temperature
    c) Coastal humid
    d) Desert soil
17. The hot arid region of India is located in:
    a) Assam b) Tamil Nadu
    c) Rajasthan d) Kerala
18. The Indo-Gangetic Plains fall under:
    a) Cold desert
    b) Hot-humid
    c) Semi-arid to sub-humid with alluvial soils
    d) Coastal saline
19. The Deccan Plateau region is mainly composed of:
    a) Alluvial soil b) Laterite soil
    c) Black cotton soil (Regur) d) Red sandy soil
20. The coastal regions are characterized by:
    a) Extreme cold b) High rainfall and humidity
    c) Desertification d) Less biodiversity
21. The AEZ maps help in:
    a) Road development
    b) Weather prediction
    c) Planning land use and agricultural practices
    d) Designing buildings
22. The map scale generally used for agroecological classification is:
    a) 1:10 b) 1:1000
    c) 1:1,000,000 d) 1:50,000

23. Which Indian region has the longest growing period?
   a) Rajasthan b) Western Ghats
   c) Ladakh d) Bundelkhand
24. The growing period of more than 270 days is classified as:
   a) Arid b) Semi-arid
   c) Humid to perhumid d) Sub-humid
25. The AEZ concept is useful in promoting:
   a) Single-crop systems
   b) Blanket fertilizer use
   c) Location-specific research and technology transfer
   d) Political reforms
26. Rice is best suited to agroecological regions with:
   a) High rainfall and humid conditions
   b) Cold deserts
   c) Dry arid conditions
   d) Less than 500 mm rainfall
27. Wheat is grown in which type of agroecological region?
   a) Arid zone
   b) Humid tropical
   c) Sub-humid with winter rainfall
   d) Perhumid
28. Millets are well adapted to:
   a) Waterlogged regions b) Arid and semi-arid zones
   c) Snowy hills d) Humid coastal belts
29. Tea is best suited for:
   a) Arid Rajasthan
   b) Gangetic plains
   c) Hilly humid zones like Assam and Nilgiris
   d) Black soil plateau
30. Pulses are widely grown in:
   a) Water-rich belts b) Low-rainfall regions
   c) Coastal saline lands d) Forest belts

31. Agroecological zoning helps in:
   a) Uniform cropping pattern
   b) Planning sustainable agriculture
   c) Urban development
   d) Taxation
32. Which is a direct benefit of agroecological classification?
   a) Higher food prices
   b) Improved marketing
   c) Better resource planning
   d) Migration control
33. AEZs support precision farming by:
   a) Random seed distribution
   b) Uniform input use
   c) Tailored crop and input planning
   d) Ignoring soil type
34. Agroecological classification aids in identifying:
   a) State boundaries
   b) Irrigation water sources
   c) Suitable crop varieties
   d) Reservoir capacity
35. Agroecological classification improves:
   a) Bureaucracy
   b) Natural farming practices based on regional suitability
   c) Industrial output
   d) Village revenue
36. A limitation of agroecological classification is:
   a) Too simple
   b) Based only on rainfall
   c) Generalized data, not at micro-level
   d) Not used in farming
37. Agroecological zones do not consider:
   a) Soil texture
   b) Crop water requirements
   c) Political will
   d) Growing period
38. Micro agroecological zoning is:
   a) Not feasible
   b) Useful for localized farming recommendations
   c) A waste of time
   d) Unrelated to climate

39. Use of remote sensing in AEZ mapping helps in:
    a) Political reforms
    b) Accurate mapping of terrain and soil
    c) Farmer behavior
    d) Livestock census
40. AEZ classification supports:
    a) Mechanization only
    b) Ecological intensification
    c) Urban sprawl
    d) Monocropping
41. Agroecological classification supports climate-smart agriculture by:
    a) Promoting fixed practices
    b) Identifying vulnerable regions
    c) Ignoring variability
    d) Fixing CO_2 levels
42. AEZs are essential for:
    a) Uniform policy
    b) Food security planning
    c) Tax collection
    d) Monsoon prediction
43. Agroecology is based on the principle of:
    a) External input maximization
    b) Resource conservation and sustainability
    c) Deforestation
    d) Minimum yield
44. What makes agroecological classification dynamic?
    a) Population shift
    b) Climate variability and land use change
    c) Political changes
    d) Export demand
45. India's agroecological classification is periodically updated based on:
    a) Market demands
    b) Changing monsoon patterns and soil surveys
    c) Political agendas
    d) Fertilizer imports

46. AEZ integrates:
   a) Soil, water, climate, and cropping systems
   b) Roads and railways
   c) Politics and economics
   d) Fisheries and mining
47. Agroecological classification is important for:
   a) Industrial planning
   b) Integrated watershed development
   c) Ocean shipping
   d) Language policy
48. AEZ maps are useful for:
   a) Tourists
   b) Agricultural researchers and planners
   c) Stock market analysts
   d) Textile engineers
49. AEZ classification helps manage:
   a) Renewable energy   b) Agro-biodiversity
   c) Public transport   d) Internet access
50. Future classification systems will likely include:
   a) Social media data
   b) Climate change projections and AI tools
   c) Political boundaries
   d) Commodity prices

Answer Key

1	c	2	c	3	a	4	c	5	c	6	c	7	c
8	b	9	c	10	c	11	c	12	c	13	c	14	b
15	b	16	b	17	c	18	c	19	c	20	b	21	c
22	c	23	b	24	c	25	c	26	a	27	c	28	b
29	c	30	b	31	b	32	c	33	c	34	b	35	c
36	c	37	c	38	b	39	b	40	b	41	b	42	b
43	b	44	b	45	b	46	a	47	b	48	b	49	b
50	b												

1. What is the primary purpose of artificial rainmaking?

a) To prevent rain b) To increase rainfall

c) To measure cloud height d) To study cloud color

2. Which of the following chemicals is most commonly used for cloud seeding?

12

Monsoon & Its Mechanism

1. What is the primary purpose of artificial rainmaking?
   a) To prevent rain
   b) To increase rainfall
   c) To measure cloud height
   d) To study cloud colors
2. Which of the following chemicals is most commonly used for cloud seeding?
   a) Sodium chloride
   b) Silver iodide
   c) Calcium carbonate
   d) Potassium nitrate
3. Artificial rainmaking is also known as:
   a) Cloud bursting
   b) Cloud harvesting
   c) Cloud seeding
   d) Rain suppression
4. Which agency first successfully carried out cloud seeding in India?
   a) ISRO
   b) IMD
   c) IITM, Pune
   d) DRDO
5. Which aircraft is commonly used for cloud seeding operations in India?
   a) Sukhoi Su-30
   b) Dornier Do-228
   c) Boeing 747
   d) Mirage 2000
6. Which of the following is NOT a method of cloud seeding?
   a) Ground-based generators
   b) Aircraft dispersion
   c) Balloon release
   d) Satellite laser beams
7. In artificial rainmaking, hygroscopic substances such as ___ are used for warm cloud seeding.
   a) Silver iodide
   b) Dry ice
   c) Sodium chloride
   d) Calcium sulfate
8. Which one is a limitation of artificial rainmaking?
   a) Increases cloud cover
   b) Only works in winter
   c) Depends on cloud availability
   d) Can cause snowfall

9. What is the role of seeding agents in cloud seeding?
   a) To disperse the clouds b) To suppress condensation
   c) To initiate nucleation d) To evaporate water

10. Which state in India has undertaken extensive cloud seeding programs?
    a) Punjab b) Maharashtra
    c) Kerala d) Odisha

11. Cold cloud seeding is most effective in clouds with temperatures below:
    a) 0°C b) 10°C
    c) 4°C d) -5°C

12. Which seeding agent is typically used in cold cloud seeding?
    a) Silver iodide b) Sodium chloride
    c) Ammonium nitrate d) Sulfur dioxide

13. The Bergeron process is associated with:
    a) Warm cloud seeding b) Cold cloud formation
    c) Cloud dissipation d) Artificial lightning

14. Warm cloud seeding primarily aims at enhancing:
    a) Ice crystal formation b) Snowfall
    c) Coalescence of water droplets d) Freezing of raindrops

15. Which of the following best describes warm cloud seeding?
    a) Uses chemicals to cool the clouds
    b) Involves dry ice and silver iodide
    c) Promotes growth of raindrops in liquid water clouds
    d) Only effective during the winter

16. Cold cloud seeding leads to rainfall by:
    a) Ice crystal growth
    b) Coalescence of water drops
    c) Evaporation of small drops
    d) Condensation on dust particles

17. Which is NOT a characteristic of cold clouds?
    a) Contain supercooled water b) Found above freezing level
    c) Contain only water vapor d) May include ice crystals

18. Dry ice used in cloud seeding works by:
   a) Heating the cloud
   b) Cooling the cloud to promote freezing
   c) Dissolving cloud particles
   d) Absorbing water vapor
19. Cold cloud seeding requires clouds to be at what altitude typically?
   a) Below 1000 m   b) 2000–3000 m
   c) Above 5000 m   d) Near sea level
20. Silver iodide works effectively because it has a crystal structure similar to:
   a) Water vapor   b) Ice
   c) Salt   d) Oxygen
21. Indian monsoon is primarily caused due to:
   a) Ocean currents
   b) Rotation of Earth
   c) Differential heating of land and sea
   d) Solar flares
22. The monsoon in India generally arrives by:
   a) February   b) May
   c) June   d) August
23. Which ocean plays a major role in the Indian monsoon?
   a) Atlantic Ocean   b) Pacific Ocean
   c) Arctic Ocean   d) Indian Ocean
24. The ITCZ (Inter-Tropical Convergence Zone) shifts northward during:
   a) Summer   b) Winter
   c) Monsoon withdrawal   d) Spring
25. Which branch of monsoon strikes Kerala coast first?
   a) Bay of Bengal   b) Arabian Sea
   c) Himalayan   d) Tibetan
26. The El Niño phenomenon generally causes:
   a) Enhanced Indian monsoon
   b) Suppressed Indian monsoon
   c) No impact
   d) Snowfall in monsoon

27. Which of the following is responsible for breaking monsoon in India?
    a) Western disturbances
    b) Madden-Julian Oscillation
    c) Cold fronts
    d) Sea breeze
28. Retreating monsoon in India occurs in:
    a) June–July
    b) August–September
    c) October–November
    d) December–January
29. Monsoon trough is a:
    a) High-pressure zone
    b) Low-pressure area
    c) Jet stream
    d) Cyclonic eye
30. Monsoon onset in India is declared by:
    a) Indian Army
    b) Indian Meteorological Department
    c) Ministry of Agriculture
    d) World Bank
31. What percentage of Indian agriculture depends on monsoon rains?
    a) 20%
    b) 40%
    c) 60%
    d) 75%
32. Deficient monsoon in India leads to:
    a) Improved yields
    b) Floods
    c) Droughts
    d) Salinity
33. Which crop is most vulnerable to monsoon failure?
    a) Wheat
    b) Maize
    c) Rice
    d) Barley
34. Kharif crops in India are sown in:
    a) October
    b) January
    c) June-July
    d) March
35. Which of the following is a Kharif crop dependent on monsoon?
    a) Mustard
    b) Wheat
    c) Groundnut
    d) Gram
36. Monsoon variability impacts:
    a) Crop selection
    b) Sowing time
    c) Yield
    d) All of the above

37. Which irrigation method becomes crucial in poor monsoon years?
a) Flood irrigation
b) Drip irrigation
c) Overhead irrigation
d) Tank irrigation

38. Excessive monsoon rains can cause:
a) Soil erosion
b) Increased yields
c) Frost
d) Cloud seeding

39. Which agro-meteorological service is used for monsoon monitoring?
a) Agro-forestry mapping
b) FASAL
c) Gramin Krishi Mausam Sewa (GKMS)
d) APEDA

40. Rainfed farming in India is practiced mostly during:
a) Rabi season
b) Kharif season
c) Zaid season
d) Winter

41. In India, cloud seeding is permitted under which environmental act?
a) Water Act 1974
b) Environmental Protection Act 1986
c) There is no specific law
d) Air Act 1981

42. Which is the best time for cloud seeding in India?
a) Before monsoon
b) Peak monsoon
c) Post monsoon
d) Winter

43. Which parameter is crucial to assess cloud seeding potential?
a) Wind speed
b) Cloud temperature and moisture
c) Soil pH
d) Atmospheric pressure

44. Monsoon prediction is currently done using:
a) Animal behavior
b) Satellite and climate models
c) Folk sayings
d) Sea wave patterns

45. What is the role of aerosols in cloud formation?
 a) Prevent rain
 b) Serve as cloud condensation nuclei
 c) Evaporate raindrops
 d) Reflect sunlight

46. Which satellite is used for Indian monsoon monitoring?
 a) INSAT-3D b) Kalpana-1
 c) GSAT-6 d) Aryabhata

47. Which Indian institution is at the forefront of cloud microphysics research?
 a) IIT Delhi b) IARI
 c) IISc Bangalore d) IITM Pune

48. Which is more uncertain—cold or warm cloud seeding?
 a) Cold b) Warm
 c) Both are equally certain d) Neither

49. A successful monsoon improves which of the following?
 a) Food security b) Farm employment
 c) GDP growth d) All of the above

50. Which is the most studied weather modification method in India?
 a) Lightning redirection b) Hailstorm suppression
 c) Cloud seeding d) Dew harvesting

Answer Key

1	b	2	b	3	c	4	c	5	b	6	d	7	c
8	c	9	c	10	b	11	a	12	a	13	b	14	c
15	c	16	a	17	c	18	b	19	c	20	b	21	c
22	c	23	d	24	a	25	b	26	b	27	b	28	c
29	b	30	b	31	d	32	c	33	c	34	c	35	c
36	d	37	b	38	a	39	c	40	b	41	c	42	a
43	b	44	b	45	b	46	a	47	d	48	b	49	d
50	c												

13

Climatic Normals for Crops and Livestock

1. Climatic normals refer to:
   a) Average crop yield
   b) Long-term average of meteorological parameters
   c) Daily weather readings
   d) Cloud patterns
2. Climatic normals are usually calculated over a period of:
   a) 5 years b) 10 years
   c) 30 years d) 50 years
3. Agroclimatic classification is primarily based on:
   a) Latitude and longitude b) Soil type
   c) Rainfall and temperature d) Crop rotation
4. Optimum temperature for C3 crop photosynthesis is:
   a) 25–30°C b) 10–15°C
   c) 40–45°C d) 5–10°C
5. C4 plants like maize grow best in temperatures of:
   a) 10–20°C b) 25–35°C
   c) 35–45°C d) 15–25°C
6. Wheat requires optimal temperature of:
   a) 35–40°C b) 20–25°C
   c) 10–15°C d) 5–10°C
7. Wheat is classified as a:
   a) Tropical crop b) Temperate crop
   c) Arid crop d) Aquatic crop

8. Paddy (rice) requires average rainfall of:
   a) 100–150 mm b) 500–700 mm
   c) 1000–1500 mm d) Over 3000 mm
9. The critical temperature range for rice flowering is:
   a) 35–40°C b) 25–30°C
   c) 15–20°C d) 10–15°C
10. Maize grows best at temperatures of:
   a) 18–22°C b) 30–35°C
   c) 12–18°C d) 40–45°C
11. Chickpea is a:
   a) Warm-season crop b) Cold-season crop
   c) Monsoon crop d) Tropical crop
12. Chickpea grows well at temperatures of:
   a) 10–15°C b) 20–30°C
   c) 30–40°C d) Above 40°C
13. Groundnut requires how much rainfall?
   a) 200–300 mm b) 500–1000 mm
   c) 1000–1500 mm d) >1500 mm
14. Optimum temperature range for sugarcane is:
   a) 10–15°C b) 18–22°C
   c) 26–32°C d) 40–45°C
15. Cotton requires how many days of frost-free weather?
   a) 50 b) 100
   c) 180–200 d) 300
16. Tomato is sensitive to:
   a) High humidity b) Temperature below 10°C
   c) Low sunlight d) Strong winds
17. Best temperature for tomato fruit setting is:
   a) 25–28°C b) 10–12°C
   c) 35–40°C d) >40°C
18. Potato grows well in which temperature range?
   a) 10–15°C b) 25–30°C
   c) 30–35°C d) >40°C

19. Mango is a:
   a) Temperate fruit b) Tropical fruit
   c) Alpine fruit d) Desert fruit
20. Citrus fruits require rainfall of:
   a) <200 mm b) 300–400 mm
   c) 750–1000 mm d) >2000 mm
21. Comfort zone temperature for dairy cattle is:
   a) 5–10°C b) 15–27°C
   c) 30–40°C d) >40°C
22. Heat stress in dairy cattle begins above:
   a) 20°C b) 25°C
   c) 30°C d) 15°C
23. Relative humidity above __% increases livestock stress:
   a) 40% b) 60%
   c) 70% d) 90%
24. Poultry birds are most comfortable at:
   a) 20–25°C b) 30–40°C
   c) 10–15°C d) >45°C
25. The temperature-humidity index (THI) is used to assess:
   a) Soil fertility b) Air quality
   c) Animal heat stress d) Milk quality
26. Goats are well adapted to:
   a) Cold and humid regions b) Arid and semi-arid climates
   c) High rainfall areas d) Flood-prone zones
27. Sheep require an annual rainfall of about:
   a) 100–200 mm b) 200–400 mm
   c) 800–1000 mm d) >1500 mm
28. Broilers are best reared at temperatures of:
   a) 10–20°C b) 21–30°C
   c) >35°C d) <10°C
29. Buffaloes are more sensitive to:
   a) Cold stress b) Heat stress
   c) Wind d) Rain

30. High humidity leads to:
a) Decreased disease b) Increased feed conversion
c) Reduced animal productivity d) Enhanced immunity

31. India is divided into how many agroclimatic zones (Planning Commission)?
a) 10 b) 15
c) 20 d) 15

32. In India, dryland agriculture is mainly practiced in:
a) Coastal zones b) Humid tropics
c) Semi-arid regions d) Wetlands

33. In arid zones, best suited crops are:
a) Rice and maize b) Wheat and pulses
c) Millets and oilseeds d) Sugarcane and banana

34. Eastern Himalayan region is suitable for:
a) Wheat b) Tea
c) Cotton d) Sorghum

35. Rainfed rice is majorly grown in:
a) Western Rajasthan b) Peninsular India
c) Punjab d) Haryana

36. Wheat cannot tolerate temperatures above:
a) 20°C b) 30°C
c) 10°C d) 5°C

37. Cold injury in paddy seedlings happens below:
a) 10°C b) 20°C
c) 25°C d) 30°C

38. Rainfed agriculture is possible with rainfall of:
a) <200 mm b) 500–750 mm
c) >2000 mm d) <100 mm

39. Sugarcane is highly sensitive to:
a) Frost b) Heat
c) Light d) Salt

40. Optimum rainfall for groundnut is:
   a) 200 mm   b) 400 mm
   c) 500–1000 mm   d) 1500 mm

41. Drought stress in crops leads to:
   a) Increased leaf area
   b) Reduced stomatal conductance
   c) Higher photosynthesis
   d) Early flowering always

42. Heat stress during flowering in cereals causes:
   a) Enhanced grain filling   b) Sterility and poor grain set
   c) Increased yield   d) No effect

43. Frost damage mostly affects:
   a) Root crops
   b) Leafy vegetables and flowers
   c) Mature grains
   d) Livestock only

44. Excessive rainfall causes:
   a) Waterlogging and root rot   b) Higher yields
   c) Increased nitrogen fixation   d) Faster maturity

45. Salinity stress affects:
   a) Photosynthesis and water uptake   b) Only root growth
   c) Fertilizer absorption only   d) Pest resistance

46. Zebu cattle are more adapted to:
   a) Cold climates   b) Hot and humid climates
   c) Mountain regions   d) Arctic regions

47. Shade provision reduces:
   a) Feed intake   b) Heat stress in animals
   c) Milk production   d) Disease resistance

48. Water requirement in livestock increases during:
   a) Winter   b) Summer
   c) Monsoon   d) Autumn

49. Evaporative cooling in animals is primarily through:
    a) Sweating and panting
    b) Drinking water
    c) Increasing feed
    d) Huddling

50. Heat stress can cause:
    a) Increased fertility
    b) Reduced milk yield and growth rate
    c) Decreased respiration
    d) Improved immunity

Answer Key

1	b	2	c	3	c	4	a	5	b	6	b	7	b
8	c	9	b	10	b	11	b	12	a	13	b	14	b
15	b	16	b	17	a	18	a	19	b	20	c	21	b
22	c	23	c	24	a	25	c	26	b	27	b	28	b
29	b	30	c	31	d	32	c	33	c	34	b	35	b
36	b	37	a	38	b	39	a	40	c	41	b	42	b
43	b	44	a	45	a	46	b	47	b	48	b	49	a
50	b												

14

Ancient Wisdom of Weather Forecasting

1. Which of the following is a traditional weather forecasting indicator in rural India?
   a) Rainbow position b) Moon halo
   c) Sunset color d) All of the above
2. Chirping of crickets during the evening is traditionally associated with:
   a) Upcoming cold weather b) Imminent rainfall
   c) Drought conditions d) High wind speeds
3. A red sky during sunset traditionally indicates:
   a) Imminent storm b) Rain the next day
   c) Fair weather d) Heavy dew
4. The halo around the moon is seen as a sign of:
   a) No change in weather b) Drought
   c) Upcoming rainfall d) Extreme heat
5. What do traditional farmers infer when ants build mounds with steep sides?
   a) The monsoon will be weak b) Heavy rain is expected
   c) Frost is coming d) No rainfall
6. In ancient Indian traditions, the croaking of frogs in large numbers often indicated:
   a) Extreme heat b) Arrival of rains
   c) Pest infestation d) Cold front
7. The flowering of the Cassia fistula tree (Amaltas) is traditionally considered a sign of:
   a) Spring b) Pre-monsoon onset
   c) Winter d) Monsoon withdrawal

8. Which constellation's position was traditionally observed by Indian farmers to time sowing?
   a) Orion b) Pleiades (Krittika)
   c) Ursa Major d) Draco
9. Dark, low-flying swallows are traditionally believed to forecast:
   a) Fair weather b) Storms
   c) Imminent rain d) Snowfall
10. Clouds that appear layered and gray in folklore often signal:
   a) Stable, dry weather b) Imminent rainfall
   c) Heat wave d) Cold weather
11. In Indian tradition, thunder in the month of Vaisakha is taken as:
   a) A blessing for crops
   b) Warning of floods
   c) A sign of drought
   d) Indicator of good rainfall in Ashadha
12. High flying dragonflies in folklore indicate:
   a) Approaching dry spell b) Clear skies
   c) Rain is unlikely d) Imminent rain
13. Cracked soil surface and dryness in May are interpreted by traditional farmers as:
   a) Upcoming good rains b) Delayed monsoon
   c) Poor crop year d) More irrigation needed
14. Heavy flowering of mango trees in ancient beliefs indicates:
   a) Heavy monsoon b) Drought year
   c) Less rainfall d) Late sowing
15. The traditional calendar used for weather predictions in India is called:
   a) Gregorian b) Hijri
   c) Panchang d) Julian
16. In ancient wisdom, continuous chirping of sparrows during the day suggests:
   a) Windstorm b) Prolonged drought
   c) Change in temperature d) Approaching rainfall

17. A sudden drop in evening temperature is traditionally interpreted as:
    a) Arrival of rain
    b) Frost risk
    c) Cloud formation
    d) Dry weather
18. According to folk knowledge, a heavy dew in the early morning indicates:
    a) High humidity
    b) No rain soon
    c) Imminent rain
    d) Cyclonic disturbance
19. Which traditional community is well known for cloud reading in India?
    a) Bhils
    b) Gonds
    c) Kalbelias
    d) Todas
20. The color of sunrise being yellowish orange is traditionally seen as a sign of:
    a) Rainy day
    b) Hazy conditions
    c) Good harvest
    d) Stable weather
21. Traditional knowledge systems are important because they are:
    a) Mythological
    b) Empirically based and community-tested
    c) Outdated
    d) Only religious
22. In ancient Chinese weather wisdom, a ring around the moon often foretells:
    a) Snow
    b) Wind
    c) Rain
    d) Earthquake
23. Shepherds' traditional rhyme, "Red sky at night, shepherd's delight" refers to:
    a) Good fishing conditions
    b) Warmer temperatures
    c) Good weather tomorrow
    d) Sunrise
24. The presence of dew in the morning is commonly interpreted as:
    a) It rained at night
    b) Clear skies ahead
    c) Rain is due
    d) Soil fertility
25. What traditional observation is made if birds stop chirping suddenly?
    a) Cold front
    b) Rainfall
    c) Predators nearby
    d) Storm or sudden change

26. What does the early blooming of Shirish (Albizia) flowers signal in ancient Indian lore?
    a) Late rainfall b) Approaching monsoon
    c) Heat wave d) Pest outbreak
27. High winds at dusk in summer are traditionally taken as a sign of:
    a) Incoming thunderstorm b) Temperature drop
    c) Rain next day d) No change in weather
28. Folklore in arid zones indicates that animal migration often predicts:
    a) Weather reversal b) Arrival of rains
    c) Soil fertility d) Cold wave
29. According to ancient traditions, cloudy nights are warmer because:
    a) Clouds trap terrestrial radiation b) Wind is stronger
    c) Moon is not visible d) Clouds radiate heat
30. Which tree's leaf movement is observed to forecast storms?
    a) Neem b) Tamarind
    c) Banyan d) Peepal
31. "If cattle sit down early in the afternoon…" is a traditional sign of:
    a) Heavy rain approaching b) Sunny next day
    c) End of monsoon d) Dust storm
32. Which ancient text refers to seasonal weather changes in India?
    a) Rigveda b) Arthashastra
    c) Manusmriti d) Ramayana
33. Heavy shedding of neem leaves in spring is associated with:
    a) Summer drought b) Upcoming rains
    c) Disease d) Pesticide requirement
34. A traditional indicator for cyclone is:
    a) Sudden calm before wind b) Rising temperature
    c) Cloudless sky d) Dust storms
35. Which Indian state's tribals are known for sky-color based weather prediction?
    a) Rajasthan b) Odisha
    c) Assam d) Maharashtra

36. Traditional weather forecasting is also called:
    a) Ethnometeorology b) Biometeorology
    c) Agroclimatology d) Paleoecology
37. A sudden increase in bird activity before sunrise may indicate:
    a) Cold night b) Upcoming rainfall
    c) Earthquake d) Pest invasion
38. Buzzing of bees louder than usual near the hive is interpreted as:
    a) Danger b) Imminent rain
    c) Pest infestation d) Lightning
39. In folklore, what does a sudden stillness in wind indicate before rain?
    a) Rain is over b) Clouds moving away
    c) Rain about to start d) Morning dew
40. Folk proverbs about rainfall timing are often based on:
    a) Observations across generations
    b) Written science
    c) Fictional texts
    d) Colonial history
41. Dogs eating grass is seen as a predictor of:
    a) Parasite infection b) Rainfall
    c) Heat stroke d) Snake presence
42. High humidity at dawn without clouds traditionally implies:
    a) Rain b) Dry spell
    c) Fog d) Thunderstorm
43. When do elders traditionally expect hailstorms?
    a) On full moon
    b) During convective summer clouds
    c) After monsoon ends
    d) Post-harvest
44. Chaitra and Vaisakha months are critical in folk forecasting for:
    a) Sowing b) Livestock breeding
    c) Rainfall prediction d) Irrigation planning

45. Which of the following is NOT part of ancient weather indicators?
   a) Mobile phone alerts b) Moon halo
   c) Bird behavior d) Ant movement

46. The term ‘Neerkuri’ in Tamil Nadu refers to:
   a) Traditional seed bank b) Indigenous water harvesting
   c) Folk rain prediction d) Wind measurement

47. Folk wisdom regards lizards making loud calls at night as a sign of:
   a) Storm b) Rainfall
   c) Earthquake d) Summer

48. According to folklore, if peacocks dance:
   a) It is going to be cold b) Rain is near
   c) Crops will fail d) Birds are mating

49. Which among these su□pports conservation of traditional weather wisdom?
   a) ICAR b) FAO
   c) WMO d) All of the above

50. Ancient wisdom in weather forecasting is now being revived for:
   a) Entertainment b) Spiritual reasons
   c) Enhancing resilience in farming d) Astrology

Answer Key

1	d	2	b	3	c	4	c	5	b	6	b	7	b
8	b	9	c	10	b	11	d	12	d	13	b	14	a
15	c	16	d	17	b	18	b	19	b	20	d	21	b
22	c	23	c	24	b	25	d	26	b	27	a	28	b
29	a	30	d	31	a	32	a	33	b	34	a	35	a
36	a	37	b	38	b	39	c	40	a	41	b	42	a
43	b	44	c	45	a	46	c	47	b	48	b	49	d
50	c												

15

Weather Forecasting

1. Weather forecasting is the prediction of:
   a) Soil fertility b) Past weather
   c) Atmospheric conditions d) Crop yield
2. The science that deals with weather forecasting is called:
   a) Climatology b) Geology
   c) Meteorology d) Agronomy
3. Which instrument is used to measure atmospheric pressure?
   a) Thermometer b) Barometer
   c) Hygrometer d) Anemometer
4. The organization responsible for weather forecasting in India is:
   a) NDMA b) IMD
   c) ICAR d) CSIR
5. Which satellite provides weather data to IMD?
   a) GSAT-1 b) INSAT-3D
   c) Aryabhata d) Mangalyaan
6. Nowcasting provides weather forecasts for a period of:
   a) Less than 12 hours b) 1–2 days
   c) 3–10 days d) Monthly
7. Short-range forecasts are valid for:
   a) 1 hour b) 1–2 days
   c) 3–5 days d) 10–15 days
8. Medium-range forecasts are issued for:
   a) Up to 3 days b) 4–10 days
   c) 10–20 days d) 1 month
9. Long-range forecasts are meant for:
   a) Next 12 hours b) 1–2 days
   c) Weeks to seasons d) Daily weather

10. Seasonal forecasts are useful for:
    a) Daily irrigation b) Sowing & cropping decisions
    c) Pesticide application d) Market planning

11. Numerical Weather Prediction (NWP) uses:
    a) Farmers' observations b) Empirical data only
    c) Mathematical models d) Folk forecasting

12. Radar is primarily used to detect:
    a) Temperature b) Humidity
    c) Rainfall and storms d) Wind direction

13. Satellites provide which type of data for forecasting?
    a) Soil data
    b) Cloud movement and temperature
    c) Crop yield data
    d) Land ownership

14. Which model is most commonly used in global weather forecasting?
    a) ICAR Model b) NWP Model
    c) GFS (Global Forecast System) d) ATM Model

15. Remote sensing is helpful in:
    a) Soil testing b) Fertilizer application
    c) Large-scale weather monitoring d) Water treatment

16. Which forecast helps in deciding irrigation schedule?
    a) Seasonal forecast b) Medium-range forecast
    c) Long-range forecast d) Historical forecast

17. Pest and disease forecasting depends on:
    a) Soil fertility
    b) Weather variables like humidity, temperature
    c) Crop residues
    d) Market demand

18. Farmers can prevent losses by:
    a) Ignoring weather data
    b) Following traditional calendars
    c) Using weather-based advisories
    d) Burning stubble

19. Weather forecasts help reduce:
    a) Water harvesting b) Input use efficiency
    c) Weather-related crop losses d) Soil salinity
20. Weather forecast helps improve:
    a) Rainfall uncertainty
    b) Market price
    c) Crop planning and risk management
    d) Pest resistance
21. Agromet Advisory Service is provided by:
    a) NDMA b) IMD
    c) FAO d) WTO
22. AAS provides:
    a) Daily market rates
    b) Crop insurance
    c) Weather-based agricultural advice
    d) Land ownership certificates
23. District Agromet Units (DAMUs) are established under:
    a) ICAR b) KVKs
    c) MoA d) ICRISAT
24. Which component is not included in AAS?
    a) Weather forecast b) Crop advisory
    c) Market support d) Livestock advisory
25. Farmers receive agromet advisories through:
    a) Newspapers only
    b) Television only
    c) Multi-channel communication including SMS, TV, and radio
    d) Email only
26. Which is not a weather parameter used in forecasting?
    a) Rainfall b) Temperature
    c) Wind speed d) Soil pH
27. Wind direction is measured using:
    a) Thermometer b) Hygrometer
    c) Wind vane d) Anemometer

28. Relative humidity is measured with a:
    a) Rain gauge b) Barometer
    c) Hygrometer d) Thermometer
29. Which of the following is a qualitative forecast?
    a) Rainfall in mm
    b) Cloud cover percentage
    c) Chance of rainfall (e.g., "likely")
    d) Wind speed in km/h
30. Pan evaporation data is used in:
    a) Forecasting soil health b) Crop damage estimation
    c) Irrigation scheduling d) Rain harvesting
31. Probability forecast expresses:
    a) Confidence in weather event b) Rain gauge accuracy
    c) Soil water level d) Forecast validity
32. Weather-based crop insurance is related to:
    a) MSP
    b) Pradhan Mantri Fasal Bima Yojana
    c) Swachh Bharat Mission
    d) NREGA
33. Forecasting helps in avoiding:
    a) Yield gains b) Timely sowing
    c) Weather-related risks d) Crop diversification
34. Rainfed farming benefits most from:
    a) Short-range forecast b) Seasonal forecast
    c) Market forecast d) Soil forecast
35. Which weather forecast helps with fertilizer application?
    a) Daily forecast b) Monthly forecast
    c) Long-range forecast d) Decadal forecast
36. One major challenge in weather forecasting is:
    a) High costs
    b) Technological reliability
    c) Inaccuracy due to chaotic atmosphere
    d) Farmer illiteracy

37. Which is a limitation of long-range forecasts?
 a) Poor availability b) Lower precision
 c) Expensive instruments d) High temperature

38. Which factor limits forecast accuracy?
 a) Large datasets
 b) Too many satellites
 c) Unpredictable natural variability
 d) Farmer cooperation

39. Forecast accuracy reduces with:
 a) Use of technology b) Larger data collection
 c) Longer time horizons d) Local observation

40. Effective forecasting needs integration of:
 a) Astrology and weather
 b) Climate models and ground data
 c) Soil testing
 d) Crop calendars only

41. Mobile apps for weather include:
 a) mKisan, Meghdoot b) Krishi Vigyan
 c) eNAM d) Soil Health Card

42. Which is not a forecasting method?
 a) Synoptic b) Numerical
 c) Statistical d) Genetic

43. Which agency collaborates with IMD for AAS?
 a) WHO b) ISRO
 c) ICAR d) FAO

44. Forecasting monsoon onset is important for:
 a) Sugarcane planting b) Kharif crop sowing
 c) Wheat irrigation d) Rabi harvest

45. Which sensor is used on satellites for weather data?
 a) GPS b) Radiometer
 c) X-ray sensor d) Altimeter

46. Use of AI in forecasting aims to:
a) Remove satellites
b) Improve forecast accuracy
c) Increase rainfall
d) Reduce temperature

47. Weather-based farming decisions lead to:
a) Increased risks
b) Delayed farming
c) Higher productivity and reduced losses
d) More input cost

48. Customized weather advisories consider:
a) Market prices only
b) Local weather and crop stages
c) Universal guidelines
d) Seed costs

49. Precision agriculture relies heavily on:
a) Historical records
b) Weather forecasts and sensors
c) Crop insurance
d) Traditional methods

50. Main goal of weather forecasting in agriculture is:
a) Marketing of inputs
b) Crop insurance selling
c) Risk management and sustainable farming
d) Seed certification

Answer Key

1	c	2	c	3	b	4	b	5	b	6	a	7	b
8	b	9	c	10	b	11	c	12	c	13	b	14	c
15	c	16	b	17	b	18	c	19	c	20	c	21	b
22	c	23	b	24	c	25	c	26	d	27	c	28	c
29	c	30	c	31	a	32	b	33	c	34	b	35	a
36	c	37	b	38	c	39	c	40	b	41	a	42	d
43	c	44	b	45	b	46	b	47	c	48	b	49	b
50	c												

16

Climate Change and Agriculture

1. Climate change refers to:
   a) Daily weather changes
   b) Seasonal variations
   c) Long-term shifts in temperature and weather patterns
   d) Annual crop cycle
2. The main greenhouse gas responsible for global warming is:
   a) Nitrogen   b) Carbon dioxide
   c) Oxygen   d) Helium
3. Which gas is most potent in terms of global warming potential?
   a) Carbon dioxide   b) Methane
   c) Oxygen   d) Nitrogen
4. Global warming is mainly caused by:
   a) Solar flares   b) Greenhouse gas emissions
   c) Plate tectonics   d) Volcanoes
5. Which sector contributes significantly to greenhouse gas emissions?
   a) Banking   b) Agriculture
   c) Education   d) IT
6. The primary source of methane in agriculture is:
   a) Fertilizer application
   b) Livestock enteric fermentation
   c) Soil erosion
   d) Wind erosion
7. Nitrous oxide is released from agricultural fields mainly due to:
   a) Burning residues   b) Use of nitrogen fertilizers
   c) Pesticide spraying   d) Water irrigation

8. Which gas has the highest global warming potential (GWP)?
   a) CO_2 b) N_2O
   c) CH_4 d) H_2O
9. Livestock farming contributes to climate change through:
   a) Methane emission b) Soil compaction
   c) Biodiversity d) Groundwater recharge
10. Which practice helps reduce methane from paddy fields?
    a) Continuous flooding b) Alternate wetting and drying
    c) Late transplanting d) Using more fertilizer
11. Climate change affects agriculture by:
    a) Improving soil fertility
    b) Increasing productivity everywhere
    c) Altering rainfall and temperature patterns
    d) Increasing water availability
12. Heat stress due to climate change can reduce:
    a) Fertilizer efficiency b) Crop pollination and yield
    c) Labour availability d) Soil erosion
13. An increase in CO_2 concentration generally leads to:
    a) Higher stomatal opening
    b) Increased photosynthesis in C3 crops
    c) Less water use efficiency
    d) Reduction in plant growth
14. Crop most sensitive to temperature rise is:
    a) Sorghum b) Rice
    c) Wheat d) Maize
15. Climate change may lead to more frequent:
    a) Cloudy days b) Droughts and floods
    c) Monsoons d) Fertility increase
16. Adaptation to climate change in agriculture includes:
    a) Carbon trading
    b) Developing drought-tolerant varieties
    c) Buying machinery
    d) Land use change

17. Mitigation means:
    a) Adjusting to new conditions
    b) Reducing causes of climate change
    c) Increasing crop diversity
    d) Building irrigation canals
18. Carbon sequestration refers to:
    a) Emitting CO_2
    b) Capturing and storing atmospheric CO_2
    c) Growing tall plants
    d) Measuring carbon in soil
19. Agroforestry helps mitigate climate change by:
    a) Increasing evapotranspiration
    b) Reducing biodiversity
    c) Absorbing atmospheric carbon dioxide
    d) Releasing greenhouse gases
20. Which farming practice is climate-smart?
    a) Slash-and-burn b) Zero tillage
    c) Mono-cropping d) Overgrazing
21. India's National Action Plan on Climate Change (NAPCC) has how many missions?
    a) 3 b) 5
    c) 8 d) 10
22. National Mission for Sustainable Agriculture (NMSA) is part of:
    a) Green Revolution
    b) NAPCC
    c) PMFBY
    d) Rashtriya Krishi Vikas Yojana
23. UNFCCC stands for:
    a) United Nations Framework Convention on Climate Change
    b) United Nations Food and Climate Committee
    c) Union National Federation of Climate Change
    d) None of these

24. The Kyoto Protocol aimed to reduce:
a) Soil erosion b) Global trade
c) Greenhouse gas emissions d) Ocean salinity

25. Paris Agreement's key goal is to limit global warming to:
a) 1.5–2°C above pre-industrial levels
b) 3°C above industrial levels
c) 2.5°C above average
d) Below 5°C always

26. Which type of crop is better suited for dry conditions?
a) Paddy b) Sugarcane
c) Sorghum d) Jute

27. Mulching helps in:
a) Increasing evaporation b) Reducing soil moisture loss
c) Enhancing soil salinity d) Water logging

28. SRI (System of Rice Intensification) helps in:
a) Using more water
b) Increasing methane emissions
c) Reducing water use and emissions
d) Growing only basmati rice

29. Crop diversification is a strategy for;
a) Disease increase
b) Mitigation of climate change risks
c) Less productivity
d) Monoculture

30. Drought-tolerant crops include:
a) Maize b) Groundnut
c) Pearl millet d) Sugarcane

31. GCMs in climate science stands for:
a) General Climate Measures b) Global Crop Models
c) General Circulation Models d) Ground Control Measures

32. Agrometeorology helps in:
    a) Assessing soil nutrition
    b) Predicting crop pests
    c) Understanding weather impact on crops
    d) Testing new machines
33. Climate scenarios are used to:
    a) Evaluate new seeds
    b) Predict market prices
    c) Assess future climate impacts
    d) Measure yield directly
34. Which is not a climate model output?
    a) Rainfall patterns
    b) CO_2 levels
    c) Pest counts
    d) Temperature trends
35. One limitation of climate models is:
    a) Too accurate
    b) Fixed assumptions
    c) No global application
    d) No scientific basis
36. Climate change increases risk of:
    a) Food security
    b) Water scarcity
    c) Better infrastructure
    d) Market stability
37. Farmers in rainfed areas are more vulnerable due to:
    a) Better irrigation
    b) Lack of climate resilience
    c) Fertile soils
    d) Access to loans
38. Extreme weather events affect:
    a) Soil pH
    b) Harvest and storage
    c) Remote sensing
    d) Seed certification
39. Migration of rural populations is linked to:
    a) Urban growth only
    b) Climate-induced livelihood losses
    c) Industrialization only
    d) Better transport
40. Gender is important in climate discussions because:
    a) Women are less educated
    b) Men are less affected
    c) Women are disproportionately impacted
    d) Only men are farmers

41. Carbon footprint in farming refers to:
    a) Use of machinery
    b) Total GHG emissions from agricultural activities
    c) Soil erosion
    d) Biodiversity loss
42. Renewable energy in agriculture includes:
    a) Diesel pumps   b) Solar dryers
    c) Electric tractors   d) Tube wells
43. Energy-efficient practices help in:
    a) Increasing emissions   b) Climate change mitigation
    c) Decreasing yield   d) Polluting water
44. Which source is not renewable?
    a) Wind   b) Coal
    c) Solar   d) Biogas
45. Energy audit in farming helps in:
    a) Financial planning
    b) Emission estimation and efficiency improvement
    c) Water conservation
    d) Soil testing
46. Climate-smart agriculture aims for:
    a) Higher input use
    b) Resilience, mitigation, and productivity
    c) Monocropping
    d) Export growth
47. Which of the following is NOT a climate-smart practice?
    a) Integrated pest management   b) Overuse of fertilizers
    c) Crop rotation   d) Rainwater harvesting
48. Which term refers to farming adapted to changing climate?
    a) Climate-resilient agriculture   b) Irrigated farming
    c) Organic farming   d) Commercial farming
49. Digital tools in climate-smart farming help in:
    a) Manual sowing   b) Real-time weather advisories
    c) Reducing technology use   d) Pest breeding

50. Which Indian mission promotes climate-resilient agriculture?
   a) National Food Security Mission b) NMSA
   c) NRLM d) MGNREGA

Answer Key

1	c	2	b	3	b	4	b	5	b	6	b	7	b
8	b	9	a	10	b	11	c	12	b	13	b	14	c
15	b	16	b	17	b	18	b	19	c	20	b	21	c
22	b	23	a	24	c	25	a	26	c	27	b	28	c
29	b	30	c	31	c	32	c	33	c	34	c	35	b
36	b	37	b	38	b	39	b	40	c	41	b	42	b
43	b	44	b	45	b	46	b	47	b	48	a	49	b
50	b												

17 Which Indian mission promotes climate-resilient agriculture?

a) National Food Security Mission b) NMSA

c) NRGM d) MGNREGA

Weather and Agriculture Relationship

1. Weather refers to:

a) Long-term atmospheric conditions

b) Daily atmospheric conditions

c) Average temperature only

d) Seasonal crop yield

2. Climate [illegible]

a) [illegible] weather conditions

b) Long-term average of weather conditions

c) [illegible]

d) [illegible]

3. Which [illegible]

a) Temperature

c) Soil pH

4. Agrometeorology is the science of:

a) [illegible]

b) Relationship between weather and crops

c) Animal health

d) [illegible]

5. Which weather element most directly affects [illegible]

a) Soil color

c) Humidity

6. The crop stage most sensitive to [illegible]

a) [illegible]

c) [illegible]

7. Low temperatures in wheat during [illegible]

a) [illegible] germination

c) [illegible]

17

Weather and Agriculture Relationship

1. Weather refers to:
   a) Long-term atmospheric conditions
   b) Daily atmospheric conditions
   c) Average temperature only
   d) Seasonal crop yield
2. Climate refers to:
   a) Temporary weather variations
   b) Long-term average of weather conditions
   c) Soil fertility
   d) Rainfall on a single day
3. Which of the following is not an element of weather?
   a) Temperature
   b) Humidity
   c) Soil pH
   d) Wind speed
4. Agrometeorology is the science of:
   a) Soil testing
   b) Relationship between weather and crop production
   c) Animal health
   d) Insecticide formulation
5. Which weather element most directly affects crop evapotranspiration?
   a) Soil color
   b) Wind speed
   c) Humidity
   d) All of the above
6. The crop stage most sensitive to adverse weather is:
   a) Vegetative
   b) Germination
   c) Flowering
   d) Ripening
7. Low night temperatures in wheat during grain filling cause:
   a) Poor germination
   b) Better grain yield
   c) Leaf curling
   d) Sterility

8. Which of the following crops is most sensitive to frost?
   a) Sorghum b) Tomato
   c) Pearl millet d) Cotton
9. Rainfall deficiency during reproductive stage of crops causes:
   a) Enhanced seed size b) Better root development
   c) Yield reduction d) Delayed maturity
10. Excessive humidity is favorable for:
   a) Drought-resistant crops b) Disease development
   c) Improved photosynthesis d) Early flowering
11. Crops that grow in high humidity are called:
   a) Xerophytes b) Hydrophytes
   c) Mesophytes d) Hygrophytes
12. Optimum temperature for wheat germination is:
   a) 10–15°C b) 20–25°C
   c) 30–35°C d) 5–10°C
13. Photosynthesis increases with:
   a) Increasing light and temperature (within limits)
   b) Decreasing CO_2
   c) High wind speed
   d) High soil moisture alone
14. A weather parameter essential for calculating growing degree days is:
   a) Humidity b) Soil moisture
   c) Temperature d) Rainfall
15. Maize is sensitive to water stress during:
   a) Germination b) Vegetative stage
   c) Silking stage d) Maturity
16. Heatwaves are particularly damaging to:
   a) Rice flowering b) Wheat grain filling
   c) Maize germination d) Sugarcane tillering
17. Hailstorms cause major damage to:
   a) Root crops b) Fruit and vegetable crops
   c) Millets d) Legumes

18. Drought conditions mainly affect:
    a) Root growth
    b) Water availability and yield
    c) Soil structure
    d) Solar radiation
19. Frost damage is primarily due to:
    a) High humidity
    b) Low temperature below freezing
    c) High wind speed
    d) Heavy rainfall
20. Stormy weather affects agriculture by:
    a) Enhancing pollination
    b) Improving soil fertility
    c) Causing lodging in crops
    d) Promoting flowering
21. Land preparation is best done during:
    a) High rainfall period
    b) Dry weather
    c) Post-harvest stage
    d) Cold waves
22. Delayed sowing due to unexpected rainfall affects:
    a) Soil structure
    b) Weed control
    c) Crop duration and yield
    d) Harvest quality
23. Harvesting in rainy weather causes:
    a) Easy threshing
    b) Crop spoilage & fungal attack
    c) High seed viability
    d) Reduced storage losses
24. Dry weather is ideal for:
    a) Sowing
    b) Harvesting and drying
    c) Irrigation
    d) Transplanting
25. Weather affects pest dynamics by:
    a) Killing them directly
    b) Modifying their life cycle and survival
    c) Altering seed variety
    d) Reducing fertilizer need

26. High ambient temperatures in livestock cause:
    a) Increased appetite
    b) Heat stress and reduced productivity
    c) Higher milk yield
    d) Lower respiration rate
27. Cold stress in poultry causes:
    a) Egg production increase b) Reduced feed intake
    c) High mortality c) Poor feathering
28. Fish production is directly affected by:
    a) Air pollution b) Wind direction
    c) Water temperature and rainfall d) Cloud cover
29. Extreme rainfall events affect livestock by:
    a) Increasing milk production
    b) Causing waterlogging and diseases
    c) Enhancing digestion
    d) Reducing fodder quality
30. Heat waves affect dairy animals by:
    a) Increasing conception rate b) Enhancing feed quality
    c) Reducing milk yield d) No impact
31. Weather data helps farmers to:
    a) Choose fertilizers b) Plan sowing and irrigation
    c) Increase subsidies d) Decide crop rotation
32. Which forecast is most useful for crop planning?
    a) Nowcast b) Medium-range forecast
    c) Seasonal forecast d) Long-term prediction
33. Dry spells after sowing affect:
    a) Seed germination b) Pest infestation
    c) Leaf shedding d) Weed suppression
34. Which crop can tolerate high rainfall?
    a) Groundnut b) Maize
    c) Rice d) Cotton

35. Weather aberrations are:
   a) Predictable temperature changes
   b) Deviations from normal weather patterns
   c) Daily fluctuations
   d) Expected seasonal shifts

36. Irrigation scheduling is best done based on:
   a) Soil color b) Temperature alone
   c) Evapotranspiration and rainfall d) Pest infestation

37. Weeding operations are best done in:
   a) Flooded conditions b) Windy weather
   c) Moist but not wet soils d) Frozen soils

38. Excess rain after fertilizer application causes:
   a) Nutrient enhancement b) Leaching losses
   c) Improved uptake d) Higher chlorophyll

39. Crop yield forecasting depends heavily on:
   a) Weather and crop models b) Fertilizer type
   c) Pest load d) Seed size

40. Cloudy weather generally results in:
   a) Higher radiation b) Reduced photosynthesis
   c) Greater transpiration d) Early maturity

41. Contingency crop planning is required for:
   a) Mechanization b) Weather aberrations
   c) Increasing subsidies d) Extending harvest

42. Crop insurance is influenced by:
   a) Soil type b) Weather risks
   c) Irrigation facility d) Market prices

43. Weather-based advisory helps in:
   a) Policy decisions only
   b) On-farm operational planning
   c) Machinery scheduling
   d) Market analysis

44. Drought-prone areas require:
a) Heavy irrigation
b) Short-duration, drought-tolerant crops
c) Transplanting rice
d) High-input farming

45. Real-time weather data helps in:
a) Historical analysis only
b) Immediate decision making on farm operations
c) Reducing soil testing
d) None of the above

46. IMD provides weather forecasts through:
a) Krishi Vigyan Kendras b) SMS and mobile apps
c) Banks d) Panchayats only

47. Which mobile app provides agromet advisories in India?
a) Arogya Setu b) Meghdoot
c) Kisan Seva d) Pusa Krishi

48. Which of these is a benefit of weather forecasting in agriculture?
a) Delay in sowing b) Efficient input use
c) Increased manual labor d) Lower seed quality

49. Farmers receive weather advisories through:
a) Radio b) SMS
c) TV d) All of the above

50. Which is an agrometeorological service?
a) Soil survey
b) Weather-based crop advisories
c) Credit schemes
d) Seed certification

Answer Key

1	b	2	b	3	c	4	b	5	d	6	c	7	b
8	b	9	c	10	b	11	c	12	a	13	a	14	c
15	c	16	b	17	b	18	b	19	b	20	c	21	b
22	c	23	b	24	b	25	b	26	b	27	c	28	c
29	b	30	c	31	b	32	b	33	a	34	c	35	b
36	c	37	c	38	b	39	a	40	b	41	b	42	b
43	b	44	b	45	b	46	b	47	b	48	b	49	d
50	b												

18

Impact of Climate Change and Adaptation Strategies in Horticulture

1. Climate change primarily affects horticulture through:
   a) Soil pH
   b) Changes in temperature and rainfall patterns
   c) Increase in seed production
   d) Reduction in pests
2. One major effect of climate change on fruit crops is:
   a) Enhanced flowering time
   b) Shift in flowering and fruiting seasons
   c) Constant yield
   d) Increased resistance to pests
3. Global warming can cause:
   a) Decreased evapotranspiration
   b) Increased incidence of heat stress in horticultural crops
   c) Lower soil temperature
   d) Longer dormancy periods
4. Increased atmospheric CO_2 concentration affects horticultural crops by:
   a) Decreasing photosynthesis
   b) Increasing photosynthesis and water use efficiency
   c) Reducing biomass
   d) Causing plant death
5. Extreme weather events under climate change can:
   a) Improve crop resilience
   b) Cause crop damage and yield loss
   c) Increase market price stability
   d) Eliminate pests

6. High temperature stress during flowering in horticultural crops causes:
   a) Increased fruit set
   b) Flower drop and poor fruit set
   c) Early harvest
   d) Enhanced fruit quality
7. Drought conditions due to climate change reduce:
   a) Fruit size and quality
   b) Photosynthesis rate only
   c) Pest incidence
   d) Root growth
8. Heat waves can lead to:
   a) Increased fruit sugar content
   b) Sunburn damage on fruits and leaves
   c) Delayed maturity
   d) Higher fruit acidity
9. Waterlogging from heavy rainfall results in:
   a) Increased root respiration
   b) Root hypoxia and disease susceptibility
   c) Better nutrient uptake
   d) Increased flowering
10. Irrigation scheduling is critical under climate change to:
   a) Prevent soil erosion
   b) Maintain optimum soil moisture
   c) Increase pest resistance
   d) Promote flowering
11. Rising temperatures generally cause:
   a) Decreased pest population
   b) Increased pest and disease outbreaks
   c) Elimination of diseases
   d) Increased natural enemies only
12. Humidity changes due to climate change can:
   a) Decrease fungal diseases
   b) Increase fungal and bacterial infections
   c) Prevent viral diseases
   d) Reduce pest infestation

13. Increased CO_2 affects pest dynamics by:
    a) Increasing pest reproduction rates
    b) Killing pests
    c) Making crops toxic
    d) Increasing pesticide efficiency
14. Warmer winters lead to:
    a) Reduced pest survival
    b) Higher overwintering survival of pests
    c) Decreased insect outbreaks
    d) Pest migration to poles
15. Climate change adaptation strategies for pest control include:
    a) Ignoring pest outbreaks
    b) Integrated Pest Management (IPM)
    c) Using chemical pesticides only
    d) Monocropping
16. Climate change can cause:
    a) Shift in flowering and fruiting time
    b) Uniform crop cycles
    c) Decrease in crop biodiversity
    d) Constant yield
17. Elevated CO_2 levels can increase:
    a) Yield potential of some horticultural crops
    b) Crop vulnerability to frost
    c) Soil salinity
    d) Pest incidence only
18. Heat stress can reduce fruit yield by:
    a) Reducing fruit set and quality b) Increasing leaf growth
    c) Extending growing season d) Increasing pollination
19. Fruit quality under climate change is often:
    a) Improved in all crops
    b) Reduced due to stress conditions
    c) Unaffected
    d) More uniform

20. Phenological shifts due to climate change affect:
    a) Water use efficiency
    b) Pest cycles and pollination timing
    c) Soil fertility
    d) Crop color only
21. Efficient water use under climate change can be achieved by:
    a) Flood irrigation
    b) Drip and micro-irrigation
    c) Increasing irrigation frequency without monitoring
    d) Rainfed only
22. Mulching helps adaptation by:
    a) Increasing soil temperature
    b) Reducing evaporation and conserving soil moisture
    c) Increasing weed growth
    d) Increasing runoff
23. Rainwater harvesting benefits horticulture by:
    a) Reducing groundwater recharge
    b) Providing supplemental irrigation water
    c) Increasing soil erosion
    d) Enhancing pest survival
24. Scheduling irrigation based on crop growth stage:
    a) Wastes water
    b) Saves water and improves yield
    c) Reduces soil fertility
    d) Increases salinity
25. Soil moisture sensors help:
    a) Monitor irrigation needs precisely b) Increase evaporation
    c) Detect pests d) Change crop variety
26. Selection of climate-resilient varieties means:
    a) Choosing drought and heat tolerant genotypes
    b) Using traditional varieties only
    c) Ignoring climate data
    d) Planting monocultures

27. Adjusting planting dates can:
    a) Avoid peak stress periods
    b) Reduce yields
    c) Increase pest outbreaks
    d) Reduce soil fertility
28. Use of shade nets in horticulture:
    a) Increases heat stress
    b) Protects crops from excessive heat and UV radiation
    c) Reduces photosynthesis
    d) Enhances wind damage
29. Crop diversification helps adaptation by:
    a) Increasing income risk
    b) Reducing vulnerability to climate stress
    c) Increasing pest outbreaks
    d) Reducing biodiversity
30. Soil health management under climate change includes:
    a) Avoiding organic amendments
    b) Using organic mulches and biofertilizers
    c) Using chemical fertilizers only
    d) Removing soil cover
31. Climate change affects post-harvest by:
    a) Increasing shelf life
    b) Increasing post-harvest losses due to higher temperatures
    c) Reducing transportation costs
    d) Improving packaging
32. Cold storage and controlled atmosphere storage help by:
    a) Accelerating spoilage
    b) Reducing post-harvest losses
    c) Increasing water loss
    d) Promoting diseases
33. Value addition and processing reduce:
    a) Market price
    b) Post-harvest losses and improve income
    c) Crop quality
    d) Farmer income

34. Developing early maturing varieties helps:
   a) Avoid late-season drought and heat stress
   b) Increase water use
   c) Increase pests
   d) Extend cropping season only
35. Crop insurance schemes help farmers by:
   a) Ignoring climate risks
   b) Providing financial support against climate-induced losses
   c) Increasing input cost
   d) Limiting crop choice
36. Climate-smart agriculture promotes:
   a) Increased use of pesticides
   b) Sustainability, productivity, and resilience
   c) Monocropping
   d) Deforestation
37. Farmer awareness and training on climate change:
   a) Has no impact
   b) Improves adoption of adaptation practices
   c) Only benefits scientists
   d) Reduces productivity
38. Access to weather forecasts helps farmers:
   a) Ignore climate variability
   b) Plan field activities and reduce risks
   c) Increase crop failures
   d) Reduce irrigation
39. Government subsidies for micro-irrigation:
   a) Discourage water saving
   b) Promote water-efficient farming
   c) Increase water wastage
   d) Are irrelevant

40. Community-based adaptation includes:
    a) Individual farming only
    b) Collective resource management and knowledge sharing
    c) Ignoring local conditions
    d) Limiting technology use
41. Use of remote sensing and GIS helps:
    a) Monitor crop stress and manage resources efficiently
    b) Increase input costs only
    c) Reduce data availability
    d) Ignore weather changes
42. Biotechnological approaches in horticulture aim to:
    a) Develop stress tolerant varieties b) Increase pesticide use
    c) Reduce genetic diversity d) Delay maturity
43. Use of protected cultivation like polyhouses:
    a) Protects crops from climate extremes
    b) Increases water loss
    c) Reduces yields
    d) Increases pest attacks
44. Precision farming helps adaptation by:
    a) Applying inputs uniformly
    b) Site-specific management based on climate and soil data
    c) Increasing waste
    d) Ignoring weather data
45. Early warning systems for pests and weather help:
    a) Increase crop damage
    b) Reduce risks by timely action
    c) Delay harvest
    d) Increase input costs
46. Diversifying income sources reduces:
    a) Climate vulnerability b) Farmer income
    c) Market access d) Food security

47. Access to credit and insurance enables:
   a) Risk taking and adaptation investments
   b) Crop failure
   c) Increased input cost
   d) Reduced productivity
48. Farmers' participation in decision-making:
   a) Decreases adaptation success
   b) Enhances relevance and uptake of adaptation strategies
   c) Limits innovation
   d) Reduces extension services
49. Gender mainstreaming in adaptation:
   a) Is irrelevant
   b) Ensures inclusive climate resilience
   c) Restricts women's role
   d) Ignores women farmers
50. Market linkages improve adaptation by:
   a) Increasing price volatility
   b) Providing stable income and access to inputs
   c) Reducing crop diversity
   d) Increasing losses

Answer Key

1	b	2	b	3	b	4	b	5	b	6	b	7	a
8	b	9	b	10	b	11	b	12	b	13	a	14	b
15	b	16	a	17	a	18	a	19	b	20	b	21	b
22	b	23	b	24	b	25	a	26	a	27	a	28	b
29	b	30	b	31	b	32	b	33	a	34	c	35	b
36	c	37	c	38	b	39	a	40	b	41	b	42	b
43	b	44	b	45	b	46	b	47	b	48	b	49	d
50	b												

19

Impact of Climate Change on Sericulture

1. Climate change affects sericulture primarily by altering:
   a) Soil fertility
   b) Temperature and humidity regimes
   c) Silkworm genetics
   d) Mulberry leaf color
2. Optimal temperature for mulberry leaf growth is around:
   a) 10–15°C b) 24–28°C
   c) 30–35°C d) 40–45°C
3. Increased temperature due to climate change can:
   a) Enhance mulberry growth indefinitely
   b) Cause heat stress reducing leaf yield
   c) Decrease silkworm growth
   d) Increase cocoon weight
4. High temperature and low humidity adversely affect:
   a) Mulberry leaf quality b) Silkworm breeding only
   c) Cocoon shell thickness d) Soil pH
5. Climate change causes shift in:
   a) Silkworm crop cycles and breeding seasons
   b) Silkworm genetic makeup
   c) Soil texture
   d) Silk market prices
6. Mulberry is sensitive to:
   a) High temperature and drought b) Cold only
   c) Waterlogging only d) Soil salinity only

7. Drought stress reduces:
   a) Leaf area and moisture content
   b) Leaf thickness only
   c) Leaf color
   d) Stem length only
8. Excessive rainfall leads to:
   a) Root rot and fungal diseases
   b) Increased leaf yield
   c) Improved leaf quality
   d) Reduced pest incidence
9. Mulberry leaves grown under heat stress show:
   a) Higher protein content
   b) Reduced nutritional quality for silkworms
   c) No change
   d) Increased fiber content
10. Mulberry yield is closely linked to:
    a) Soil pH only
    b) Temperature and rainfall patterns
    c) Pest control only
    d) Fertilizer type only
11. Silkworms are most sensitive to temperature during:
    a) Egg incubation and larval growth
    b) Cocoon spinning only
    c) Adult moth stage
    d) None of the above
12. Ideal temperature for silkworm larval rearing is:
    a) 15–20°C
    b) 23–28°C
    c) 30–35°C
    d) >35°C
13. High temperature (>30°C) causes:
    a) Faster larval development but poor cocoon quality
    b) Larger cocoons
    c) Longer larval period
    d) Increased silk quality
14. Low humidity (<70%) during silkworm rearing causes:
    a) Better cocoon shell formation
    b) Larval dehydration and mortality
    c) Faster larval growth
    d) Increased cocoon weight

15. Fluctuations in temperature cause:
    a) Stable silkworm growth
    b) Stress leading to lower silk yield
    c) Improved cocoon quality
    d) None of the above
16. Climate change can increase incidence of:
    a) Viral and fungal diseases in silkworms
    b) Only bacterial diseases
    c) No diseases
    d) Only pest infestations
17. High humidity favors:
    a) Bacterial diseases in silkworms
    b) Fungal infections such as grasserie
    c) Reduced disease incidence
    d) Increased cocoon production
18. Extreme temperatures can:
    a) Reduce silkworm immunity, increasing disease susceptibility
    b) Increase resistance to disease
    c) Have no effect on diseases
    d) Kill all pathogens
19. Grasserie disease is aggravated by:
    a) High temperature and humidity b) Low temperature only
    c) Dry conditions only d) None of the above
20. Disease management under climate stress requires:
    a) Frequent chemical sprays only
    b) Integrated disease management including environment control
    c) Ignoring weather changes
    d) Increasing silkworm density
21. Drought-tolerant mulberry varieties help by:
    a) Increasing water requirement
    b) Reducing crop failure under water stress
    c) Increasing pest incidence
    d) Reducing leaf quality

22. Mulberry mulching:
    a) Increases soil moisture loss
    b) Conserves soil moisture and reduces temperature stress
    c) Has no effect on climate stress
    d) Increases weed growth

23. Use of drip irrigation in mulberry cultivation:
    a) Saves water and improves leaf yield
    b) Wastes water
    c) Increases waterlogging
    d) Reduces leaf quality

24. Changing planting dates in mulberry:
    a) Avoids peak heat and drought periods
    b) Increases pest attack
    c) Reduces leaf quality
    d) None of the above

25. Soil organic matter management helps:
    a) Improve water retention and nutrient availability
    b) Increase soil erosion
    c) Reduce fertility
    d) Increase pest incidence

26. Climate-controlled rearing houses help:
    a) Maintain optimum temperature and humidity
    b) Increase disease incidence
    c) Increase water consumption
    d) Reduce cocoon quality

27. Use of improved silkworm breeds:
    a) Enhances tolerance to temperature fluctuations
    b) Decreases yield
    c) Increases disease susceptibility
    d) None of the above

28. Regular monitoring of microclimate in rearing houses:
    a) Helps early detection of stress conditions
    b) Is unnecessary
    c) Increases costs only
    d) Reduces yield
29. Improved disease management under climate stress:
    a) Uses bio-pesticides and sanitation
    b) Relies on chemicals only
    c) Ignores environmental control
    d) None of the above
30. Adjusting feeding schedules helps to:
    a) Reduce heat stress in silkworms
    b) Increase labor cost only
    c) Have no effect on silkworm health
    d) Reduce silk quality
31. Climate change impacts on sericulture can lead to:
    a) Increased farmer income
    b) Reduced cocoon production and farmer livelihoods
    c) Stable markets
    d) Increased exports
32. Farmers' awareness of climate risks in sericulture:
    a) Is not important
    b) Helps adoption of adaptation practices
    c) Increases costs only
    d) None of the above
33. Access to credit for climate-resilient technologies:
    a) Facilitates better adaptation   b) Has no impact
    c) Reduces adoption   d) Increases vulnerability
34. Diversification in sericulture includes:
    a) Mono cropping only
    b) Intercropping mulberry with other crops
    c) Ignoring climate data
    d) Increasing silkworm density only

35. Government policies supporting climate-smart sericulture:
  a) Increase vulnerability
  b) Promote resilience and sustainability
  c) Limit farmer options
  d) Are irrelevant

36. Development of heat-tolerant silkworm breeds:
  a) Is essential for climate change adaptation
  b) Reduces silk quality
  c) Increases disease incidence
  d) Is not possible

37. Use of mulberry varieties tolerant to abiotic stresses:
  a) Enhances sustainability b) Has no effect on yield
  c) Increases input cost only d) Is irrelevant

38. Remote sensing in sericulture helps to:
  a) Monitor mulberry crop health and water stress
  b) Increase labor cost only
  c) Reduce leaf quality
  d) Have no practical use

39. Biotechnological approaches include:
  a) Genetic improvement of silkworm and mulberry
  b) Only chemical use
  c) Ignoring environmental factors
  d) None of the above

40. Protected cultivation for mulberry:
  a) Minimizes climate stress effects b) Increases water loss
  c) Reduces leaf yield d) Increases pest attack

41. Climate change may alter pest species composition in sericulture by:
  a) Reducing pest diversity
  b) Shifting pest populations and emergence of new pests
  c) Eliminating all pests
  d) None of the above

42. Maintaining biodiversity in mulberry plantations:
    a) Helps ecological balance and pest control
    b) Increases disease risk
    c) Reduces yields
    d) Has no effect
43. Soil erosion due to extreme rainfall can:
    a) Reduce mulberry productivity b) Improve soil quality
    c) Have no effect d) Increase leaf size
44. Climate change can lead to:
    a) Increased soil salinity in some regions affecting mulberry growth
    b) Decreased soil temperature only
    c) Soil fertility increase
    d) None of the above
45. Conservation of water and soil in mulberry gardens:
    a) Is crucial for climate resilience b) Has no benefit
    c) Increases production cost only d) None of the above
46. Integrated management for climate-resilient sericulture includes:
    a) Crop, pest, and water management combined
    b) Chemical use only
    c) Ignoring climate factors
    d) No changes
47. Climate adaptation in sericulture requires:
    a) Only farmer knowledge
    b) Coordination among researchers, extension, and farmers
    c) No research
    d) Increased costs only
48. Monitoring climatic parameters in sericulture helps:
    a) Ignore weather changes
    b) Take timely corrective measures
    c) Increase risks
    d) Reduce yields

49. Climate change mitigation in sericulture involves:
   a) Reducing greenhouse gas emissions and carbon sequestration
   b) Increasing chemical fertilizers only
   c) Expanding cultivation into fragile areas
   d) Ignoring environmental impact

50. Future sericulture sustainability depends on:
   a) Technological innovations and adaptive management
   b) Traditional practices only
   c) Ignoring climate data
   d) Increasing monocropping

Answer Key

1	b	2	b	3	b	4	a	5	a	6	a	7	a
8	a	9	b	10	b	11	a	12	b	13	a	14	b
15	b	16	a	17	b	18	a	19	a	20	b	21	b
22	b	23	a	24	a	25	a	26	a	27	a	28	a
29	a	30	a	31	b	32	b	33	a	34	b	35	b
36	a	37	a	38	a	39	a	40	a	41	b	42	a
43	a	44	a	45	a	46	b	47	b	48	b	49	a
50	a												

20

Agricultural Meteorology: An Essential Associate for Food and Nutrition Security

1. Agricultural Meteorology primarily deals with:
   a) Soil fertility
   b) Weather impacts on crops and livestock
   c) Farm mechanization
   d) Market trends
2. The main aim of agricultural meteorology is to:
   a) Improve rainfall patterns
   b) Study diseases in livestock
   c) Enhance food and nutrition security through weather-informed practices
   d) Increase landholdings
3. Which of the following is a key atmospheric element in agrometeorology?
   a) Soil color b) Wind direction
   c) Seed variety d) Fertilizer type
4. Which organization provides agromet advisories in India?
   a) NABARD
   b) FSSAI
   c) IMD (India Meteorological Dept)
   d) WTO
6. Which stage of crop is most vulnerable to weather variability?
   a) Vegetative b) Flowering
   c) Maturity d) Storage

7. Prolonged drought during the cropping season can lead to:
   a) Reduced pest attack b) Higher yield
   c) Crop failure d) Delayed flowering
8. Solar radiation directly influences:
   a) Leaf senescence b) Crop photosynthesis
   c) Soil acidity d) Harvest index
9. Evapotranspiration is the sum of evaporation and:
   a) Infiltration b) Rainfall
   c) Transpiration d) Irrigation
10. Which crop is more sensitive to low temperature stress?
   a) Pearl millet b) Wheat
   c) Sorghum d) Sugarcane
11. Food security means:
   a) Adequate availability of food only
   b) Access to junk food
   c) Access to sufficient, safe and nutritious food
   d) Free food supply
12. Malnutrition can result from:
   a) Balanced diet
   b) Weather-driven food production losses
   c) Reduced rainfall variability
   d) Pest control
13. Weather-induced crop failure impacts nutrition by:
   a) Increasing calorie consumption
   b) Enhancing food diversity
   c) Reducing food availability and quality
   d) Increasing soil fertility
14. Climate-resilient crops are promoted to:
   a) Increase dependence on imports
   b) Maintain food supply under changing climates
   c) Reduce productivity
   d) Make farming more expensive

15. Food insecurity is highest in:
    a) Coastal cities
    b) Mountain towns
    c) Drought-prone and flood-prone rural areas
    d) Industrial zones
16. Agricultural meteorology plays a major role in combating:
    a) Waterlogging
    b) Climate change impacts on agriculture
    c) Market failures
    d) Land reforms
17. Global warming primarily affects:
    a) Soil fertility
    b) Weather extremes
    c) Machinery usage
    d) Seed prices
18. Increased CO_2 levels may lead to:
    a) Better nutrition in all crops
    b) Reduced crop yields under stress
    c) Lower photosynthesis
    d) Immediate rainfall
19. Mitigation of climate change through agriculture includes:
    a) Burning residues
    b) Precision farming and reduced emissions
    c) Flood irrigation
    d) Excess fertilizer use
20. Which of the following is an adaptation strategy?
    a) Switching to longer duration varieties
    b) Use of weather-based advisories
    c) Ignoring weather data
    d) Monocropping
21. Erratic weather can cause:
    a) Stable food production
    b) Global food price volatility
    c) Soil formation
    d) Water desalination

22. The main driver of global hunger is:
    a) Food storage issues
    b) Political conflict only
    c) Climate extremes and poor access
    d) Internet issues
23. Which continent is most vulnerable to food insecurity from weather change?
    a) Europe b) North America
    c) Africa d) Australia
24. Extreme rainfall events can cause:
    a) Improved soil aeration b) Waterlogging & crop damage
    c) Higher nitrogen use d) Better storage conditions
25. Resilient agriculture aims to:
    a) Maintain productivity despite weather challenges
    b) Depend on old methods
    c) Avoid forecasts
    d) Use more chemicals
26. Which global body addresses food security and weather science?
    a) FAO b) WHO
    c) NASA d) WTO
27. WMO provides leadership in:
    a) Market prices
    b) Meteorological science and services
    c) Soil analysis
    d) Agroforestry
28. IPCC reports are crucial for:
    a) Banking sector b) Climate policy and action
    c) Fish export d) Fertilizer licensing
29. Agrometeorological research helps in:
    a) Fuel development
    b) Improved climate resilience in crops
    c) Increased pesticide resistance
    d) Minimizing harvest size

30. Policy for food security must integrate:
    a) Weather and climate science
    b) Marketing agents
    c) Loan repayment strategies
    d) Branding efforts
31. Weather-smart agriculture includes:
    a) Ignoring forecasts
    b) Rainfed monocropping
    c) Use of advisories, sensors, and resilient crops
    d) Dependence on old varieties
32. Soil moisture stress can be reduced by:
    a) Heavy tillage
    b) Mulching & timely irrigation
    c) High fertilizer use
    d) Removing shade
33. Integrated farming reduces:
    a) Weather risks to income
    b) Number of crops
    c) Government support
    d) Irrigation need
34. Diversification in cropping helps combat:
    a) Soil erosion
    b) Single crop failure due to weather
    c) Water pollution
    d) Air pollution
35. Rainwater harvesting is a method to:
    a) Reduce cloud formation
    b) Increase local humidity
    c) Store water during dry spells
    d) Avoid fertilization
36. A career in agricultural meteorology involves work with:
    a) Museums
    b) Meteorological services and agriculture departments
    c) Sports management
    d) Financial institutions
37. Agromet advisory preparation requires knowledge of:
    a) Carpentry
    b) Weather, crops, and local practices
    c) Banking rules
    d) Marketing skills

38. Agrometeorology helps in:
a) Predicting earthquakes
b) Planning farm operations with weather insight
c) Building dams
d) Conducting veterinary surgery

39. Crop modeling under weather scenarios is used for:
a) TV programs
b) Predicting yield and losses
c) Air quality testing
d) Advertising

40. Future food systems must rely on:
a) Traditional weather beliefs only
b) Weather science and innovation
c) Imports only
d) Elimination of local crops

41. Resilient agriculture includes practices that:
a) Depend only on traditional knowledge
b) Ignore forecast data
c) Adapt to weather variability
d) Promote water wastage

42. Early warning systems help in:
a) Price prediction
b) Preparing for weather extremes
c) Plant breeding
d) Soil testing

43. Climate-smart agriculture integrates:
a) Traditional farming alone
b) Livestock without feed planning
c) Productivity with adaptation and mitigation
d) Only irrigation techniques

44. ICT in agrometeorology helps in:
a) Weather manipulation
b) Dissemination of weather-based advisories
c) Fertilizer mixing
d) Crop coloring

45. Seasonal forecast helps in:
    a) Water harvesting
    b) Crop planning and input management
    c) Seed multiplication
    d) Irrigation design
46. Which factor does not directly influence weather?
    a) Latitude
    b) Altitude
    c) Fertilizer application
    d) Distance from sea
47. Weather parameters crucial during seed germination:
    a) Rainfall and wind speed
    b) Soil moisture and temperature
    c) Sunshine hours and cloud cover
    d) Fog and thunderstorm
48. Agrometeorological field units (AMFUs) provide:
    a) Fertilizer subsidies
    b) Weather-based agromet advisories
    c) Seed distribution
    d) Land records
49. Weather's role in animal production is evident through:
    a) Improved meat color
    b) Influence on feed intake and productivity
    c) Better manure quality
    d) Ear size
50. Overall, weather serves agriculture by:
    a) Reducing labor cost
    b) Guiding timely and efficient farm decisions
    c) Fixing prices
    d) Promoting imports

Answer Key

1	b	2	c	3	b	4	c	5	??	6	b	7	c
8	b	9	c	10	b	11	c	12	b	13	c	14	b
15	c	16	b	17	b	18	b	19	b	20	b	21	b
22	c	23	c	24	b	25	a	26	a	27	b	28	b
29	b	30	a	31	c	32	b	33	a	34	b	35	c
36	b	37	b	38	b	39	b	40	b	41	c	42	b
43	c	44	b	45	b	46	c	47	b	48	b	49	b
50	b												

21

Indigenous Technical Knowledge for Weather Forecasts and Its Validity

1. Indigenous Technical Knowledge (ITK) for weather forecasting is primarily based on:
   a) Quantitative data from advanced meteorological instruments.
   b) Generations of acute observation and intimate understanding of the local environment.
   c) Complex mathematical models run on supercomputers.
   d) Global satellite imagery analysis.
2. Which of the following is NOT typically an observational indicator used in ITK for weather forecasting?
   a) Animal behavior. b) Plant phenology.
   c) Economic market trends. d) Atmospheric signs.
3. According to ITK, low-flying birds before a storm can indicate:
   a) Rising atmospheric pressure.
   b) Falling atmospheric pressure, making it harder to gain altitude.
   c) Abundant food sources.
   d) A clear, sunny day ahead.
4. If ants are observed building unusually high mounds or sealing their entrances, ITK might interpret this as a sign of:
   a) Impending drought. b) A very mild winter.
   c) Impending heavy rain or floods.
   d) A stable high-pressure system.
5. Unusual timing or routes of migratory birds in ITK might suggest:
   a) A change in wind direction for the next day.
   b) Long-term seasonal shifts or more severe weather in their usual destinations.

c) A specific lunar phase.

d) Increased local insect populations.

6. Plant phenology, as an ITK indicator, typically provides insights for:

a) Immediate, hourly weather changes.

b) Short-term (daily) forecasts.

c) Seasonal or medium-range forecasts.

d) Predicting volcanic eruptions.

7. If a wild plant flowers significantly earlier than its historical average, ITK might interpret this as a sign of:

a) A very cold, harsh upcoming season.

b) An unusually mild or warmer upcoming season.

c) Impending strong winds.

d) Increased soil salinity.

8. The proverb „Red sky at night, sailor‘s delight; Red sky in morning, sailor‘s warning“ has a basis in:

a) Pure superstition with no scientific correlation.

b) The scattering of light by particles in the atmosphere and typical weather system movement.

c) Astronomical alignments that dictate ocean tides.

d) The behavior of nocturnal animals.

9. A halo appearing around the Moon or Sun is often interpreted in ITK as a sign of:

a) Extremely clear and stable weather.

b) Approaching precipitation (rain or snow).

c) Decreased atmospheric humidity.

d) A solar flare.

10. The scientific basis for a halo around the Moon or Sun involves:

a) Lunar magnetism.

b) Refraction of light through ice crystals in high-altitude clouds.

c) Absorption of light by water droplets in the lower atmosphere.

d) The Moon‘s gravitational pull on clouds.

11. What does increased or rapid twinkling of stars typically indicate in ITK for weather forecasting?
    a) Very stable and calm atmospheric conditions.
    b) Turbulent, unstable air in the upper atmosphere, potentially preceding unsettled weather.
    c) Decreased atmospheric moisture.
    d) A sign of good harvest.
12. Traditional ecological calendars are distinct from conventional calendars because they:
    a) Only track lunar cycles.
    b) Organize the year based on astronomical or Gregorian dates only.
    c) Divide the year by significant ecological and meteorological events.
    d) Are used exclusively by meteorologists.
13. The ''Mackerel sky'' (small, rippled, high-level clouds) in ITK is often linked to:
    a) Immediate clear skies.
    b) Prolonged periods of drought.
    c) Unsettled weather or rain within a short period.
    d) A strong, consistent high-pressure system.
14. Weather proverbs are best described as:
    a) Complex mathematical equations.
    b) Concise, memorable phrases encapsulating empirical weather observations.
    c) Detailed scientific reports.
    d) Instrumental readings.
15. The proverb ''When smoke from a chimney goes straight up, fair weather it will be. When smoke descends to the ground, foul weather it will be found'' relates to ITK's understanding of:
    a) Wind direction only.
    b) Atmospheric pressure and stability.
    c) The amount of fuel in the chimney.
    d) Cloud temperature.

16. Which observation is an example of a hydrometeorological indicator in ITK?

    a) Bird migration patterns. b) Cloud formations.

    c) Dew formation. d) Star twinkling.

17. Heavy dew at dawn is typically interpreted in ITK as a sign of:

    a) Impending heavy rainfall.

    b) A clear, calm night and fair weather ahead.

    c) Very strong winds.

    d) High humidity leading to immediate fog.

18. If springs are unusually low or dry for a particular time of year, ITK might interpret this as an indicator of:

    a) An upcoming period of abundant rainfall.

    b) Prolonged drought conditions or poor seasonal recharge.

    c) Increased groundwater availability.

    d) A shift in tidal patterns.

19. The absence of dew on a morning when it would typically be expected can signal:

    a) Perfect sunny weather for the entire day.

    b) Significant cloud cover or strong winds preventing condensation.

    c) Decreased atmospheric moisture.

    d) An imminent rise in air temperature.

20. What is a key strength of ITK weather forecasts?

    a) Their ability to provide precise quantitative predictions globally.

    b) Their perfect reliability under all conditions, including rapid climate change.

    c) Their deep contextual relevance within specific local microclimates.

    d) Their independence from any human observation.

21. A major limitation of ITK weather forecasts, particularly in the face of rapid climate change, is their:

    a) High cost of implementation.

    b) Inability to be passed down through generations.

    c) Potential disruption of traditional indicators due to unprecedented shifts.

    d) Exclusive focus on short-term predictions.

22. What does an integrated approach (combining ITK and modern science) to weather forecasting aim to achieve?
    a) To replace ITK with scientific methods entirely.
    b) To solely rely on ITK for all weather predictions.
    c) To enhance agricultural resilience through comprehensive and locally relevant information.
    d) To make weather forecasting more complex and less accessible.
23. The observation that specific plants flower earlier or later than usual due to weather changes is an example of which ITK indicator?
    a) Zoological indicator.
    b) Astronomical indicator.
    c) Botanical/Phenological indicator.
    d) Hydro-meteorological indicator.
24. A distinct „earthy" smell just before rain is attributed in ITK to:
    a) Increased wind speed.
    b) Geosmin, a chemical released by soil bacteria activated by humidity.
    c) The presence of a rainbow.
    d) A sudden drop in air pressure.
25. While ITK is primarily qualitative, what benefit does it offer to smallholder farmers?
    a) Access to global long-range climate models.
    b) High-precision numerical forecasts.
    c) Low-cost, actionable insights integrated with local practices.
    d) Advanced statistical analysis of weather data.
26. The traditional belief that „When the grass is dry at morning light, look for rain before the night" relates to the absence of:
    a) Wind. W5w b) Clouds.
    c) Dew. d) Sunlight.
27. The concept of „hungry season" in some traditional ecological calendars is often defined by:
    a) A specific astronomical alignment.
    b) The period before harvest when food stores are low.
    c) The blooming of a rare flower.
    d) A particular wind direction.

28. Which of the following is a direct observation of terrestrial signs in ITK for weather forecasting?
   a) The color of the sunset.
   b) Fish jumping out of water.
   c) Soil dampness or „sweating" rocks.
   d) The timing of bird migration.
29. The „scientific basis" of many ITK observations suggests that:
   a) They are purely coincidental.
   b) They reflect genuine physiological or atmospheric responses to precursor meteorological changes.
   c) They are only valid in the past.
   d) They contradict all modern scientific findings.
30. The primary challenge in integrating ITK with modern scientific weather predictions is often:
   a) The high cost of ITK.
   b) The lack of any data from ITK.
   c) Bridging the gap between qualitative, localized traditional knowledge and quantitative, large-scale scientific data.
   d) Farmers' unwillingness to accept new information.

Answer Key

1	b	2	c	3	b	4	c	5	c	6	c	7	b
8	b	9	b	10	b	11	b	12	c	13	c	14	b
15	b	16	c	17	b	18	b	19	b	20	c	21	c
22	c	23	c	24	b	25	c	26	c	27	b	28	c
29	b	30	c										

22

Crop Weather Calendars

1. Crop Weather Calendars primarily synthesize understanding from:
   a) Economic market analysis and global trade routes.
   b) Meteorological information and crop-specific data.
   c) Soil microbial activity and plant genetics only.
   d) Historical rainfall patterns and pest outbreaks exclusively.
2. A key distinction of Crop Weather Calendars from traditional ecological calendars is their:
   a) Reliance solely on animal behavior.
   b) More formalized and systematically organized compilation of data.
   c) Lack of connection to agricultural practices.
   d) Exclusive use of qualitative observations.
3. Which type of weather data is not typically integrated into Crop Weather Calendars?
   a) Historical weather patterns.
   b) Real-time meteorological data.
   c) Future weather forecasts.
   d) Paleoclimatic data from ice cores.
4. One of the core objectives of Crop Weather Calendars is to:
   a) Promote a single, uniform cropping system globally.
   b) Optimize resource use efficiency, particularly for water and nutrients.
   c) Predict global food prices with high accuracy.
   d) Replace all traditional farming knowledge.
5. By identifying critical weather thresholds for each growth stage, Crop Weather Calendars primarily help in:
   a) Determining the exact market value of the crop.
   b) Enabling early warnings and implementing preventive measures for adverse conditions.

c) Calculating the total biomass produced irrespective of stress.

d) Designing new agricultural machinery.

6. Crop Weather Calendars contribute to enhancing farm productivity by:

a) Promoting random planting dates.

b) Ensuring crops experience favorable environments during sensitive stages.

c) Reducing the need for any kind of fertilizer.

d) Ignoring pest and disease risks.

7. For which crucial farm operation do Crop Weather Calendars provide guidance, ensuring proper soil moisture and expected rainfall?

a) Post-harvest storage. b) Land preparation.

c) Marketing of produce. d) Financial accounting.

8. The input data for Crop Weather Calendars is expected to be comprehensive, covering which domains?

a) Social, political, and cultural.

b) Economic, legal, and regulatory.

c) Meteorological, agronomic, and edaphic (soil).

d) Geological, astronomical, and marine.

9. For historical weather data, what is the ideal duration of daily or weekly records required for a robust Crop Weather Calendar?

a) 1-2 years. b) 5-10 years.

c) 20-30+ years d) Less than 1 year.

10. Which specific meteorological parameter is crucial for calculating Growing Degree Days (GDD) and identifying heat/cold stress periods in a Crop Weather Calendar?

a) Wind speed.

b) Relative humidity.

c) Daily maximum and minimum temperatures.

d) Atmospheric pressure.

11. Crop Coefficients (Kc) are an important crop-specific input to Crop Weather Calendars, as they help determine:

a) The crop's sensitivity to pest attacks.

b) The crop's water requirements at different growth stages.

c) The optimal planting density.

d) The amount of solar radiation intercepted.

12. The maximum effective rooting depth of a crop is a soil/crop input that influences:

a) Its sensitivity to heat stress.

b) Its susceptibility to lodging.

c) Its water extraction capacity from the soil.

d) Its nutrient application rate.

13. On a Crop Weather Calendar, the horizontal axis typically represents:

a) Specific weather parameters like temperature or rainfall.

b) The progression of time and crop developmental stages.

c) The various recommended farm operations.

d) Different types of soil.

14. If a calendar uses "Vegetative,""Reproductive," and "Grain Filling" as its primary horizontal divisions, it is organized by:

a) Calendar weeks.

b) Days After Sowing (DAS).

c) Crop developmental stages.

d) Standard Meteorological Weeks (SMW).

15. The vertical axis of a Crop Weather Calendar typically provides:

a) A singular historical yield average.

b) Detailed meteorological parameters, crop requirements and recommended actions.

c) A general overview of global weather patterns.

d) Economic forecasts for crop prices.

16. Which type of information is found in the "Recommended Agricultural Operations / Advisories" section of a Crop Weather Calendar?

a) Details on the genetic makeup of the crop.

b) Precise timing and type of fertilizer application.

c) The history of agricultural policy.

d) Global trade agreements for commodities.

17. What distinguishes Dynamic Crop Weather Calendars from static ones?
    a) They only use historical averages.
    b) They continuously adapt using real-time weather observations and updated forecasts.
    c) They are always printed on paper.
    d) They are exclusively used for subsistence farming.
18. The "dynamic" nature of these calendars is largely enabled by technologies such as:
    a) Hand tools and manual irrigation.
    b) Traditional rain gauges and physical notebooks.
    c) Automatic Weather Stations (AWS) and remote sensing.
    d) Manual observation of animal behavior.
19. A key benefit of Dynamic Crop Weather Calendars is their:
    a) Reduced need for any kind of weather data.
    b) Increased accuracy and relevance of advisories tailored to current conditions.
    c) Fixed and unchanging recommendations throughout the season.
    d) Sole reliance on expert intuition.
20. When an unexpected rainfall event occurs, a dynamic crop weather calendar would typically:
    a) Ignore the event and stick to the original plan.
    b) Automatically recalculate and potentially postpone or reduce irrigation recommendations.
    c) Issue a warning about heat stress.
    d) Advise increasing fertilizer application.
21. The India Meteorological Department (IMD) initially developed Crop Weather Calendars based on:
    a) Daily satellite imagery.
    b) Long-term historical climatic normals for districts and crops.
    c) Real-time sensor networks in every field.
    d) Farmer feedback only.

22. What information is found in the "Weather Warnings and Pest/Disease Conditions" section of traditional IMD CWCs?
    a) Global market prices for pesticides.
    b) Favorable meteorological conditions for pest/disease incidence and types of warnings to be issued.
    c) Detailed chemical composition of fertilizers.
    d) Historical crop yield statistics only.
23. How are IMD's Crop Weather Calendar insights primarily disseminated to farmers in India?
    a) Through international news channels.
    b) Via the Gramin Krishi Mausam Sewa (GKMS) program and Agromet Advisories.
    c) Directly by supercomputer models.
    d) Through academic journals.
24. A challenge in implementing dynamic crop weather calendars is:
    a) The simplicity of their underlying models.
    b) The widespread availability of high-quality, real-time data in all regions.
    c) The need for robust technological infrastructure and data quality.
    d) Farmers' immediate and universal adoption of new technologies without training.
25. The ultimate goal of Crop Weather Calendars in modern agriculture is to:
    a) Eliminate all risk from farming.
    b) Increase reliance on a single crop variety.
    c) Foster greater resilience and enhance productivity in a changing climate.
    d) Centralize all agricultural decision-making away from farmers.

Answer Key

1	b	2	b	3	d	4	b	5	b	6	b	7	b
8	c	9	c	10	c	11	b	12	c	13	b	14	c
15	b	16	b	17	b	18	c	19	b	20	b	21	b
22	b	23	b	24	c	25	c						

23

Agroadvisory Based on Weather Forecast

1. What is the primary purpose of an agroadvisory based on weather forecasts?
   a) To predict global economic trends affecting agriculture.
   b) To transform meteorological data into actionable farm-level advice.
   c) To replace traditional farming knowledge completely.
   d) To solely report historical climate patterns.
2. The conceptual framework of agroadvisory services views them primarily as a:
   a) Data storage repository.
   b) Social media platform.
   c) Decision-support system.
   d) Historical documentation tool.
3. Which of the following is not one of the four interconnected pillars of the agroadvisory conceptual framework?
   a) High-quality weather information.
   b) Agronomic expertise and crop-weather relationships.
   c) Global market analysis.
   d) Effective dissemination and feedback.
4. Nowcasting in weather forecasting typically provides predictions for a period of:
   a) 1-3 months. b) 0-6 hours.
   c) 3-10 days. d) 1-2 years.

5. Which type of forecast is most suitable for informing strategic choices about crop selection and rotation planning?
   a) Nowcasting.
   b) Short-range forecast.
   c) Medium-range forecast.
   d) Long-range/Seasonal forecast.
6. Agronomic expertise in the agroadvisory framework primarily focuses on:
   a) Designing new farm machinery.
   b) Interpreting meteorological information in the context of specific crops.
   c) Predicting global food prices.
   d) Developing new crop varieties through genetic engineering.
7. Understanding the precise developmental stages of crops and their weather sensitivities is termed:
   a) Climatology.
   b) Pedology.
   c) Phenology.
   d) Hydrology.
8. For nutrient management, an agroadvisory might recommend top-dressing fertilizer based on expected:
   a) Wind speed for the entire season.
   b) Light rainfall to enhance dissolution and uptake.
   c) High temperatures to accelerate decomposition.
   d) Long dry spells to prevent leaching.
9. Which of these is an essential component found in a comprehensive agroadvisory?
   a) Local political commentary.
   b) General weather forecast for the advisory period.
   c) International commodity prices.
   d) Detailed farm financial statements.
10. The period of validity in a weather forecast component of an agroadvisory indicates:
    a) The date of issuance.
    b) The duration for which the forecast is applicable.

c) The historical accuracy rate of the forecast.

d) The frequency of advisories.

11. Why is information on wind speed and direction crucial in an agroadvisory?

a) It indicates the overall climate type.

b) It influences spraying efficacy and lodging risk.

c) It predicts soil erosion rates.

d) It determines soil temperature.

12. In the „Interpretation in Local Context" section, an agroadvisory translates expected weather into:

a) Scientific research hypotheses.

b) Its likely effect on specific crop growth and potential stress.

c) Global atmospheric circulation patterns.

d) Historical weather anomaly data.

13. An actionable recommendation in an agroadvisory for water management might involve:

a) A general statement about climate change impacts.

b) Advice on irrigation scheduling with specific water amounts.

c) Historical rainfall averages for the region.

d) Global water scarcity statistics.

14. What distinguishes a „Customized Agroadvisory" from a general one?

a) It is only issued once per season.

b) It provides advice tailored to individual farm/field-level conditions and specific cultivars.

c) It is valid for an entire agro-climatic zone without variation.

d) It focuses solely on historical data, not forecasts.

15. Which piece of information is most crucial for formulating a truly customized agroadvisory?

a) The national agricultural policy.

b) The exact GPS coordinates and sowing date of a farmer's field.

c) The average rainfall for the past 50 years in the country.

d) The global market price of fertilizers.

16. How do Crop Simulation Models (CSMs) primarily contribute to agroadvisory formulation?
    a) By generating marketing strategies for agricultural produce.
    b) By physically growing crops under controlled conditions.
    c) By predicting crop growth, development, and yield under varying conditions.
    d) By solely collecting real-time weather data.
17. CSMs can accurately predict phenological stages by calculating:
    a) Humidity levels. b) Wind chill factors.
    c) Growing Degree Days (GDD). d) Barometric pressure.
18. What kind of „what-if" scenario analysis can CSMs facilitate for agroadvisories?
    a) Predicting political stability in agricultural regions.
    b) Testing different planting dates or fertilizer rates under various climate scenarios.
    c) Simulating global trade impacts on local prices.
    d) Forecasting new agricultural machinery innovations.
19. Decision Support Systems (DSS) in agroadvisory formulation primarily act as:
    a) Raw weather data collection devices.
    b) Advanced farm machinery.
    c) Integrated platforms for data analysis and recommendation generation.
    d) Communication networks for farmers.
20. A DSS might incorporate „expert systems" to:
    a) Store historical rainfall data.
    b) Codify agronomic knowledge to trigger specific advisories.
    c) Broadcast weather forecasts on radio.
    d) Analyze farmer feedback directly from the field.
21. What is a key benefit of using CSMs and DSS in agroadvisory formulation?
    a) Reduced need for any weather data.
    b) Increased reliance on manual labor.
    c) Enhanced precision, accuracy, and proactive risk management.
    d) Elimination of all agricultural risks.

22. What is a significant challenge in delivering highly customized agroadvisories?
    a) Lack of demand from farmers.
    b) Low cost of implementation.
    c) Requirement for vast amounts of granular, accurate data.
    d) Oversupply of skilled personnel.

23. Which service provider would be most interested in an alert about the likely overall demand for specific crop varieties in the upcoming season?
    a) A food processing industry.
    b) An agricultural input supplier (seeds).
    c) A custom hire service.
    d) A local grocery store.

24. For agro-based industries like sugar mills, what kind of agroadvisory alert is critical?
    a) Daily local temperature swings.
    b) Precise harvest window forecasts based on dry spells.
    c) Global fertilizer price trends.
    d) Historical data on pest infestations.

25. What is a primary concern for food processing industries when receiving agroadvisories?
    a) The exact planting method used by farmers.
    b) Raw material supply consistency and quality degradation due to weather.
    c) The type of irrigation system employed.
    d) The historical yield of a single demonstration plot.

26. Custom hire services would find which type of alert most useful for their operations?
    a) Warnings about national agricultural policy changes.
    b) Notifications on soil workability and optimal spraying windows.
    c) Long-range forecasts for global commodity prices.
    d) Reports on farmer income levels in the previous year.

27. Why is building „confidence and trust" crucial for agroadvisory services?
    a) It is a regulatory requirement.
    b) It directly correlates with the adoption rate ofAAS
    c) It reduces the need for accurate forecasts.
    d) It simplifies the data collection process.
28. The most direct way to build farmer trust in agroadvisories is through:
    a) Aggressive marketing campaigns.
    b) Consistently accurate and reliable forecasts.
    c) Reducing the frequency of advisories.
    d) Using highly technical language.
29. Timeliness in agroadvisory dissemination refers to:
    a) The advisory being available for public record.
    b) The advisory reaching farmers well in advance of the recommended action.
    c) The speed of data processing at the meteorological center.
    d) The time taken to print the advisory bulletin.
30. Which strategy enhances the „specificity and local relevance" of an agroadvisory?
    a) Providing a generalized national weather outlook.
    b) Tailoring advice to individual field conditions, crop varieties, and sowing dates.
    c) Focusing only on broad climatic zones.
    d) Using only historical average data.
31. To build trust, agroadvisories should be based on:
    a) Personal knowledge and intuition of experts.
    b) Anecdotal evidence from local farmers.
    c) Rigorous scientific support and verifiable evidence.
    d) Financial market speculation.
32. The primary role of human meteorologists in the data flow pipeline is to:
    a) Conduct farmer surveys.
    b) Physically collect soil samples.
    c) Interpret NWP model outputs and refine forecasts.
    d) Design new mobile applications.

33. Which component of an agroadvisory provides a brief summary of recent weather?

a) General weather forecast. b) Current weather status.

c) Actionable recommendations. d) Contingency measures.

34. A farmer receives an alert about „high probability of fungal disease." This is most likely generated by integrating weather data with:

a) Global economic models

b) Pest and disease forecasting models

c) Livestock management software

d) Farm machinery usage logs

35. For agricultural insurance companies, what kind of weather-related alerts are particularly vital?

a) Daily wind direction changes.

b) Alerts on specific weather parameters triggering potential policy payouts.

c) Monthly average temperatures.

d) Historical data on crop types.

36. Providing feedback mechanisms where farmers can report on the utility and clarity of advisories primarily helps in:

a) Increasing the number of advisories issued.

b) Continuous improvement and building trust.

c) Reducing the need for extension workers.

d) Automating all farming operations.

37. Which of these is a key output of Crop Simulation Models (CSMs) relevant to agroadvisories?

a) Prediction of social media engagement.

b) Estimation of potential yield under various scenarios.

c) Development of new fertilizer compounds.

d) Design of irrigation pumps.

38. The process of taking raw meteorological data and environmental data from various sources is known as:

a) Data Visualization. b) Data Acquisition.

c) Data Archiving. d) Data Dissemination.

39. If an agroadvisory suggests postponing pesticide application due to strong winds, this advice originates from the integration of weather data with:
   a) Soil moisture sensors.
   b) Crop protection efficacy guidelines.
   c) Market demand forecasts.
   d) Post-harvest storage protocols.

40. When considering the ethical aspects of customized agroadvisories, a significant challenge is:
   a) The simplicity of the underlying models.
   b) Ensuring farmer digital literacy.
   c) Data privacy concerns related to individual farm data.
   d) The lack of suitable communication channels.

Answer Key

1	b	2	c	3	c	4	b	5	d	6	b	7	c
8	b	9	b	10	b	11	b	12	b	13	b	14	b
15	b	16	c	17	c	18	b	19	c	20	b	21	c
22	c	23	b	24	b	25	b	26	b	27	b	28	b
29	b	30	b	31	c	32	b	33	b	34	b	35	b
36	b	37	b	38	b	39	b	40	c				

24

Dissemination of Agrometeorological Advisories

1. What is the primary goal of disseminating agrometeorological advisories to farmers?
   a) To provide raw weather data for research.
   b) To convert weather forecasts into actionable, location-specific advice.
   c) To inform policy decisions at the national level only.
   d) To track global climate patterns.
2. Which Indian scheme is a prominent example of disseminating agrometeorological advisories?
   a) Swachh Bharat Abhiyan
   b) Pradhan Mantri Fasal Bima Yojana
   c) Gramin Krishi Mausam Sewa (GKMS)
   d) Digital India
3. What is a key benefit of timely and effective agro advisory dissemination for farmers?
   a) Increased reliance on traditional farming methods.
   b) Reduced need for modern agricultural technology.
   c) Enhanced efficiency, reduced risk, and increased productivity.
   d) Promotion of only one type of crop.
4. Which of the following communication channels is most effective for reaching farmers in remote rural areas with agro advisories?
   a) International scientific journals
   b) Local community radio and public address systems
   c) High-speed internet conferences
   d) Urban newspapers

5. What role do mobile applications (like IMD's Meghdoot app) play in agro advisory dissemination?
   a) They only provide historical weather data.
   b) They act as a direct channel for localized, real-time advisories.
   c) They are used exclusively by meteorologists.
   d) They measure soil moisture directly.
6. Beyond weather forecasts, what essential non-meteorological information is often integrated into value-added agro advisories?
   a) Global stock market trends.
   b) Crop growth stages, pest life cycles, and market prices.
   c) Urban traffic conditions.
   d) International political news.
7. What does the „localization" aspect of agro advisories imply?
   a) Advisories are only available in English.
   b) Advisories are generic for an entire continent.
   c) Advice is tailored to specific microclimates, crop types, and farming practices.
   d) Advisories are only for government officials.
8. Which type of weather forecast provides the most immediate and actionable information for day-to-day farm operations via advisories?
   a) Seasonal forecasts
   b) Long-range climate projections
   c) Short-range and nowcasting
   d) Decadal forecasts
9. What is a potential challenge in the effective dissemination of agro advisories to all farmers?
   a) Farmers always have access to smartphones and internet.
   b) High literacy rates among all farmers.
   c) Language barriers, digital divide, and lack of awareness among some farmers.
   d) Weather forecasts are always perfectly accurate.

10. When an agro advisory recommends a „spraying window," what weather parameters are typically considered?
    a) Only temperature.
    b) Only humidity.
    c) Wind speed and direction, and likelihood of rain.
    d) Soil pH level.
11. Why is a „feedback loop" important in the dissemination of agro advisories?
    a) To tell farmers what they did wrong.
    b) To allow farmers to send their own forecasts to meteorologists.
    c) To collect user experiences and suggestions for improving future advisories.
    d) To measure the popularity of the advisory service.
12. What role do agricultural extension services play in agro advisory dissemination?
    a) They produce the initial weather forecasts.
    b) They act as intermediaries, interpreting advisories and explaining them to farmers.
    c) They are responsible for collecting raw weather data.
    d) They design and maintain the IT infrastructure for dissemination.
13. An agro advisory warning of a „potential fungal blight outbreak" based on forecast humidity and temperature is an example of value-added information for:
    a) Irrigation scheduling.
    b) Pest and disease management.
    c) Crop harvesting.
    d) Livestock care.
14. What does „actionable intelligence" in the context of agro advisories mean?
    a) Raw data that requires further interpretation.
    b) Information that directly tells a farmer what specific action to take.
    c) Forecasts that are only for academic research.
    d) Data that is only useful for large-scale commercial farms.

15. Beyond advising farmers, who else benefits from the effective dissemination of agro advisories?
    a) Only urban dwellers.
    b) Agricultural policymakers, input suppliers, and agricultural insurance companies.
    c) International climate scientists only.
    d) Automobile manufacturers.

Answer Key

1	b	2	c	3	c	4	b	5	b	6	b	7	c
8	c	9	c	10	c	11	c	12	b	13	b	14	b
15	b												

25

Evaluation of Crop Responses to Weather

1. Crop growth, representing biomass accumulation, is fundamentally the net result of:
   a) Transpiration minus Respiration
   b) Gross Photosynthesis minus Transpiration
   c) Gross Photosynthesis minus Total Respiration
   d) Light Interception minus Nutrient Uptake
2. Which part of the solar radiation spectrum is primarily utilized by plants for photosynthesis?
   a) Infrared radiation
   b) Ultraviolet radiation
   c) Photosynthetically Active Radiation (PAR)
   d) X-rays
3. High night temperatures are generally detrimental to crop growth because they:
   a) Promote excessive water uptake
   b) Increase maintenance respiration, depleting carbohydrates
   c) Lead to chilling injury
   d) Reduce light interception
4. How does severe water stress primarily reduce photosynthesis?
   a) By increasing stomatal opening and CO_2 uptake
   b) By directly denaturing photosynthetic enzymes
   c) By inducing stomatal closure, limiting CO_2 entry
   d) By increasing soil oxygen levels

5. The ‚CO_2 fertilization effect' is generally more pronounced in which type of plants?
   a) C4 plants b) CAM plants
   c) C3 plants d) Both C3 and C4 equally
6. Moderate wind speeds can positively influence crop growth by:
   a) Directly increasing leaf temperature
   b) Accelerating the onset of water stress
   c) Increasing the supply of carbon dioxide to the plants
   d) Causing physical damage to the plant canopy
7. Which evaluation method offers the highest precision and control over environmental parameters, making it ideal for studying fundamental physiological responses?
   a) Field Experiments
   b) Historical Weather-Yield Correlations
   c) Growth Chambers / Phytotrons
   d) Remote Sensing
8. The main limitation of historical weather-yield correlations is that they:
   a) Are too expensive to conduct
   b) Cannot be replicated in different locations
   c) Show correlation, not necessarily causation
   d) Require real-time data, which is often unavailable
9. Free Air CO_2 Enrichment (FACE) experiments are primarily designed to:
   a) Simulate frost damage
   b) Measure the CO_2 fertilization effect under realistic field conditions
   c) Analyze long-term phenological shifts
   d) Control soil moisture levels precisely
10. Which method provides large-scale, non-destructive monitoring of crop responses, often using Vegetation Indices (VIs)?
   a) Growth Chambers b) Field Experiments
   c) Process-Based Crop Models d) Satellite Imagery

11. What is a key advantage of process-based crop models?
    a) They are completely free of uncertainty.
    b) They only require minimal historical data.
    c) They provide mechanistic insights into why weather affects crop performance.
    d) They eliminate the need for any field validation.
12. Empirical methods primarily rely on:
    a) Simulations of physiological processes
    b) Direct observation and statistical analysis of historical data
    c) Precise control of all environmental variables
    d) Genetic engineering to test weather responses
13. In statistical weather-yield regression, if the coefficient for ‚July rainfall' is positive and significant, it implies:
    a) July rainfall directly causes increased yield.
    b) Higher July rainfall is statistically associated with higher yields.
    c) July rainfall is the only factor affecting yield.
    d) The relationship is always linear.
14. What is a significant drawback of purely statistical crop-weather models?
    a) They are too complex to interpret.
    b) They require extensive computational power.
    c) They cannot reliably extrapolate to novel climate conditions.
    d) They only work for a single crop type.
15. Which statistical technique is used to measure the strength and direction of a linear association between two variables?
    a) Regression Analysis
    b) Time Series Analysis
    c) Correlation Analysis
    d) Principal Component Analysis
16. Analyzing yield deviations from a long-term trend in historical data helps to:
    a) Account for changes in pest and disease incidence.
    b) Remove the influence of technological advancements and management improvements.

c) Directly measure the impact of soil fertility.

d) Predict future market prices.

17. A limitation of agro-climatological indices and zonation is that they can:

a) Be too complex to calculate for large areas.

b) Oversimplify complex interactions and mask daily weather effects.

c) Only apply to perennial crops.

d) Directly predict economic returns.

18. When dealing with numerous inter-correlated weather variables, which multivariate statistical technique can synthesize them into fewer, uncorrelated components?

a) Simple Linear Regression

b) Principal Component Analysis (PCA)

c) Cluster Analysis

d) Time Series Analysis

19. Which of the following is NOT a core principle of empirical methods?

a) Observation-driven from historical data

b) Statistical foundation for relationships

c) Explicit representation of biological mechanisms

d) Often treats the crop as a „black box“

20. What is a key requirement for reliable statistical analysis of weather effects on crops?

a) Data from only one growing season

b) Short-term forecasts rather than historical data

c) Long-term, consistent, high-quality records for both weather and crop outcomes

d) Exclusion of all non-weather-related variables

21. Analytical methods for evaluating crop response primarily aim to:

a) Find statistical correlations between yield and weather.

b) Simulate the underlying biological and physical processes.

c) Determine the economic impact of weather on farmers.

d) Classify climate zones for crop suitability.

22. In a process-based crop model, which component is typically calculated by considering Leaf Area Index (LAI) and light extinction coefficients?
   a) Respiration Rate
   b) Nutrient Uptake
   c) Light Interception by Canopy
   d) Root Water Uptake

23. The carbon lost by a plant for maintaining existing tissues and synthesizing new ones is accounted for by:
   a) Gross Photosynthesis
   b) Transpiration
   c) Respiration
   d) Light Use Efficiency

24. What does a process-based crop model do with assimilated carbon (net growth)?
   a) It assumes it‘s all converted to yield immediately.
   b) It allocates it dynamically among different plant organs.
   c) It releases it back into the atmosphere.
   d) It only considers carbon gained by roots.

25. What critical process does a process-based model meticulously track between the soil, plant, and atmosphere?
   a) Wind patterns
   b) Hail formation
   c) Water balance and Transpiration
   d) Solar flare activity

26. A key advantage of analytical (mechanistic) crop models over statistical models is their ability to:
   a) Be simpler to calibrate
   b) Provide mechanistic explanations (the ‚why‘)
   c) Require less input data
   d) Be less computationally demanding

27. When using process-based models for „what-if“ scenarios, what kind of inputs are typically varied?
   a) Only historical yield data
   b) Combinations of weather parameters, soil types, or management practices
   c) Economic market prices only
   d) Genetic sequences of pests

28. Which of the following is a major limitation of analytical crop models?
    a) They cannot simulate physiological processes.
    b) They are too simplistic for real-world applications.
    c) They require vast amounts of high-quality input data for parameterization and validation.
    d) They can only be used for short-term forecasting.
29. The concept of „optimum weather conditions“ for a crop is:
    a) A universal constant for all crops globally.
    b) Independent of the crop cultivar or region.
    c) Highly region-specific, crop-specific, and even cultivar-specific.
    d) Determined solely by temperature.
30. Why is determining optimum weather conditions a complex task?
    a) Weather parameters never interact.
    b) Crops have uniform sensitivities throughout their life cycle.
    c) It involves interacting factors, temporal dynamics, and genotype-environment interactions.
    d) It only requires average annual data.
31. In analyzing long-term historical data, comparing GDD accumulation with known crop requirements helps to:
    a) Determine soil nutrient levels.
    b) Assess if a region has sufficient heat units for a crop to mature reliably.
    c) Predict pest outbreaks.
    d) Evaluate market demand for the crop.
32. What is a primary contribution of controlled environment studies (like growth chambers) to determining optimum weather conditions?
    a) They provide large-scale yield forecasts.
    b) They allow for precise determination of cardinal temp for specific processes.
    c) They assess economic viability directly.
    d) They predict global climate change impacts.

33. When using process-based crop models to determine optimal planting windows, what is the typical approach?

a) Only using current year's weather forecast.

b) Simulating yields for different planting dates over many yrs of historical weather.

c) Observing phenological events visually.

d) Performing laboratory nutrient analysis.

34. Agro-climatic zonation, as a macro-level application, primarily helps in:

a) Predicting daily weather fluctuations.

b) Delineating regions based on climatic suitability for specific crops.

c) Measuring individual grain weight.

d) Controlling pest populations.

35. Which term refers to the natural, short-term fluctuations in climatic parameters around their long-term average?

a) Climate Change b) Global Warming

c) Climate Variability d) Anthropogenic Climate

36. An increase in the frequency and intensity of heatwaves over several decades is an example of:

a) Normal climate variability b) Climate change

c) Seasonal weather anomaly d) Microclimate effect

37. What is a key characteristic of the current climate change with respect to extreme events?

a) A decrease in their frequency.

b) A shift in their type but not intensity.

c) Changes in their frequency, intensity, duration, and spatial extent.

d) No impact on extreme events.

38. Which of the following is a potential effect of rising average temperatures due to climate change on crops?

a) Prolonged growing seasons and delayed maturity everywhere.

b) Accelerated crop development and shorter growing seasons.

c) Decreased pest pressure globally.

d) Guaranteed increase in nutritional quality.

39. The, CO_2 fertilization effect‘ is a positive impact of climate change, but its benefits can be offset by:
   a) Increased rainfall.
   b) Concurrent heat and water stress.
   c) Decreased solar radiation.
   d) Reduced pest populations.
40. Evaluating climate change impacts on crops primarily relies on:
   a) Long-term historical yield-weather correlations only.
   b) Short-term weather forecasts.
   c) Forward-looking, sophisticated process-based crop models driven by future climate projections.
   d) Field observations of isolated weather events.
41. What is the fundamental difference in effect on crops between climate variability and climate change?
   a) Variability causes irreversible shifts, while change causes annual fluctuations.
   b) Variability causes only positive impacts, while change causes only negative impacts.
   c) Variability refers to fluctuations around a mean, while change refers to a persistent shift in the mean itself and altered extremes.
   d) Variability is human-induced, while change is purely natural.
42. The primary goal of incorporating ‚weather response traits‘ in crop breeding is to enhance:
   a) Post-harvest processing efficiency
   b) Resilience, stability, and productivity under diverse climatic conditions
   c) Crop aesthetic appeal
   d) Market access for farmers
43. Which of the following is a key weather response trait targeted for heat tolerance?
   a) Deep rooting
   b) Aerenchyma formation
   c) Efficient stomatal regulation for evaporative cooling
   d) Increased chilling hours

44. Breeding for ‚drought escape' involves selecting cultivars that:
   a) Can maintain high water use efficiency throughout the season.
   b) Complete their life cycle before severe drought sets in.
   c) Develop very deep root systems.
   d) Accumulate solutes for osmotic adjustment.

45. Why is ‚photoperiod sensitivity' an important trait for breeders to consider for light response?
   a) It directly impacts individual grain weight.
   b) It ensures flowering and maturity occur at the optimal time for a given latitude.
   c) It improves soil nutrient uptake.
   d) It reduces wind damage.

46. What does ‚lodging resistance' primarily address in cereals?
   a) Damage from hailstorms
   b) Resistance to pests
   c) Prevention of crops falling over due to strong winds
   d) Tolerance to waterlogging

47. Which advanced molecular technique helps identify specific genes associated with desirable weather response traits, accelerating the selection process?
   a) Traditional Cross-breeding
   b) Manual Phenotyping
   c) Marker-Assisted Selection (MAS)
   d) Direct Weather Forecasting

48. A severe reduction in plant population is most likely caused by adverse weather during which stage?
   a) Grain filling
   b) Flowering/Anthesis
   c) Germination and emergence
   d) Early senescence

49. High temperatures around flowering (anthesis) primarily reduce yield by impacting which component?
   a) Individual grain weight
   b) Plant population
   c) Number of grains/seeds per reproductive organ
   d) Number of tillers

50. Prolonged cloudy weather during the grain filling period is most likely to reduce:
   a) Plant population
   b) Number of tillers
   c) Individual grain/seed weight
   d) Number of reproductive organs

51. Waterlogging during the early vegetative stage most directly impacts which yield component?
   a) Individual grain weight
   b) Number of grains per reproductive organ
   c) Stunted growth and reduced tillering/branching, limiting potential reproductive organs
   d) Pollen viability

52. Frost occurring during the grain filling period is likely to cause:
   a) Increased individual grain weight
   b) Premature termination of grain filling, reducing individual grain weight
   c) Increased plant population
   d) Enhanced photosynthesis

53. If a crop experiences severe drought stress during flowering, which yield component is most likely to be significantly reduced?
   a) Plant Population
   b) Number of Grains/Seeds per Reproductive Organ
   c) Individual Grain/Seed Weight (with no impact on number)
   d) Root biomass

54. The most critical and often devastating impact of a heatwave on cereal crops occurs during:
   a) Early vegetative growth   b) Tillering
   c) Flowering/Anthesis   d) Post-harvest

55. How do strong winds primarily reduce crop yield?
   a) By increasing soil temperature.
   b) By causing lodging, defoliation, and stem breakage.
   c) By enhancing nutrient uptake.
   d) By reducing atmospheric CO_2 concentration.

56. Flooding or waterlogging severely impacts plant roots primarily due to:
    a) Excessive light exposure
    b) Oxygen deprivation (anaerobiosis)
    c) Increased soil pH
    d) Accelerated nutrient absorption
57. A hailstorm causes direct physical damage to crops, which leads to:
    a) Enhanced photosynthesis and growth
    b) Shredded leaves, broken stems, and bruised produce
    c) Increased soil organic matter
    d) Improved nutrient translocation
58. What is a „compound extreme event"?
    a) A single, very intense weather event.
    b) Multiple extreme weather events occurring simultaneously or in close succession.
    c) An extreme event that only affects one type of crop.
    d) A long-term shift in average climate.
59. If a late spring frost occurs, which part of a fruit tree is most susceptible to damage leading to reduced fruit set?
    a) Dormant woody stems
    b) Mature leaves
    c) Developing flower buds, open flowers, and newly formed fruits
    d) Deep roots
60. Which type of extreme event can lead to an accumulation of toxic compounds in the root zone due to anaerobic conditions?
    a) Heatwave   b) Drought
    c) Waterlogging/Flood   d) Hailstorm

Answer Key

1	c	2	c	3	b	4	c	5	c	6	c	7	c
8	c	9	b	10	d	11	c	12	b	13	b	14	c
15	c	16	b	17	b	18	b	19	c	20	c	21	b
22	c	23	c	24	b	25	c	26	b	27	b	28	c
29	c	30	c	31	b	32	b	33	b	34	b	35	c
36	b	37	c	38	b	39	b	40	c	41	c	42	b

43	c	44	b	45	b	46	c	47	c	48	c	49	c
50	c	51	c	52	b	53	b	54	c	55	b	56	b
57	b	58	b	59	c	60	c						

26

Elementary Crop Growth Models

1. Elementary crop growth models are primarily characterized by their:
   a) Extreme complexity and detailed cellular representations.
   b) Simplicity, ease of use, and focus on the main weather factors.
   c) Exclusive reliance on genetic sequencing data.
   d) Ability to predict long-term global climate shifts.
2. What is a main function of elementary crop growth models?
   a) To perform highly precise mechanistic simulations of all plant processes.
   b) To provide an initial, quick estimate of crop performance.
   c) To manage international agricultural trade policies.
   d) To eliminate the need for any field observations.
3. Which statement accurately describes a characteristic of elementary crop growth models?
   a) They explicitly simulate nutrient uptake kinetics.
   b) They require vast computational power for daily runs.
   c) They typically focus on the influence of one or two dominant weather variables.
   d) They offer perfect predictions under all stress conditions.
4. Thermal Time Models, often represented by Growing Degree Days (GDD), are commonly used to predict:
   a) The total amount of biomass produced by a crop.
   b) Changes in soil water content over time.
   c) The timing of a crop's phenological developmental stages.
   d) The market price of agricultural commodities.

5. Thermal Time Models (Growing Degree Days - GDD) primarily use which weather input for their core calculation of developmental progress?
   a) Total daily solar radiation.
   b) Daily maximum and minimum temperatures.
   c) Wind speed and relative humidity.
   d) The total amount of rainfall.
6. In a Thermal Time Model, if the average daily temperature is below the crop's base temperature, how much developmental progress (GDD) is typically accumulated for that day?
   a) A negative amount.
   b) The full potential for that day.
   c) Zero.
   d) An amount equal to the maximum temperature.
7. A significant limitation of Thermal Time (GDD) models is that they:
   a) Are too difficult for farmers to understand.
   b) Do not typically account for the direct influence of factors like solar radiation or water stress on development rate.
   c) Can accurately predict final crop yield directly.
   d) Are only suitable for crops grown in tropical climates.
8. Radiation Use Efficiency (RUE) models estimate total dry matter production based on the concept that it's proportional to:
   a) The plant's genetic potential and soil type.
   b) The amount of photosynthetically active radiation (PAR) intercepted by the crop canopy.
   c) The daily average wind speed.
   d) The total amount of applied fertilizer.
9. What is a major drawback of Radiation Use Efficiency (RUE) models?
   a) They are overly complex to set up.
   b) They require too many specialized weather instruments.
   c) They assume a constant RUE value, ignoring how environmental stresses can reduce it.
   d) They can accurately predict individual grain weight.

10. Simple water-limited yield models are designed to assess the impact of:
    a) Soil temperature on root growth.
    b) The availability of water on overall crop yield.
    c) Air pollution on plant health.
    d) Light intensity on chlorophyll content.
11. In simple water-limited yield models, how is the actual crop yield typically determined?
    a) As a direct measure of seasonal rainfall totals.
    b) By adjusting a potential yield based on how well the crop's water demand is met.
    c) Exclusively through the plant's maximum daily temperature.
    d) Based solely on the crop's inherent genetic yield potential.
12. A key advantage of simple water-limited yield models is their ability to:
    a) Mechanistically simulate every water transport pathway in the plant.
    b) Provide a basic but important way to include the critical effect of water availability on yield.
    c) Precisely predict the economic returns from irrigation.
    d) Function without any weather data inputs.
13. When empirical regression models are categorized as elementary growth models, their primary role is to:
    a) Fully explain the biochemical reasons behind crop growth.
    b) Establish quantifiable relationships from historical data for predictive purposes.
    c) Conduct multi-century simulations of climate change impacts.
    d) Discover entirely new plant species.
14. A significant limitation when relying on empirical regression models for crop growth prediction is their:
    a) Ease of interpretation by non-experts.
    b) Difficulty in extrapolating reliably to novel or unprecedented weather conditions.
    c) Requirement for only a single year of historical data.
    d) Capacity to precisely model sub-daily weather fluctuations.

15. Beyond phenological forecasting, what is another practical application of GDD models in agriculture?
    a) Determining the precise amount of nutrients in the soil.
    b) Forecasting the optimal timing for critical field operations like harvest.
    c) Predicting the emergence of new insect pests.
    d) Calculating the efficiency of solar panels in the field.
16. Elementary models prove particularly useful in situations where:
    a) The highest level of scientific precision in predicting crop physiology is required.
    b) Extensive and detailed physiological or soil data are readily available.
    c) Detailed physiological or soil data are either limited or completely unavailable.
    d) The main objective is to design new genetic crop modifications.
17. Which of the following represents an inherent oversimplification within many elementary crop growth models?
    a) Their capability to dynamically adjust plant morphology.
    b) Their explicit modeling of complex carbon partitioning processes.
    c) Their assumption of linear responses to environmental factors within certain ranges.
    d) Their ability to accurately predict the impact of all extreme weather events.
18. Compared to more complex, process-based models, elementary models often lack:
    a) Any representation of temperature effects.
    b) The explicit representation of intricate physiological feedback mechanisms.
    c) Outputs such as phenological dates or total biomass.
    d) A connection to observed crop responses in the field.

19. When dealing with environmental stress, a major limitation of elementary models is that they:
    a) Are designed to perfectly predict threshold-based responses to extreme events.
    b) Often rely on simple, empirically derived reduction factors that may not capture complex physiological realities.
    c) Can precisely simulate changes in stomatal function under severe drought conditions.
    d) Require no adjustment for variability in soil properties.
20. Elementary crop growth models are considered valuable educational tools primarily because of their:
    a) Advanced mathematical formulations and computational requirements.
    b) Capacity to model global food production systems.
    c) Simplicity and clarity in illustrating fundamental crop-weather relationships.
    d) Unmatched accuracy in long-term climate predictions.

Answer Key

1	b	2	b	3	c	4	c	5	b	6	c	7	b
8	b	9	c	10	b	11	b	12	b	13	b	14	b
15	b	16	c	17	c	18	b	19	b	20	c		

27

Calibration, Validation, Verification, and Sensitivity of Elementary Crop Models

1. What is the primary purpose of calibration in elementary crop models?
   a) To prove the model's theoretical correctness.
   b) To adjust model parameters to match observed data for specific conditions.
   c) To assess the model's performance on entirely new datasets.
   d) To simplify the model's equations.
2. Why is calibration necessary for a crop model?
   a) To make it universally applicable without change.
   b) To account for cultivar specificity and local environmental nuances.
   c) To reduce its computational requirements.
   d) To eliminate all future sources of error.
3. In Thermal Time (GDD) models, which parameters are typically adjusted during calibration?
   a) Daily rainfall totals.
   b) The base temperature (Tbase) and accumulated GDD for phenological stages.
   c) Solar radiation intensity.
   d) Wind speed coefficients.
4. If a GDD model consistently predicts flowering too late compared to observations, which parameter might be adjusted during calibration?
   a) Increase the daily maximum temperature.
   b) Reduce the required GDD sum for the flowering stage.
   c) Increase the total growing season length.
   d) Change the soil type in the model input.

5. What is the core parameter calibrated in Radiation Use Efficiency (RUE) models?
   a) Leaf Area Index (LAI)   b) Water Holding Capacity
   c) Radiation Use Efficiency (ϵ)   d) Number of tillers per plant
6. The calibration process is typically:
   a) A one-time, simple calculation.
   b) An iterative process involving data collection, simulation, adjustment, and refinement.
   c) Conducted only by programming experts.
   d) Done without any need for observed field data.
7. What is the main purpose of validation in elementary crop models?
   a) To fine-tune model parameters.
   b) To rigorously test the model's predictive accuracy on independent datasets.
   c) To debug coding errors.
   d) To identify the most sensitive input variables.
8. Which type of data is essential for validation?
   a) Economic market data.
   b) Data used repeatedly during the calibration process.
   c) Independent datasets not used during calibration.
   d) Genetic sequences of crop pests.
9. If a scatter plot of observed vs. simulated values shows points consistently above the 1:1 line during validation, it suggests:
   a) Perfect model performance.
   b) The model has a systematic positive bias (overprediction).
   c) The model has a systematic negative bias (underprediction).
   d) The model is perfectly calibrated.
10. Which statistical metric measures the proportion of variance in observed data explained by the model?
   a) Root Mean Square Error (RMSE) b) Mean Absolute Error (MAE)
   c) Coefficient of Determination (R^2) d) Bias

11. A Normalized Root Mean Square Error (nRMSE) of less than 10% for a model's prediction is generally considered:
    a) Poor performance. b) Fair performance.
    c) Good performance. d) Excellent performance.
12. What does a high R^2 value in validation NOT guarantee by itself?
    a) That the model explains a large proportion of variability.
    b) That there is a systematic bias in predictions.
    c) That the model is perfectly accurate.
    d) That the observed data is reliable.
13. Verification of an elementary crop model focuses on:
    a) Adapting the model to new cultivars.
    b) Assessing the model's predictive accuracy against field data.
    c) The internal logic and computational correctness of the model itself.
    d) Determining economic returns of crop production.
14. Verification helps answer which question?
    a) „Are we building the right model?"
    b) „Is the model performing as intended, free from coding errors?"
    c) „Is the model economically viable?"
    d) „Is the model applicable to all global regions?"
15. What technique is used in verification to check if individual equations or sub-routines produce correct numerical results for simple cases?
    a) Statistical regression.
    b) Analytical solutions / Benchmarking.
    c) Sensitivity analysis.
    d) Validation with large datasets.
16. Running a model with input values at the extreme ends of their expected range (e.g., very high or very low temperatures) is a technique used in:
    a) Calibration.
    b) Routine prediction.
    c) Boundary and Extreme Value Testing (part of verification).
    d) Model simplification.

17. Which of the following is an ideal order for crop model development and assessment?
    a) Validation →Calibration →Verification
    b) Calibration →Validation →Verification
    c) Verification →Calibration →Validation
    d) Sensitivity →Verification →Calibration
18. Sensitivity analysis for elementary crop models systematically assesses:
    a) The overall accuracy of the model after calibration.
    b) How the model's outputs change in response to variations in its input parameters or driving variables.
    c) The internal logical consistency of the model.
    d) The ethical implications of using the model.
19. What is a primary benefit of sensitivity analysis?
    a) It eliminates all uncertainty in model predictions.
    b) It identifies which inputs or internal coefficients have the most significant influence on model predictions.
    c) It directly optimizes irrigation schedules.
    d) It guarantees successful crop breeding programs.
20. If a crop model's output (e.g., yield) changes disproportionately with a small change in one input parameter (e.g., temperature), the model is said to be:
    a) Insensitive to that input. b) Overfitted.
    c) Highly sensitive to that input. d) Perfectly calibrated.
21. Which type of sensitivity analysis involves varying one input parameter at a time while keeping all others constant?
    a) Global Sensitivity Analysis.
    b) One-at-a-Time (OAT) Sensitivity Analysis.
    c) Monte Carlo Simulation.
    d) Variance-Based Sensitivity Analysis.
22. Sensitivity analysis helps in prioritizing data collection efforts by:
    a) Showing which data are easiest to collect.
    b) Identifying inputs to which model is highly sensitive, thus requiring accurate measurement.
    c) Demonstrating which data have no impact on the model.
    d) Reducing the overall amount of data needed.

23. A disadvantage of the One-at-a-Time (OAT) sensitivity analysis is that it:
   a) Is computationally very demanding.
   b) Does not account for interactions between parameters.
   c) Requires too much expert knowledge.
   d) Can only be applied to very complex models.

24. For a water-limited yield model, which parameter's sensitivity might be tested to understand a crop's response to water deficit?
   a) Photosynthetically Active Radiation (PAR)
   b) Base Temperature (Tbase)
   c) Yield Response Factor (Ky)
   d) Plant population density

25. If sensitivity analysis reveals that a model's predicted yield is highly sensitive to the exact value of daily maximum temperature during flowering, this suggests:
   a) That daily maximum temperature is irrelevant to yield.
   b) That accurate measurement of this temperature is crucial for model reliability, and the real crop is vulnerable to heat at this stage.
   c) That the model is flawed and should be discarded.

Answer Key

1	b	2	b	3	b	4	b	5	c	6	b	7	b
8	c	9	b	10	c	11	d	12	b	13	c	14	b
15	b	16	c	17	c	18	b	19	b	20	c	21	b
22	b	23	b	24	c	25	b						

28

Agrometeorological Observatory

1. The main purpose of an agrometeorological observatory is:
   a) Tax assessment
   b) Crop marketing
   c) Observation and recording of weather data for agriculture
   d) Soil testing only
2. Agrometeorological observatories are primarily used for:
   a) Military communication
   b) Weather forecasting and agricultural planning
   c) Satellite launching
   d) Transport services
3. The observations in an agromet observatory help in:
   a) Import decisions
   b) Urban development
   c) Weather-based agricultural advisories
   d) Export promotion
4. IMD stands for:
   a) Indian Market Department
   b) Indian Meteorological Department
   c) Institute of Meteorology Development
   d) Indian Monsoon Division
5. The standard agrometeorological observatory in India follows the guidelines of:
   a) WHO b) IPCC
   c) WMO and IMD d) ISRO
6. How many types of agrometeorological observatories are there?
   a) 1 b) 2 (Principal and Auxiliary)
   c) 3 d) 5

7. A principal observatory records:
   a) Only rainfall
   b) All major meteorological parameters
   c) Only wind data
   d) Fertilizer content
8. An auxiliary observatory records:
   a) Rainfall only
   b) A few selected weather elements
   c) Cloud cover only
   d) Satellite data
9. Agro-met observatories are located at:
   a) Airports only
   b) Railway stations
   c) Agricultural universities and research stations
   d) Parliament buildings
10. Who manages agrometeorological observatories at Krishi Vigyan Kendras (KVKs)?
   a) MHRD b) Indian Army
   c) ICAR/IMD d) Ministry of Transport
11. The instrument used to measure rainfall is:
   a) Thermometer b) Barometer
   c) Rain gauge d) Evaporimeter
12. The instrument to measure air temperature is:
   a) Wind vane
   b) Maximum-minimum thermometer
   c) Rain gauge
   d) Barograph
13. A Stevenson screen is used for:
   a) Observing the sky
   b) Housing thermometers to measure air temperature
   c) Measuring rainfall
   d) Measuring wind speed

14. Relative humidity is measured using:
    a) Hygrometer or psychrometer b) Rain gauge
    c) Wind vane d) Evaporimeter
15. The wind direction is measured using:
    a) Cup anemometer b) Barometer
    c) Wind vane d) Sunshine recorder
16. Wind speed is measured by:
    a) Wind vane b) Barometer
    c) Cup anemometer d) Evaporimeter
17. Bright sunshine hours are recorded using:
    a) Wind vane
    b) Thermometer
    c) Campbell-Stokes sunshine recorder
    d) Barometer
18. Evaporation is measured using:
    a) Anemometer b) Class A pan evaporimeter
    c) Hygrometer d) Wind vane
19. Soil temperature is measured using:
    a) Rain gauge b) Soil thermometer
    c) Cup anemometer d) Barometer
20. Solar radiation is measured with a:
    a) Thermograph b) Pyranometer
    c) Wind vane d) Barometer
21. The standard height of the rain gauge above ground is:
    a) 5 m b) 10 m
    c) 0.3 to 0.5 m d) 2 m
22. Stevenson screen is installed at:
    a) Ground level b) 2 meters above ground
    c) 10 feet d) 10 meters above surface
23. The open pan evaporimeter is placed:
    a) Under a tree
    b) Indoors
    c) In an open area, away from obstructions
    d) Inside Stevenson screen

24. The standard exposure for weather instruments is:
   a) Shaded and enclosed
   b) Inside buildings
   c) In open field away from buildings and trees
   d) Near water bodies

25. The instrument shelter (Stevenson screen) should be painted:
   a) Black b) Green
   c) White d) Red

26. Meteorological data is recorded:
   a) Weekly b) Monthly
   c) Daily at fixed observation hours d) Annually

27. Standard observation times in India are:
   a) 5 AM and 5 PM b) 7 AM and 2 PM IST
   c) 6 PM and 10 PM d) 10 AM and 4 PM

28. Rainfall is usually recorded:
   a) Once in a month
   b) Twice daily or after every rain event
   c) Once a year
   d) Randomly

29. Temperature extremes (max and min) are noted:
   a) Hourly b) Only at night
   c) Daily at specific time d) Weekly

30. Wind direction is reported in:
   a) Degrees
   b) Radians
   c) Compass directions (N, NE, E, etc.)
   d) Meters per second

31. Agro-met observatories support:
   a) Crop insurance and yield forecasting
   b) Fertilizer production
   c) Political decisions
   d) Textile exports

31. Agro-advisories are generated based on:
   a) Random decisions
   b) Historical rainfall only
   c) Observed and forecasted weather
   d) Subsidy availability
32. Real-time weather data is essential for:
   a) Printing newspapers
   b) Advising farmers on irrigation, spraying, and harvesting
   c) Export-import regulations
   d) Classroom teaching only
33. Drought monitoring is possible through:
   a) Wind speed
   b) Rainfall and evapotranspiration records
   c) Soil pH
   d) Number of tractors
34. Which data is crucial for pest and disease forecasting?
   a) Rainfall and temperature b) Soil color
   c) Seed price d) Landholding size
36. AWS stands for:
   a) Agricultural Water System b) Automatic Weather Station
   c) Agro-Water Storage d) Automatic Wind Speed
37. AWSs record data:
   a) Manually b) Only during rain
   c) Automatically and continuously d) Once a month
38. Which system is used to send data to central servers in real time?
   a) SMS only
   b) Manual logbooks
   c) GSM/GPRS and satellite telemetry
   d) Postal mail
39. Automatic weather stations are installed in India by:
   a) WHO b) IMD and ICAR
   c) RBI d) CBSE

40. Advantage of AWS is:
   a) Cheaper than manual observatories
   b) Error-free, continuous, real-time data
   c) Manual input needed
   d) Only for research
41. The minimum area required for a standard observatory is about:
   a) 10 sq. m b) 25 sq. m
   c) 50 x 50 ft (approx. 2500 sq. ft) d) 5 hectares
42. Which weather element is crucial for sowing decisions?
   a) Wind b) Rainfall
   c) Humidity d) Sunshine
43. Which of the following is NOT a weather parameter recorded in agromet observatories?
   a) Temperature b) Rainfall
   c) Soil nutrient status d) Wind speed
44. Manual observations are generally taken:
   a) Every 6 hours b) Once daily
   c) Twice a day d) Only during summer
45. Evaporation rate data is used to estimate:
   a) Pest incidence b) Irrigation requirement
   c) Fertilizer needs d) Land price
46. Data from agromet observatories is used in:
   a) AI-based yield models b) Film making
   c) Road transport d) Hotel management
47. Farmers can access observatory data through:
   a) Radio
   b) Agro-advisory apps and portals
   c) Post office
   d) None
48. Agrometeorology combines:
   a) Physics and philosophy b) Agriculture and meteorology
   c) Chemistry and engineering d) Law and social science

49. Soil moisture observations support:
    a) Sowing decisions b) Harvest only
    c) Marketing d) Pesticide procurement

50. The future of agrometeorological observatories will involve:
    a) Manual labor only
    b) Fully automated, AI and IoT integrated systems
    c) Fossil-fuel dependent tools
    d) Weather balloons only

Answer Key

1	c	2	b	3	b	4	b	5	c	6	b	7	b
8	b	9	c	10	c	11	c	12	b	13	b	14	a
15	c	16	c	17	c	18	b	19	b	20	b	21	c
22	b	23	c	24	c	25	c	26	c	27	b	28	b
29	c	30	c	31	a	32	c	33	b	34	b	35	a
36	b	37	c	38	c	39	b	40	b	41	c	42	b
43	c	44	c	45	b	46	a	47	b	48	b	49	a
50	b												

B. Meteorological Applications in Allied Disciplines/Sciences

1

Agricultural Biotechnology

1. Agricultural meteorology supports agri-biotechnology by:
   a) Predicting genetic traits
   b) Providing environmental data for studying gene-environment interactions
   c) Creating hybrid seeds
   d) Determining microbial load in water
2. Which meteorological factor is most important for evaluating stress-tolerant transgenic crops?
   a) Solar eclipse frequency
   b) Temperature & moisture stress
   c) Soil color
   d) Air pressure
3. Weather data helps agri-biotechnologists in:
   a) Sequencing DNA
   b) Testing gene expression under abiotic stress conditions
   c) Labeling food products
   d) Enhancing pesticide activity
4. Which biotechnology trait is most associated with drought-prone meteorological conditions?
   a) Cold resistance
   b) Glyphosate resistance
   c) Drought tolerance genes (e.g., DREB genes)
   d) Color enhancement genes
5. Field trials for genetically modified crops require agrometeorological data to:
   a) Estimate market demand
   b) Correlate environmental variables with trait performance
   c) Enhance soil acidity
   d) Reduce biodiversity

6. Temperature and humidity conditions are critical for testing:
   a) Disease resistance genes in crops
   b) Seed storage in biobanks
   c) Animal cloning efficiency
   d) Pesticide efficacy only
7. Which weather-related challenge is addressed using biotechnological interventions?
   a) Sowing calendar
   b) Development of stress-resilient crop varieties
   c) Manual harvesting techniques
   d) Cost of irrigation equipment
8. Agrometeorology is essential in biotech-based phenotyping for:
   a) Studying weather-resistant traits under field conditions
   b) Editing the DNA of animals
   c) Conducting laboratory chemical analysis
   d) Estimating import taxes
9. Weather forecasts assist agri-biotech industries in:
   a) Pricing hybrid seeds
   b) Scheduling trials for stress evaluation of modified crops
   c) Designing laboratory SOPs
   d) Setting up irrigation norms
10. Integration of weather models with biotechnology is crucial in:
   a) Predicting seed shelf life
   b) Breeding climate-smart crops for future climate scenarios
   c) Classifying weeds
   d) Managing subsidies

Answer Key

1	b	2	b	3	b	4	c	5	b	6	a	7	b
8	b	9	a	10	b								

2

Agri-Business Management

1. Agricultural meteorology supports agri-business management by:
   a) Designing packaging material
   b) Offering climate-based risk assessment for farm enterprises
   c) Determining tractor efficiency
   d) Creating subsidies
2. Weather forecasts help agribusinesses in:
   a) Fixing international tariffs
   b) Scheduling climate-sensitive operations like harvesting and logistics
   c) Reducing pesticide effectiveness
   d) Changing product branding
3. Crop yield forecasting using agrometeorological data is crucial for:
   a) Creating slogans
   b) Managing input supply chains and marketing strategies
   c) Labeling products
   d) Reducing export taxes
4. Agrometeorology helps in agribusiness risk management by:
   a) Reducing customer complaints
   b) Forecasting weather-related losses and planning contingencies
   c) Providing legal advice
   d) Fixing minimum wages
5. Which agri-business component is most influenced by long-range weather forecasts?
   a) Commodity pricing b) Seed color enhancement
   c) Agrochemical branding d) Microbial testing

6. Weather-based crop insurance schemes rely on:
   a) Market surveys
   b) Historical and forecasted weather data
   c) Seed packaging details
   d) Soil type information only
7. Logistics and supply chain in agri-business are sensitive to:
   a) Plant spacing
   b) Weather disruptions like heavy rains or heat waves
   c) Harvest index
   d) Seed moisture content only
8. Which tool is used in agribusiness to assess crop prospects under variable weather?
   a) Agro-microphone
   b) Crop simulation models using weather inputs
   c) Plant genome scanner
   d) Soil pH meter
9. Which of the following is a key agromet-based decision support application for agribusinesses?
   a) Genetic mapping
   b) Weather-based market forecasting and input planning
   c) Seed germination testing
   d) Biofertilizer culturing
10. Failure to incorporate weather information in agri-business decisions may lead to:
   a) Brand enhancement
   b) Increased customer loyalty
   c) Financial losses due to unanticipated crop failures
   d) Higher product quality

Answer Key

1	b	2	b	3	b	4	b	5	a	6	b	7	b
8	b	9	b	10	c								

3

Agricultural Economics

1. Agricultural meteorology contributes to agricultural economics mainly by:
   a) Estimating soil nutrient content
   b) Forecasting market prices directly
   c) Reducing uncertainty in weather-dependent farm decisions
   d) Designing crop varieties
2. Weather-based crop yield forecasts are crucial for:
   a) Making trade agreements
   b) Agricultural credit planning and food policy formulation
   c) Calculating soil carbon
   d) Estimating fertilizer prices
3. Which of the following is an economic benefit of early weather forecasts to farmers?
   a) Delayed sowing
   b) Optimized input use and reduced losses
   c) Increased loan interest
   d) Decreased subsidy support
4. Agrometeorological data is used in crop insurance schemes primarily to:
   a) Fix fertilizer subsidies
   b) Determine premium on rainfall variability
   c) Guide export taxes
   d) Assess farm mechanization needs

5. The Minimum Support Price (MSP) decisions can be better informed by:
   a) Remote sensing of forests
   b) Long-range rainfall forecasts affecting crop production estimates
   c) Annual government surveys only
   d) Import and export balance sheets
6. Weather anomalies such as droughts and floods influence agricultural economics by:
   a) Lowering farmer income and increasing risk
   b) Improving rural employment
   c) Enhancing biodiversity
   d) Increasing food subsidies
7. Weather-based agroadvisory services can lead to:
   a) Higher land prices
   b) Improved profitability through timely farm operations
   c) Reduction in extension services
   d) Increased input costs
8. In economic terms, a good monsoon typically results in:
   a) Increased interest rates
   b) Lower agricultural productivity
   c) Higher rural spending and economic growth
   d) Decreased employment in agriculture
9. Crop failure due to extreme weather events increases:
   a) Export potential
   b) Farmer debts and demand for relief packages
   c) Fertilizer application
   d) Soil microbial activity
10. Which economic planning tool uses agrometeorological input for forecasting food grain availability?
   a) Farm mechanization index b) GDP estimation
   c) Food security monitoring systems d) Land ceiling regulation

Answer Key

1	c	2	b	3	b	4	b	5	b	6	a	7	b
8	c	9	b	10	c								

4

Agricultural Engineering

1. Which of the following meteorological parameters is most important in designing irrigation systems?
   a) Soil pH b) Evapotranspiration rate
   c) Wind direction d) Solar radiation intensity
2. Rainfall data is crucial in agricultural engineering for the design of:
   a) Biogas plants b) Tractors
   c) Water harvesting structures d) Poultry sheds
3. Which meteorological factor significantly affects the structural design of greenhouses?
   a) Dew point b) Rainfall intensity
   c) Wind speed and direction d) Relative humidity
4. Agrometeorology supports agricultural mechanization by providing:
   a) Soil nutrient levels
   b) Optimal sowing depth
   c) Weather windows for field operations
   d) Genetic data of crops
5. Solar radiation data is most directly used in:
   a) Drip irrigation layout
   b) Solar-powered cold storage system design
   c) Terracing of land
   d) Trench digging
6. Which parameter is essential for determining the runoff potential of a watershed?
   a) Wind chill index b) Maximum temperature
   c) Rainfall intensity and duration d) Cloud type

7. Agrometeorological inputs are used in post-harvest engineering to:
   a) Select fertilizer rates
   b) Optimize drying and storage systems
   c) Improve seed germination
   d) Determine planting dates
8. The design of farm drainage systems relies primarily on:
   a) Minimum temperature
   b) Relative humidity
   c) Rainfall frequency and distribution
   d) Sunshine hours
9. In precision agriculture, agrometeorological data is used to:
   a) Manually control ploughing
   b) Determine historical crop prices
   c) Drive automated decision-making on irrigation and fertilization
   d) Estimate market demand
10. Which meteorological element affects the structural safety of grain silos and warehouses?
   a) Solar elevation angle b) Wind load and humidity
   c) Soil organic matter d) Daylength

Answer Key

1	b	2	c	3	c	4	c	5	b	6	c	7	b
8	c	9	c	10	b								

5

Agronomy

1. Agricultural meteorology contributes to agronomy by:
   a) Creating new fertilizer products
   b) Providing weather-based data for crop planning and management
   c) Monitoring insect behavior
   d) Determining tractor horsepower
2. Which meteorological factor is most critical in determining the sowing time of kharif crops?
   a) Wind direction
   b) Onset of monsoon rainfall
   c) Soil temperature
   d) Cloud cover
3. Evapotranspiration data is used in agronomy for:
   a) Seed rate determination
   b) Crop spacing
   c) Irrigation scheduling and water requirement estimation
   d) Fertilizer selection
4. Which agrometeorological factor primarily affects seed germination in field crops?
   a) Cloud type
   b) Dew point
   c) Soil temperature and moisture
   d) Wind speed
5. Crop growth models used in agronomy rely on:
   a) Market surveys
   b) Weather and soil data inputs
   c) Government subsidies
   d) Manual weeding records
6. Drought monitoring in agronomy is supported by:
   a) Soil taxonomy
   b) Rainfall and evapotranspiration data
   c) Wind erosion data
   d) Nutrient uptake curves

7. Long-range weather forecasts are useful in agronomy for:
   a) Export decisions
   b) Machinery design
   c) Seasonal crop planning and input allocation
   d) Herbicide development
8. Which cropping system benefits most from agrometeorological data in terms of optimizing planting time and input use?
   a) Mono-cropping b) Mixed farming
   c) Rainfed farming d) Hydroponics
9. Which weather parameter is most closely linked to nitrogen loss via volatilization in fields?
   a) Relative humidity
   b) Temperature and wind speed
   c) Cloud cover
   d) Atmospheric pressure
10. Which agronomic operation is most sensitive to rainfall forecasting?
   a) Seed treatment
   b) Ploughing
   c) Harvesting and post-harvest handling
   d) Soil classification

Answer Key

1	b	2	b	3	c	4	c	5	b	6	b	7	c
8	c	9	b	10	c								

6

Animal Sciences

1. Agricultural meteorology contributes to animal sciences by:
   a) Replacing animal feed
   b) Providing weather-based insights for managing livestock health, shelter, and productivity
   c) Designing meat packaging
   d) Enhancing wool color
2. High ambient temperatures can affect livestock by:
   a) Increasing appetite
   b) Causing heat stress and reducing milk and meat yield
   c) Promoting wool growth
   d) Enhancing reproductive efficiency
3. Wind chill is a significant factor in livestock comfort because it:
   a) Enhances digestion
   b) Increases risk of cold stress in open housing systems
   c) Improves muscle development
   d) Makes animals more fertile
4. Meteorological data supports animal housing design by:
   a) Determining roof color
   b) Ensuring proper ventilation and thermal regulation
   c) Selecting grass species
   d) Avoiding animal feed use
5. Agrometeorological forecasts help livestock farmers by:
   a) Increasing feed cost
   b) Preparing for extreme weather events like heatwaves and cold spells
   c) Reducing water availability
   d) Encouraging overgrazing

6. Heat stress in animals is aggravated by:
   a) Low humidity and wind
   b) High temperature and humidity
   c) Dry feed only
   d) Winter rainfall
7. Rainfall and humidity are important in animal science for:
   a) Breeding programs
   b) Managing shelter hygiene and controlling disease outbreaks
   c) Determining wool texture
   d) Reducing animal body weight
8. Livestock diseases often correlate with weather because:
   a) Pathogens are influenced by climatic conditions like temperature and moisture
   b) Soil moisture increases meat tenderness
   c) Fertilizer use rises
   d) Feed conversion improves
9. Temperature-Humidity Index (THI) is used to:
   a) Measure hay quality
   b) Assess heat stress levels in dairy and beef animals
   c) Identify animal age
   d) Estimate manure output
10. Climate-smart livestock practices include:
   a) Ignoring weather forecasts
   b) Adjusting feeding, watering, and housing based on weather conditions
   c) Feeding only in open fields
   d) Reducing animal shelter sizes

Answer Key

1	b	2	b	3	b	4	b	5	b	6	b	7	b
8	a	9	b	10	b								

7

Apiculture

1. Which meteorological factor most directly influences nectar secretion in flowering plants?
   a) Wind speed
   b) Soil temperature
   c) Relative humidity
   d) Solar radiation
2. Optimum temperature range for maximum honeybee activity is:
   a) 10–15°C
   b) 16–21°C
   c) 22–35°C
   d) Above 40°C
3. Rainfall during flowering period primarily affects honey production by:
   a) Increasing pollen viability
   b) Enhancing nectar concentration
   c) Washing away nectar and hindering bee flight
   d) Stimulating hive temperature
4. Which of the following weather conditions is unfavorable for honeybee foraging activity?
   a) Calm and sunny
   b) Light wind with clear sky
   c) Cloudy with drizzle
   d) Warm and dry afternoon
5. Agricultural meteorology supports apiculture by forecasting:
   a) Swarming events only
   b) Pollen quality
   c) Weather conducive for bee flights and nectar flow
   d) Soil moisture content

6. Extended drought during peak flowering period impacts honey production by:
   a) Promoting honey preservation
   b) Increasing nectar flow
   c) Reducing floral nectar secretion
   d) Improving bee lifespan
7. Which agrometeorological tool can help beekeepers plan seasonal hive placement for maximum honey yield?
   a) Soil nutrient map
   b) Long-range weather forecast
   c) Agromet advisory bulletin
   d) Crop calendar only
8. Relative humidity above 80% can affect honey quality by:
   a) Making honey thicker
   b) Promoting fermentation in hive
   c) Increasing bee foraging
   d) Preserving nectar
9. During which time of the day is bee activity highest under favorable weather?
   a) Early morning (5–7 AM)
   b) Mid-morning to early afternoon (9 AM–2 PM)
   c) Late afternoon (3–5 PM)
   d) Night (8 PM–12 AM)
10. Weather-based decision support for migratory beekeeping includes information on:
   a) Hive construction methods
   b) Floral calendars and weather suitability of target areas
   c) Bee species diversification
   d) Pesticide formulations

Answer Key

1	d	2	c	3	c	4	c	5	c	6	c	7	b
8	b	9	b	10	b								

8

Basic Sciences

1. Agricultural meteorology connects with basic sciences by:
   a) Only supporting farm mechanization
   b) Providing physical and biological data for understanding plant-environment interactions
   c) Replacing chemistry in crop research
   d) Avoiding mathematical models
2. Which branch of basic science is most directly involved in studying heat and energy flow in meteorology?
   a) Biology b) Physics
   c) Zoology d) Sociology
3. In chemistry, agricultural meteorology helps by:
   a) Determining soil carbon and nitrogen cycles under varying weather conditions
   b) Studying insecticide branding
   c) Enhancing fuel efficiency
   d) Identifying minerals only
4. Weather data contributes to biological sciences by:
   a) Mapping aquifers
   b) Understanding how temperature and humidity affect plant physiology and disease development
   c) Regulating rainfall
   d) Sequencing genes
5. Mathematical models in agrometeorology are used to:
   a) Predict farm income
   b) Simulate crop growth based on weather variables
   c) Design warehouses
   d) Enhance irrigation motors

6. Which of the following is a basic science concept applied in agrometeorology?
   a) Law of supply and demand
   b) Laws of thermodynamics in energy exchange between soil, plant, and atmosphere
   c) Consumer behavior theory
   d) Photoshop editing tools
7. Solar radiation, as studied in physics, is important in agrometeorology because it:
   a) Promotes seed color changes
   b) Drives photosynthesis and plant development
   c) Enhances pesticide effects
   d) Affects tractor weight
8. Biological processes like transpiration are influenced by:
   a) Weather variables such as temperature, wind, and humidity
   b) Storage conditions
   c) Loan availability
   d) Marketing channels
9. Which physical parameter is commonly monitored in agrometeorology for basic science research?
   a) Leaf taste
   b) Air temperature and relative humidity
   c) Soil price
   d) Fertilizer brand
10. Integration of basic sciences with agrometeorology helps in:
    a) Designing advertisements
    b) Deepening understanding of crop-environment relationships for better predictions and innovations
    c) Reducing seed rates
    d) Improving fuel prices

Answer Key

1	b	2	b	3	a	4	b	5	b	6	b	7	b
8	a	9	b	10	b								

9

Community Sciences

1. Meteorology supports community science by:
   a) Promoting high-input farming
   b) Empowering communities with weather-based knowledge for sustainable living
   c) Eliminating traditional practices
   d) Supplying hybrid seeds
2. Community science uses meteorological data primarily to:
   a) Track satellite launches
   b) Design irrigation equipment
   c) Enhance resilience to climate variability in rural livelihoods
   d) Engineer new fertilizers
3. Weather-based advisories are essential for community-level decisions in:
   a) Classroom scheduling
   b) Crop selection, planting time, and disaster preparedness
   c) Media content planning
   d) Voting processes
4. Which of the following is a key benefit of agromet services in community science?
   a) Improved access to subsidies
   b) Better weather-risk preparedness and livelihood security
   c) Reduced need for education
   d) Elimination of indigenous knowledge
5. Climate literacy at the community level is enhanced through:
   a) Pesticide promotion
   b) Mobile-based weather advisory systems and local extension outreach

c) Market advertisement

d) Patent registration

6. Which group benefits most from location-specific agromet information in rural communities?

a) Urban consumers

b) Commercial airlines

c) Smallholder farmers and women in agriculture

d) Industrial workers

7. Community-based disaster risk management uses agrometeorology for:

a) Calculating population density

b) Forecasting floods, droughts, and extreme events

c) Managing e-commerce

d) Conducting exams

8. Traditional weather forecasting practices are:

a) Replaced by agrometeorology

b) Combined with scientific forecasts to build community resilience

c) Irrelevant in modern agriculture

d) Unscientific and avoided

9. In nutrition-sensitive agriculture, weather data supports community well-being by:

a) Enhancing junk food production

b) Planning seasonal cultivation of nutrient-rich crops

c) Replacing home gardens

d) Removing dietary diversity

10. Agrometeorology in community science promotes:

a) Climate-smart village models and participatory planning

b) Centralized seed control

c) High energy food dependency

d) Urban expansion

Answer Key

1	b	2	c	3	b	4	b	5	b	6	c	7	b
8	b	9	b	10	a								

10

Crop Physiology

1. Which meteorological factor has the most direct impact on photosynthesis in plants?
   a) Wind speed
   b) Soil moisture
   c) Solar radiation
   d) Atmospheric pressure
2. Temperature affects crop physiology primarily by:
   a) Enhancing soil texture
   b) Regulating enzymatic and metabolic activities
   c) Increasing nitrogen fixation
   d) Reducing transpiration
3. The term "growing degree days (GDD)" is used to:
   a) Measure rainfall intensity
   b) Predict crop yield
   c) Estimate crop development stages based on temperature
   d) Determine humidity levels
4. Which crop physiological process is most sensitive to water stress?
   a) Seed germination
   b) Flowering and grain filling
   c) Leaf color change
   d) Senescence
5. Agricultural meteorology helps in scheduling irrigation by providing data on
   a) Soil pH
   b) Relative humidity
   c) Evapotranspiration
   d) Wind chill factor
6. How does high relative humidity affect crop physiology?
   a) Enhances transpiration
   b) Reduces stomatal conductance
   c) Promotes respiration
   d) Increases water loss

7. Which of the following is used to assess heat stress effects on crop physiology?
   a) NDVI index
   b) Wind rose diagram
   c) Temperature Humidity Index (THI)
   d) Soil salinity index
8. The effect of day length on flowering is called:
   a) Phototropism b) Photoperiodism
   c) Photosynthesis d) Photolysis
9. Crop canopy temperature is an indicator of:
   a) Soil fertility
   b) Heat stress and water status
   c) Nutrient deficiency
   d) Pest infestation
10. Which meteorological parameter directly affects transpiration rate in plants?
   a) Barometric pressure b) Dew point
   c) Wind speed d) Cloud cover

Answer Key

1	c	2	b	3	c	4	b	5	c	6	b	7	c
8	b	9	b	10	c								

11

Data Science

1. Agricultural meteorology contributes to data science by:
   a) Providing structured and unstructured weather datasets for predictive analytics in agriculture
   b) Creating new tractors
   c) Promoting fossil fuel use
   d) Analyzing soil color manually
2. Which data science tool is commonly used in agrometeorology to forecast weather patterns?
   a) Photoshop
   b) Machine learning models
   c) Spreadsheets only
   d) Manual thermometers
3. Big data in agrometeorology refers to:
   a) Soil sample labels
   b) Large volumes of real-time weather, soil, and crop data used for modeling and decision-making
   c) Price tags on seeds
   d) Manual labor records
4. What is the role of remote sensing in agrometeorological data science?
   a) Measuring seed moisture content
   b) Capturing spatial weather and crop condition data from satellites
   c) Marketing agri-products
   d) Estimating tractor fuel consumption
5. Data visualization in agrometeorology helps stakeholders to:
   a) Paint graphs
   b) Understand complex weather trends and communicate risk effectively
   c) Color weather balloons
   d) Harvest crops faster

6. A key application of agrometeorological data science is:
   a) Crop modeling and yield forecasting using historical and real-time weather inputs
   b) Seed packaging design
   c) Manual irrigation scheduling
   d) Human health testing

7. Which platform is widely used for handling agrometeorological datasets in data science?
   a) MS Paint
   b) Python or R programming with data libraries
   c) WordPad
   d) Audio editing software

8. Predictive analytics in agricultural meteorology supports:
   a) Market fluctuation predictions
   b) Advanced warnings of droughts, floods, and crop pests
   c) Coloring of satellite images
   d) Book publishing

9. Integration of IoT (Internet of Things) in agrometeorology enables:
   a) Better handwriting recognition
   b) Real-time collection of field weather and soil data for analytics
   c) Manual seed germination
   d) Enhancing plant height visually

10. Artificial Intelligence (AI) in agrometeorological data science is used to:
    a) Make fictional stories
    b) Optimize decision-making in weather forecasting and agri-advisory services
    c) Increase food coloring
    d) Eliminate natural farming

Answer Key

1	a	2	b	3	b	4	b	5	b	6	a	7	b
8	b	9	b	10	b								

12

Dairy Sciences

1. Agricultural meteorology supports dairy sciences by:
   a) Promoting artificial coloring of milk
   b) Providing climate data to manage heat stress and optimize milk production
   c) Enhancing milk flavor with additives
   d) Designing milking machines
2. High Temperature-Humidity Index (THI) in dairy animals leads to:
   a) Increased feed intake
   b) Heat stress and reduced milk yield
   c) Better fat content in milk
   d) Faster growth of calves
3. Which meteorological factor is most crucial for managing dairy cattle comfort?
   a) Soil texture
   b) Temperature and humidity
   c) Rainfall pattern only
   d) Wind speed alone
4. During heat waves, dairy farmers should:
   a) Increase lighting in shelters
   b) Provide shade, water sprinkling, and adjust feeding times
   c) Reduce ventilation
   d) Restrict animal movement
5. Agrometeorological forecasts help dairy management by:
   a) Improving fodder marketing
   b) Preparing for extreme weather and adjusting housing and feeding schedules
   c) Changing animal breeds
   d) Decreasing milking frequency

6. Cold stress in dairy cattle can result in:
   a) Higher fertility
   b) Decreased milk yield and increased disease susceptibility
   c) Improved feed efficiency
   d) Longer lactation periods

7. Meteorological data is useful for scheduling fodder cultivation by:
   a) Indicating seed prices
   b) Aligning sowing and harvesting with optimal rainfall and temperature conditions
   c) Selecting tractor types
   d) Controlling milk pricing

8. Increased humidity in dairy shelters may cause:
   a) Better hoof strength
   b) Risk of mastitis and other infections
   c) Improved milk letdown
   d) Lower body temperature

9. Climate-resilient dairy practices include:
   a) Ignoring seasonal weather trends
   b) Installing cooling systems, insulation, and weather-based feeding plans
   c) Avoiding any shelter modifications
   d) Switching to non-lactating animals

10. Which tool is commonly used to assess weather impact on dairy animals?
   a) Soil penetrometer
   b) Temperature-Humidity Index (THI) calculator
   c) Refractometer
   d) Lactometer only

Answer Key

1	b	2	b	3	b	4	b	5	b	6	b	7	b
8	b	9	b	10	b								

13

Desert Agriculture

1. Which meteorological factor is most critical for scheduling irrigation in desert agriculture?

   a) Wind speed b) Dew point
   c) Evapotranspiration rate d) Barometric pressure

2. In desert agriculture, agrometeorological advisories help mainly in:

   a) Enhancing mechanization
   b) Improving rainfall harvesting and water-use efficiency
   c) Increasing fertilizer input
   d) Managing crop rotation cycles

3. Which meteorological parameter is key to designing microclimate modification strategies (like windbreaks) in desert areas?

   a) Rainfall intensity b) Solar angle
   c) Wind direction and speed d) Relative humidity

4. Crop selection for desert areas using agrometeorology is mainly based on:

   a) Soil salinity
   b) Wind erosion rates
   c) Temperature extremes and rainfall patterns
   d) Fertilizer response curves

5. What role does agrometeorology play in protected cultivation in deserts?

   a) Controls soil fertility
   b) Monitors underground water table
   c) Manages temperature and humidity inside greenhouses
   d) Reduces pest infestations

6. Thermal time (growing degree days) in desert regions helps in:
   a) Determining pest spray intervals
   b) Forecasting flowering and maturity stages of crops
   c) Improving rainfall simulation models
   d) Estimating soil erosion
7. Which of the following is a suitable agro-climatic adaptation for desert agriculture?
   a) Monsoon rice farming
   b) Zero tillage
   c) Agroforestry with drought-resistant species
   d) Submerged rice paddies
8. High temperatures in deserts primarily affect crops by:
   a) Increasing leaf chlorophyll
   b) Enhancing soil moisture retention
   c) Reducing photosynthetic efficiency and yield
   d) Promoting fungal growth
9. Forecasting dust storms using agrometeorology helps farmers by:
   a) Improving seed germination
   b) Reducing disease spread
   c) Preventing damage to young seedlings and infrastructure
   d) Enhancing organic matter in soil
10. Solar radiation data in desert agriculture is important for:
   a) Predicting pest outbreaks
   b) Planning sowing during cloudy weather
   c) Managing photoperiod-sensitive crops and solar-powered irrigation
   d) Reducing transpiration rates

Answer Key

1	c	2	b	3	c	4	c	5	c	6	b	7	c
8	c	9	c	10	c								

14

Desert Locust Management

1. Which meteorological condition is most favorable for desert locust breeding?
   a) Cold and dry conditions
   b) Hot and dry conditions
   c) Warm temperatures with moist soil from recent rains
   d) Low temperatures with high humidity
2. Which wind system plays a major role in the long-distance migration of desert locusts?
   a) Monsoon winds b) Westerlies
   c) Trade winds d) Jet streams
3. Agrometeorological monitoring helps in desert locust control primarily by:
   a) Increasing pesticide efficacy
   b) Forecasting favorable breeding and migration conditions
   c) Enhancing soil fertility
   d) Measuring leaf chlorophyll content
4. What is the minimum rainfall threshold (~mm) generally required to trigger locust breeding in desert areas?
   a) 5 mm b) 10 mm
   c) 25 mm d) 50 mm
5. Which temperature range is optimal for rapid desert locust development?
   a) 10–15°C b) 16–20°C
   c) 25–35°C d) 35–45°C

6. Remote sensing and weather data together are useful for:
   a) Estimating fertilizer application
   b) Locating underground water sources
   c) Mapping potential locust breeding sites
   d) Identifying crop nutrient deficiencies
7. High humidity after rainfall contributes to locust outbreaks by:
   a) Killing the hoppers
   b) Enhancing egg desiccation
   c) Supporting egg hatching and hopper survival
   d) Preventing adult swarm formation
8. Which organization uses agrometeorological models to predict locust movements globally?
   a) WMO
   b) FAO Locust Watch
   c) IPCC
   d) ICAR
9. The combination of weather anomalies and vegetation greening is a signal for:
   a) Pest-resistant crop breeding
   b) Locust population decline
   c) Possible locust breeding and swarm formation
   d) Improved groundwater recharge
10. Wind direction and speed data help in:
    a) Reducing pesticide resistance
    b) Predicting locust migration paths
    c) Selecting crop varieties
    d) Managing irrigation

Answer Key

1	c	2	a	3	b	4	c	5	c	6	c	7	c
8	b	9	c	10	b								

15

Dryland/Rainfed Agriculture

1. Agricultural meteorology is essential in dryland farming because it:
   a) Replaces irrigation systems
   b) Provides critical weather information for managing limited water resources
   c) Eliminates pests
   d) Improves machinery speed
2. In rainfed agriculture, rainfall variability mainly affects:
   a) Seed color
   b) Crop yield, sowing time, and soil moisture availability
   c) Tractor performance
   d) Grain size only
3. Which agrometeorological input is most vital for deciding sowing in dryland areas?
   a) Soil texture
   b) Onset and amount of monsoon rainfall
   c) Wind speed
   d) Cloud shape
4. Contingency crop planning in dryland agriculture is guided by:
   a) Fertilizer cost trends
   b) Weather forecasts and seasonal rainfall outlooks
   c) Market surveys
   d) Export demand

5. Which technique relies on weather data for improving dryland productivity?
   a) Strip cropping
   b) Rainwater harvesting and moisture conservation practices
   c) Increased tillage
   d) Frequent ploughing
6. Weather-based agromet advisories in rainfed regions aim to:
   a) Promote deforestation
   b) Minimize climate risk and optimize agricultural operations
   c) Encourage fallow lands
   d) Delay planting
7. Drought-prone areas benefit from agricultural meteorology by:
   a) Avoiding seed use
   b) Receiving early warnings for water stress and drought management
   c) Reducing plant growth
   d) Improving fertilizer residues
8. Which crop is best suited to variable rainfall as advised through agrometeorology?
   a) Sugarcane b) Pearl millet (bajra)
   c) Paddy d) Jute
9. Temperature and humidity data in dryland areas are important for:
   a) Pest and disease forecasting in rainfed crops
   b) Estimating seed cost
   c) Transport logistics
   d) Fuel price management
10. The success of dryland agriculture depends on:
   a) Heavy mechanization
   b) Timely agrometeorological advisories and weather-based decision-making
   c) Export subsidies
   d) Use of synthetic colors

Answer Key

1	b	2	b	3	b	4	b	5	b	6	b	7	b
8	b	9	a	10	b								

16

Environmental Science

1. Agricultural meteorology contributes to environmental science by:
   a) Promoting plastic use in agriculture
   b) Providing data on weather–climate interactions affecting ecosystems & sustainability
   c) Replacing organic matter
   d) Ignoring carbon emissions
2. Which meteorological element is most critical in assessing climate change impacts on agriculture?
   a) Soil color
   b) Temperature and precipitation trends
   c) Wind direction only
   d) Fertilizer composition
3. Agrometeorology helps monitor greenhouse gas emissions by:
   a) Using satellites to count plants
   b) Tracking temperature and soil moisture to understand emissions from agriculture
   c) Measuring seed length
   d) Forecasting food taste
4. Which of the following is a key environmental benefit of integrating agrometeorology?
   a) Increasing pesticide use
   b) Enhancing monoculture
   c) Supporting climate-resilient and resource-efficient farming systems
   d) Encouraging industrial waste
5. Weather data helps in environmental planning by:
   a) Designing fashion wear
   b) Assessing risk of droughts, floods, and land degradation

c) Improving plastic production

d) Managing online stores

6. Deforestation impacts local climate by:

a) Reducing sunlight

b) Altering rainfall patterns and increasing surface temperatures

c) Increasing snow

d) Decreasing wind erosion

7. Which environmental problem is directly monitored using agrometeorological data?

a) Ozone hole in urban areas

b) Soil erosion due to rainfall intensity and land use

c) Food packaging waste

d) Urban congestion

8. Seasonal forecasts assist in:

a) Advertising climate apps

b) Planning sustainable land use and reducing environmental risks

c) Designing farm uniforms

d) Importing livestock

9. Agrometeorological advisories support environmental conservation by:

a) Encouraging excessive tillage

b) Promoting efficient water and nutrient management

c) Limiting crop diversity

d) Increasing carbon footprint

10. The linkage of agrometeorology with environmental science is vital for:

a) Short-term yield boosts only

b) Long-term sustainability, ecosystem balance, and adaptation to climate variability

c) Export of fertilizers

d) Reducing tree cover

Answer Key

1	b	2	b	3	b	4	c	5	b	6	b	7	b
8	b	9	b	10	b								

17

Entomology

1. Which weather factor most influences the development and multiplication of insect pests?
   a) Soil pH
   b) Air temperature
   c) Wind direction
   d) Soil type
2. Agricultural meteorology aids entomology mainly by:
   a) Releasing biocontrol agents
   b) Providing subsidies for pesticide use
   c) Forecasting insect pest outbreaks based on weather parameters
   d) Designing insect-proof nets
3. High humidity and moderate temperatures generally favor the outbreak of which type of insect pest?
   a) Stem borers
   b) Aphids
   c) White grubs
   d) Termites
4. Which meteorological condition may help in suppressing the activity of most insect pests?
   a) Warm and humid
   b) Cloudy and windless
   c) Cool and dry
   d) Hot and wet
5. Which of the following pests shows migratory behavior highly influenced by wind patterns?
   a) Rice stem borer
   b) Armyworm
   c) Aphid
   d) Mealybug
6. The insect life cycle acceleration is most associated with:
   a) Low rainfall
   b) High wind velocity
   c) Increase in temperature within optimal range
   d) Decrease in soil moisture

7. Degree-day models in entomology are used to:
   a) Estimate fertilizer use
   b) Predict insect development stages
   c) Measure rainfall distribution
   d) Assess pesticide residue
8. Which meteorological element is crucial for predicting locust swarming behavior?
   a) Soil pH b) Wind and temperature
   c) Fog intensity d) Soil color
9. Weather-based pest forecasting helps farmers by:
   a) Promoting crop rotation
   b) Avoiding pesticide use altogether
   c) Timely application of pest control measures
   d) Estimating market prices
10. Sudden population explosion of insects like thrips and mites often follows:
   a) Heavy continuous rain
   b) Cold winter spells
   c) Dry spells followed by light rains and high temperature
   d) Flooding events

Answer Key

1	b	2	c	3	b	4	c	5	b	6	c	7	b
8	b	9	c	10	c								

18

Extension Education

1. Agricultural meteorology enhances extension education by:
   a) Providing crop marketing services
   b) Delivering location-specific weather-based advisories to farmers
   c) Supplying farm machinery
   d) Promoting only traditional knowledge
2. Weather-based agromet advisories help extension workers in:
   a) Assessing machinery efficiency
   b) Planning pesticide marketing
   c) Educating farmers on weather-responsive decision-making
   d) Identifying soil microflora
3. Which of the following tools is commonly used by extension personnel to communicate weather-based advisories?
   a) Cloud seeding
   b) Farm budget analysis
   c) SMS, mobile apps, and radio
   d) Genetic engineering
4. The Agromet Advisory Services (AAS) under IMD is aimed at:
   a) Exporting agricultural commodities
   b) Providing employment to scientists
   c) Advising farmers on weather-based farm operations
   d) Developing new crop varieties
5. Extension education uses seasonal weather forecasts to:
   a) Delay cropping patterns
   b) Frame customized agro-advisories and contingency plans
   c) Create artificial rainfall
   d) Promote mono-cropping

6. One of the major challenges in using agrometeorological data in extension is:
   a) Lack of radio communication
   b) Language and comprehension barriers among farmers
   c) Overuse of fertilizers
   d) Inadequate rainfall
7. Agro-met Field Units (AMFUs) play a role in extension by:
   a) Regulating food prices
   b) Certifying organic products
   c) Translating and disseminating weather-based advisories
   d) Conducting crop breeding trials
8. Integrating agrometeorology into extension education leads to:
   a) Greater dependence on chemical inputs
   b) Better climate resilience and informed decision-making by farmers
   c) Higher seed prices
   d) Less use of digital tools
9. Farmer awareness about weather and climate risks is improved through:
   a) Crop modeling only
   b) Field visits and weather-based extension campaigns
   c) Laboratory experiments
   d) Mechanization drives
10. A key extension strategy in agricultural meteorology is to:
   a) Promote international trade
   b) Forecast pest and disease outbreaks for timely advisories
   c) Subsidize weather stations
   d) Monitor soil erosion rate

Answer Key

1	b	2	c	3	c	4	c	5	b	6	b	7	c
8	b	9	b	10	b								

19

Hill Agriculture

1. Agricultural meteorology supports hill agriculture by:
   a) Promoting mechanization only
   b) Providing location-specific weather data for crop planning in hilly terrains
   c) Encouraging mono-cropping
   d) Ignoring slope-based farming systems
2. Which meteorological factor is most important for managing frost risk in hill agriculture?
   a) Rainfall only
   b) Minimum temperature and humidity
   c) Wind speed only
   d) Soil pH
3. Weather-based crop advisories help hill farmers to:
   a) Choose wrong crop combinations
   b) Select altitude- and season-appropriate crops and planting windows
   c) Avoid irrigation planning
   d) Reduce vegetation cover
4. In hill agriculture, sudden changes in weather patterns can lead to:
   a) Stable crop yield
   b) Landslides, hailstorms, and unseasonal frosts
   c) Higher temperatures year-round
   d) Decreased rainfall
5. Rainfall variability in hills affects:
   a) Fishing productivity
   b) Terrace farming stability, water harvesting, and crop productivity
   c) Number of livestock only
   d) Market arrival of grains

6. Agrometeorological forecasts help prevent:
   a) Labor shortages
   b) Crop loss due to untimely snowfall, hail, or temperature dips
   c) Fertilizer storage
   d) Seed import
7. Solar radiation data is useful in hill farming for:
   a) Enhancing leaf size
   b) Planning greenhouse structures and crop selection at different altitudes
   c) Choosing tractor brands
   d) Increasing deforestation
8. Slope and altitude-specific weather data are vital for:
   a) Export decisions
   b) Designing microclimate-based agricultural practices
   c) Urban farming
   d) Industrial expansion
9. Cold wave advisories are important in hill agriculture to:
   a) Promote chemical sprays
   b) Protect horticultural crops from frost damage
   c) Enhance wind speed
   d) Delay planting
10. Agrometeorology supports sustainable hill farming by:
   a) Encouraging overgrazing
   b) Assisting in climate-smart agriculture practices like contour farming and water conservation
   c) Replacing traditional knowledge
   d) Boosting non-agricultural land use

Answer Key

1	b	2	b	3	b	4	b	5	b	6	b	7	b
8	b	9	b	10	b								

20

Horticultural Science

1. Agricultural meteorology supports horticultural sciences mainly by:
   a) Developing new irrigation pumps
   b) Studying plant DNA
   c) Providing weather-based information to manage growth, yield, and quality
   d) Preparing hybrid seeds
2. Which meteorological factor most directly affects fruit set in horticultural crops?
   a) Wind direction b) Solar radiation
   c) Temperature during flowering d) Soil compaction
3. Frost forecasting in horticulture is critical because:
   a) It helps schedule harvesting
   b) It prevents nutrient leaching
   c) Frost can damage sensitive crops like citrus and grapes
   d) It promotes flowering
4. Which weather parameter is most important for predicting sunburn in fruits like apples and mangoes?
   a) Humidity
   b) Wind speed
   c) Intense solar radiation and high temperature
   d) Rainfall
5. Weather-based irrigation scheduling in horticulture is commonly guided by:
   a) Pest population
   b) Evapotranspiration estimates
   c) Market prices
   d) Labor availability

6. Which horticultural operation is highly sensitive to wind speed?
   a) Fertilizer application
   b) Pesticide spraying
   c) Transplanting
   d) Soil tilling
7. In floriculture, temperature and day length influence:
   a) Fertilizer choice
   b) Flower initiation and blooming
   c) Pest control frequency
   d) Leaf size only
8. High humidity combined with moderate temperature favors the development of:
   a) Sunscald
   b) Blossom end rot
   c) Fungal diseases in fruits and vegetables
   d) Leaf curling
9. Agricultural meteorology helps in protected horticulture (e.g., greenhouses) by:
   a) Replacing fertilizers
   b) Modifying and monitoring microclimate conditions
   c) Changing crop varieties
   d) Avoiding plant breeding
10. Heat units (growing degree days) are useful in horticulture to:
   a) Calculate soil salinity
   b) Predict flowering and fruit maturity stages
   c) Estimate rainfall
   d) Assess carbon sequestration

Answer Key

1	c	2	c	3	c	4	c	5	b	6	b	7	b
8	c	9	b	10	b								

21

Farm Forestry

1. Agricultural meteorology contributes to farm forestry by:
   a) Determining timber pricing
   b) Providing weather data for species selection, planting, and management
   c) Monitoring forest crimes
   d) Replacing agroforestry systems
2. Which meteorological factor is most important for selecting tree species in farm forestry?
   a) Soil pH
   b) Rainfall and temperature regime
   c) Market price of timber
   d) Leaf color
3. Strong winds can cause which of the following problems in farm forestry?
   a) Improved rooting b) Enhanced canopy growth
   c) Tree lodging and breakage d) Increased seed germination
4. Which climatic factor most influences the growth rate of tree species?
   a) Atmospheric pressure b) Wind direction
   c) Rainfall and solar radiation d) Soil texture
5. Agroforestry systems benefit from agricultural meteorology by:
   a) Reducing shade
   b) Forecasting weather conditions to schedule pruning and intercropping
   c) Avoiding tree plantation
   d) Limiting fertilizer application

6. High evapotranspiration in dry regions can:
   a) Promote tree germination
   b) Lead to moisture stress and poor survival of tree seedlings
   c) Increase tree height
   d) Improve leaf quality

7. Meteorological data helps in designing shelterbelts by assessing:
   a) Soil salinity
   b) Wind speed and direction
   c) Timber density
   d) Tree age

8. Seasonal weather forecasting helps farm forestry by:
   a) Improving soil porosity
   b) Predicting optimal planting windows
   c) Eliminating pests
   d) Enhancing carbon sequestration immediately

9. Which tree species is commonly recommended in arid regions based on meteorological data?
   a) *Eucalyptus globulus*
   b) Tectona grandis
   c) Acacia tortilis
   d) Mangifera indica

10. Extreme temperatures in farm forestry can lead to:
   a) Enhanced bark quality
   b) Flowering at uniform time
   c) Stunted growth and leaf scorching
   d) Uniform height

Answer Key

1	b	2	b	3	c	4	c	5	b	6	b	7	b
8	b	9	c	10	c								

22

Food Science

1. Agricultural meteorology supports food sciences by:
   a) Enhancing packaging designs
   b) Providing climate data that influences crop quality, food safety, and nutrition
   c) Increasing food coloring agents
   d) Deciding food prices
2. Which weather parameter significantly affects the nutritional quality of food crops?
   a) Soil depth
   b) Temperature and rainfall patterns
   c) Crop label color
   d) Tractor type
3. High humidity during harvesting and storage can lead to:
   a) Higher protein content
   b) Fungal contamination and reduced shelf life
   c) Increased vitamin levels
   d) Stronger seed coats
4. Which agrometeorological condition is most likely to increase the risk of aflatoxin contamination in food grains?
   a) Very low humidity
   b) Alternating drought and humidity
   c) Constant rainfall
   d) Cold spells
5. Weather forecasts are useful in food sciences for:
   a) Estimating flavor
   b) Planning harvest and post-harvest operations to reduce spoilage
   c) Reducing nutritional value
   d) Improving product color

6. Temperature and relative humidity play a key role in:
   a) Selecting food additives
   b) Designing nutrition plans
   c) Ensuring proper drying and storage of food products
   d) Enhancing aroma
7. Food security is influenced by agrometeorology through:
   a) Climate-resilient farming and stable food production
   b) Crop aesthetics
   c) Export marketing
   d) Label design
8. Climate variability may impact food sciences by:
   a) Enhancing shelf life
   b) Affecting nutrient composition, flavor, and contamination levels
   c) Removing allergens
   d) Improving packaging speed
9. Weather-based crop production forecasts are essential for:
   a) Determining cooking time
   b) Estimating food availability and planning food processing operations
   c) Improving refrigeration
   d) Reducing recipe complexity
10. Solar radiation data in agrometeorology is useful in food sciences for:
   a) Heating warehouses
   b) Designing solar dryers for fruits, vegetables, and grains
   c) Enhancing food dyes
   d) Avoiding transportation

Answer Key

1	b	2	b	3	b	4	b	5	b	6	c	7	a
8	b	9	b	10	b								

23

Marine Sciences

1. Meteorology contributes to marine sciences primarily by:
   a) Measuring soil fertility
   b) Monitoring ocean-atmosphere interactions that affect fisheries and coastal farming
   c) Managing fish breeding in tanks
   d) Analyzing seed genetics
2. Which of the following weather parameters significantly influence marine fish catch?
   a) Solar radiation and dew point
   b) Wind speed and sea surface temperature
   c) Soil pH and salinity
   d) Humidity and soil texture
3. Monsoon variability affects marine sciences by:
   a) Promoting desertification
   b) Impacting ocean currents, fish migration, and coastal agriculture
   c) Decreasing atmospheric CO_2
   d) Enhancing mountain erosion only
4. Cyclone warnings issued by meteorological departments are vital for:
   a) Seed storage management
   b) Protecting coastal fishers and marine assets
   c) Enhancing inland crop yield
   d) Increasing fertilizer use
5. The El Niño phenomenon is monitored in marine-agrometeorological studies because it:
   a) Increases snowfall in mountains
   b) Alters ocean temperatures and disrupts marine ecosystems

c) Promotes soil erosion inland

d) Enhances seed viability

6. Satellite-based agrometeorological observations help in:

a) Measuring groundwater levels

b) Mapping chlorophyll concentration and predicting fish abundance zones

c) Determining plant spacing

d) Locating warehouses

7. Sea surface temperature (SST) data is important in marine sciences because it:

a) Affects photosynthesis in crops

b) Influences fish behavior, breeding, and distribution

c) Increases seed hardiness

d) Determines farm mechanization cost

8. Coastal aquaculture planning benefits from meteorological data by:

a) Selecting salt-tolerant vegetables

b) Avoiding high-risk periods for stocking due to storm forecasts

c) Reducing land degradation

d) Increasing forest cover

9. The Indian National Centre for Ocean Information Services (INCOIS) provides:

a) Soil health reports

b) Weather advisories for marine fishers and ocean conditions

c) Genetic data for rice

d) Groundwater maps

10. Ocean-atmosphere models integrated with agricultural meteorology help in:

a) Pricing marine products

b) Forecasting extreme weather events that affect both marine and coastal agricultural livelihoods

c) Generating rainfall manually

d) Enhancing urban development

Answer Key

1	b	2	b	3	b	4	b	5	b	6	b	7	b
8	b	9	b	10	b								

24

Mushroom Farming

1. Agricultural meteorology supports mushroom cultivation by:
   a) Improving seed coatings
   b) Providing weather and microclimate data essential for optimal growth conditions
   c) Selecting mushroom packaging designs
   d) Enhancing spore visibility
2. Which two meteorological parameters are most crucial for successful mushroom cultivation?
   a) Wind speed and soil texture
   b) Temperature and relative humidity
   c) Sunlight hours and slope
   d) Rainfall and seed size
3. Mushroom yields are highly sensitive to:
   a) Day length only
   b) Changes in temperature and humidity during spawn run and fruiting stages
   c) Soil pH
   d) Wind erosion
4. High humidity in mushroom houses helps in:
   a) Enhancing vitamin content
   b) Maintaining moisture needed for fruiting body development
   c) Reducing microbial activity
   d) Drying the substrate
5. Temperature above the optimum range for mushroom species can cause:
   a) Faster growth
   b) Reduced yield and poor fruiting body quality

c) Better shelf life

d) Enhanced spore formation

6. Meteorological monitoring inside mushroom growing chambers is essential to:

a) Market mushrooms online

b) Control condensation, ventilation, and air exchange

c) Change mushroom color

d) Avoid harvesting

7. Which mushroom variety thrives best under cool and humid conditions, making weather data vital?

a) Button mushroom (*Agaricus bisporus*)

b) Paddy straw mushroom

c) Oyster mushroom

d) Shiitake mushroom

8. `Excess rainfall and poor weather control in mushroom units may lead to:

a) Increased production

b) Contamination and pest issues

c) Longer storage life

d) Higher vitamin content

9. Solar radiation data is indirectly important in mushroom cultivation for:

a) Improving mushroom flavor

b) Managing indoor light and temperature for certain species like *shiitake*

c) Enhancing spore shape

d) Making compost

10. Agrometeorological forecasts help mushroom growers by:

a) Timing cultivation cycles during favorable seasons

b) Marketing international varieties

c) Avoiding labor scheduling

d) Selecting mushroom dyes

Answer Key

1	b	2	b	3	b	4	b	5	b	6	b	7	a
8	b	9	b	10	a								

25

Natural Farming

1. Agricultural meteorology supports natural farming by:
   a) Promoting chemical pesticide use
   b) Providing weather-based guidance for ecological and input-free farming practices
   c) Advising on GM crop selection
   d) Encouraging monocropping systems
2. In natural farming, rainfall data is essential for:
   a) Selecting tractors
   b) Determining sowing time and managing soil moisture without irrigation
   c) Controlling seed color
   d) Enhancing fertilizer use
3. Which of the following is a weather-sensitive practice in natural farming?
   a) Synthetic nutrient spraying
   b) Zero tillage only
   c) Mulching to conserve soil moisture and regulate temperature
   d) Hybrid seed sowing
4. Weather-based forecasts help natural farmers in:
   a) Selecting chemical herbicides
   b) Timing operations like sowing, mulching, and protective measures
   c) Increasing export value
   d) Replacing native crop varieties
5. In natural farming, which weather factor most influences soil microbial activity and nutrient cycling?
   a) Wind direction b) Air pressure
   c) Temperature and moisture d) Cloud type

6. Drought prediction using agrometeorological data helps natural farmers to:
   a) Intensify irrigation
   b) Prepare crop choices and conservation strategies in advance
   c) Increase chemical inputs
   d) Extend harvest duration
7. Weather-based advisories support natural farming by:
   a) Encouraging pesticide use
   b) Helping minimize crop stress through timely eco-practices
   c) Promoting commercial seed suppliers
   d) Supporting fertilizer subsidies
8. Natural farming systems prefer cropping patterns based on:
   a) Import data
   b) Weather and seasonal rainfall predictions
   c) Fertilizer cost
   d) Tractor availability
9. Which weather condition is most favorable for preparing Jeevamrit (a natural bio-input)?
   a) Very low humidity
   b) Hot and dry conditions
   c) Mild temperatures and moderate humidity
   d) Heavy winds
10. Which agrometeorological tool is most useful for natural farming planning?
   a) Pesticide calculator
   b) Long-range weather forecast and local agromet advisory
   c) GMO selector
   d) Mechanical weeder guide

Answer Key

1	b	2	b	3	c	4	b	5	c	6	b	7	b
8	b	9	c	10	b								

26

Nematology

1. Which weather factor most significantly influences the activity and survival of plant-parasitic nematodes?
   a) Solar radiation
   b) Soil moisture and temperature
   c) Wind speed
   d) Atmospheric pressure
2. Agricultural meteorology supports nematology by:
   a) Designing crop calendars
   b) Predicting nematode population dynamics based on environmental conditions
   c) Improving fertilizer formulations
   d) Providing mechanical control methods
3. Soil temperature directly affects nematodes by:
   a) Stimulating their above-ground movement
   b) Enhancing their reproduction and life cycle speed
   c) Reducing their oxygen requirement
   d) Making them dormant permanently
4. High soil moisture combined with warm temperatures generally leads to:
   a) Decline in nematode populations
   b) Ideal conditions for nematode multiplication
   c) Increased resistance in plants
   d) Fungicide degradation
5. Which nematode species thrives in moist, warm soil conditions and affects vegetables like tomato and brinjal?
   a) Heterodera avenae
   b) Radopholus similis

c) Meloidogyne incognita (Root-knot nematode)
d) Xiphinema index

6. During drought or dry spells, nematode activity usually:
a) Increases rapidly
b) Is unaffected
c) Decreases due to desiccation stress
d) Converts to a fungal phase

7. Which of the following meteorological parameters is most useful in modeling nematode population growth?
a) Cloud cover
b) Air pressure
c) Soil temperature and moisture
d) UV radiation

8. Weather-based forecasting in nematology helps in:
a) Seed rate calculation
b) Predicting nematode attack timing for timely intervention
c) Harvesting schedule planning
d) Nutrient budgeting

9. Prolonged waterlogging conditions can result in:
a) Reduced nematode survival due to oxygen deficiency
b) Increased nematode mobility
c) Higher root-knot formation
d) Genetic mutation in nematodes

10. Remote sensing and soil temperature maps are useful in nematology for:
a) Identifying nematode species
b) Estimating organic matter in soil
c) Locating potential nematode hot spots in fields
d) Classifying weed infestation

Answer Key

1	b	2	b	3	b	4	b	5	c	6	c	7	c
8	b	9	a	10	c								

27

Organic Farming

1. Agricultural meteorology supports organic farming by:
   a) Recommending chemical inputs
   b) Providing weather-based advisories for natural input use and stress management
   c) Promoting monoculture
   d) Supporting synthetic seed development
2. Weather data in organic farming is essential for:
   a) Choosing pesticide application dates
   b) Managing composting and irrigation schedules
   c) Deciding hybrid seed treatments
   d) Increasing tillage frequency
3. Which meteorological factor is most important for composting in organic farming?
   a) Cloud cover
   b) Rainfall and temperature
   c) Wind direction
   d) Soil salinity
4. Agrometeorological forecasts help organic farmers to:
   a) Apply chemical sprays
   b) Schedule sowing, intercultural operations, and natural pest control
   c) Select transgenic varieties
   d) Reduce use of biological inputs
5. In organic farming, rainfall forecasting is vital for:
   a) Promoting fertilizer leaching
   b) Deciding on irrigation-free crop schedules and green manuring
   c) Harvesting solar energy
   d) Enhancing herbicide efficiency

6. Organic farming relies on weather-based data to:
   a) Increase pesticide residue
   b) Monitor and manage crop stress naturally
   c) Select synthetic micronutrients
   d) Promote chemical weed control
7. Soil health in organic farming is closely linked with:
   a) Mechanical tillage only
   b) Soil temperature and moisture influenced by weather
   c) Synthetic fertilizers
   d) GPS-based planting
8. Drought monitoring in organic farming systems supports:
   a) Use of growth regulators
   b) Planning mulching, crop selection, and moisture conservation practices
   c) Expansion of mono-cropping
   d) Switching to GM crops
9. Organic disease and pest management depends on:
   a) Timing of weather events for deploying natural deterrents
   b) Import of pesticides
   c) Use of nano-particles
   d) Fertilizer subsidies
10. Weather-based advisories help organic farmers to:
    a) Plan chemical applications
    b) Time eco-friendly practices like neem sprays and trap cropping
    c) Use genetically modified organisms (GMOs)
    d) Increase soil erosion

Answer Key

1	b	2	b	3	b	4	b	5	b	6	b	7	b
8	b	9	a	10	b								

28

Plant Breeding

1. Agricultural meteorology contributes to plant breeding mainly by:
   a) Studying soil nutrients
   b) Providing environmental data for genotype evaluation
   c) Controlling seed storage
   d) Increasing mutation frequency
2. The interaction of genotype with environment in plant breeding is referred to as:
   a) Environmental resistance
   b) Genotype-by-environment (G × E) interaction
   c) Phenotypic correlation
   d) Genetic drift
3. Which meteorological factor is most important when screening genotypes for drought tolerance?
   a) Wind speed
   b) Rainfall and evapotranspiration
   c) Cloud cover
   d) Fog frequency
4. Heat units or Growing Degree Days (GDD) are used in plant breeding to:
   a) Evaluate soil temperature
   b) Estimate the thermal time requirement of crop genotypes
   c) Calculate irrigation needs
   d) Assess nutrient uptake
5. Which of the following meteorological tools is used in selecting climate-resilient crop varieties?
   a) Wind tunnel b) Infrared thermometer
   c) Crop-weather modeling systems d) Soil auger

6. Agroclimatic zoning is useful in plant breeding for:
   a) Determining pesticide doses
   b) Selecting suitable breeding sites and genotype testing zones
   c) Studying pest migration
   d) Designing irrigation systems
7. In plant breeding programs, photoperiod data is essential for developing:
   a) Cold-tolerant varieties
   b) Day-neutral or photoperiod-sensitive cultivars
   c) Salt-tolerant plants
   d) Pesticide-resistant hybrids
8. Plant breeders rely on agrometeorological data for:
   a) Predicting market demand
   b) Enhancing fertilizer response
   c) Identifying genotype adaptability and stability
   d) Calculating input costs
9. Which weather variable most influences pollen viability and fertilization success in breeding trials?
   a) Wind direction   b) Temperature and humidity
   c) Cloud cover   d) Soil moisture content
10. Stress breeding in crops is most effective when:
   a) Grown under optimal weather conditions
   b) Conducted in controlled environments only
   c) Exposed to real-time weather extremes during sensitive growth stages
   d) Conducted only during the rainy season

Answer Key

1	b	2	b	3	b	4	b	5	c	6	b	7	b
8	c	9	b	10	c								

29

Plant Pathology

1. Which of the following meteorological factors most influences the outbreak of fungal diseases in crops?
   a) Solar radiation
   b) High humidity and leaf wetness
   c) Wind speed
   d) Atmospheric pressure
2. Agricultural meteorology contributes to plant pathology by:
   a) Controlling pests
   b) Identifying weed species
   c) Forecasting disease outbreaks based on weather parameters
   d) Developing fungicides
3. The most critical combination of factors favoring the development of late blight in potatoes includes:
   a) High temperature and low humidity
   b) Low rainfall and high wind
   c) Cool, moist conditions with prolonged leaf wetness
   d) Hot and dry weather
4. Disease forecasting models often use which of the following meteorological inputs?
   a) Soil texture and slope
   b) Temperature, humidity, and rainfall
   c) Seed rate and row spacing
   d) Light intensity and UV radiation
5. Which airborne pathogen is commonly spread through wind under favorable meteorological conditions?
   a) Fusarium
   b) Ustilago (Smut fungi)
   c) Puccinia (Rust fungi)
   d) Pythium

6. The concept of a "disease triangle" includes host, pathogen, and:
   a) Soil type
   b) Genetic resistance
   c) Environment (weather conditions)
   d) Fertilizer level
7. Which of the following weather conditions enhances the development of bacterial leaf blight in rice?
   a) Cold and dry
   b) High temperature and wind-driven rain
   c) Frosty nights
   d) Continuous bright sunshine
8. Agrometeorological tools such as remote sensing and GIS are used in plant pathology for:
   a) Soil classification
   b) Monitoring and mapping disease spread over large areas
   c) Breeding resistant varieties
   d) Determining seed dormancy
9. Plant disease epidemics are most likely to occur when weather is:
   a) Highly variable with extreme cold
   b) Unfavorable for plant growth
   c) Continuously favorable for pathogen development
   d) Constantly hot and dry
10. The timing of fungicide application can be optimized using:
   a) Crop calendar
   b) Soil test data
   c) Weather-based disease prediction models
   d) Visual observation of weeds

Answer Key

1	b	2	c	3	c	4	b	5	c	6	c	7	b
8	b	9	c	10	c								

30

Plantation Crops

1. Agricultural meteorology supports plantation crop management by:
   a) Designing labels for export
   b) Providing weather data for long-term planning and productivity
   c) Improving packaging materials
   d) Coloring leaves for aesthetic appeal
2. Which meteorological factor is most critical for tea and coffee plantations?
   a) Soil color
   b) Rainfall distribution and humidity
   c) Market demand
   d) Leaf shape
3. Weather anomalies like unseasonal rains affect plantation crops by:
   a) Enhancing flavor
   b) Causing flower drop and disease outbreaks
   c) Increasing fruit size
   d) Improving pest control
4. Solar radiation data helps plantation crop growers in:
   a) Determining coffee roast levels
   b) Managing shade requirements for crops like cocoa and coffee
   c) Replacing pruning cycles
   d) Enhancing soil erosion
5. Wind speed and direction are crucial for:
   a) Harvest calendar design
   b) Planning windbreaks in rubber and coconut plantations
   c) Coloring fruits
   d) Fertilizer storage

6. Agrometeorological forecasts assist plantation farmers in:
   a) Advertising techniques
   b) Planning harvesting and disease management operations
   c) Setting export taxes
   d) Improving tree height
7. High humidity and rainfall can lead to:
   a) Enhanced seed storage
   b) Fungal diseases like blight and rot in plantation crops
   c) Reduction in caffeine content
   d) Longer shelf life
8. Temperature thresholds are particularly important in:
   a) Designing drip systems
   b) Determining cold sensitivity of crops like arecanut and black pepper
   c) Adjusting pesticide labels
   d) Marketing organic labels
9. Drought monitoring in plantations helps in:
   a) Coloring leaves for export
   b) Scheduling irrigation and reducing water stress impacts on perennial crops
   c) Removing mulch
   d) Avoiding shade management
10. Agrometeorology aids sustainable plantation crop production by:
   a) Reducing biodiversity
   b) Supporting climate-resilient practices like intercropping and soil moisture conservation
   c) Promoting deforestation
   d) Ignoring traditional methods

Answer Key

1	b	2	b	3	b	4	b	5	b	6	b	7	b
8	b	9	b	10	b								

31

Poultry Science

1. Which of the following environmental factors is most critical in poultry heat stress?

   a) Wind speed b) Relative humidity
   c) Ambient temperature d) Solar radiation

2. The Temperature-Humidity Index (THI) in poultry science is used to assess:

   a) Egg quality b) Feed conversion efficiency
   c) Thermal comfort or stress levels d) Disease prevalence

3. During high ambient temperatures, poultry generally exhibit:

   a) Increased feed intake b) Increased egg production
   c) Panting and reduced activity d) Improved growth rate

4. What role does wind speed play in poultry houses in hot climates?

   a) Promotes disease spread b) Increases humidity
   c) Helps evaporative cooling d) Reduces light intensity

5. Which agrometeorological tool helps forecast heat waves affecting poultry farms?

   a) Doppler radar b) Heat Index charts
   c) Agromet advisories d) Soil moisture sensors

6. Sudden cold weather can lead to which problem in poultry?

   a) Heatstroke
   b) Feed poisoning
   c) Respiratory distress and reduced immunity
   d) Increased hatching rate

7. Optimal temperature for brooding day-old chicks is typically around:

   a) 18–20°C b) 22–24°C
   c) 28–30°C d) 32–35°C

8. Which weather condition can significantly increase the risk of fungal infections in poultry feed?
   a) High temperature with low humidity
   b) Cold and dry conditions
   c) High humidity and poor ventilation
   d) Strong sunlight
9. Poultry production is most efficient when microclimatic conditions are:
   a) Monitored manually only
   b) Not considered significant
   c) Closely regulated using sensors and climate controllers
   d) Left to natural adaptation
10. Weather-based early warning systems in poultry science help in:
   a) Reducing feed cost
   b) Predicting bird color variations
   c) Planning vaccinations and stress management
   d) Enhancing feather growth

Answer Key

1	c	2	c	3	c	4	c	5	c	6	c	7	d
8	c	9	c	10	c								

32

Protected Cultivation

1. Agricultural meteorology contributes to protected cultivation by:
   a) Advising on export taxes
   b) Providing microclimate data for optimizing crop growth in greenhouses and polyhouses
   c) Designing farm buildings
   d) Selecting pesticide packaging
2. Which weather parameter is most crucial to manage inside protected structures?
   a) Soil depth
   b) Temperature and relative humidity
   c) Wind direction outside
   d) Soil type
3. Solar radiation data in protected cultivation is used for:
   a) Coloring greenhouse walls
   b) Managing light intensity for photosynthesis
   c) Enhancing irrigation pump size
   d) Determining sowing depth
4. Temperature extremes inside polyhouses can lead to:
   a) Faster seed packaging
   b) Heat stress, flower drop, and poor fruit set
   c) Improved soil drainage
   d) Reduced fertilizer requirement

5 Humidity control in protected cultivation is important to:
   a) Increase air conditioning
   b) Prevent fungal diseases and maintain optimal transpiration
   c) Reduce plant size
   d) Boost weed growth

6. Wind speed and direction data are important in protected cultivation for:
   a) Painting greenhouse frames
   b) Designing proper ventilation and structural safety
   c) Choosing crop names
   d) Monitoring crop taste
7. Agrometeorological data helps in scheduling operations like:
   a) Fertilizer marketing
   b) Sowing, fertigation, and pest control inside protected structures
   c) Market inspections
   d) Label printing
8. Climate-controlled cultivation systems require continuous monitoring of:
   a) Soil compaction
   b) Inside temperature, humidity, and CO_2 concentration
   c) Rainfall alone
   d) Pest populations only
9. Radiation balance in protected cultivation affects:
   a) Water storage tanks
   b) Photosynthetic efficiency and energy use
   c) Tractor use
   d) Soil type selection
10. Weather forecasting supports protected cultivation by:
   a) Designing outdoor irrigation canals
   b) Planning ventilation and temperature control in advance
   c) Enhancing leaf color
   d) Identifying greenhouse locations

Answer Key

1	b	2	b	3	b	4	b	5	b	6	b	7	b
8	b	9	b	10	b								

33

Seed Science

1. Agricultural meteorology supports seed science primarily by:
   a) Enhancing seed color
   b) Providing weather data for ideal seed production conditions
   c) Changing seed genetic structure
   d) Determining seed packaging material
2. Which meteorological factor most affects seed germination in the field?
   a) Cloud cover b) Soil moisture & temperature
   c) Wind speed d) Sunshine duration
3. High relative humidity during seed storage can lead to:
   a) Better seed hardening
   b) Increased seed longevity
   c) Faster seed drying
   d) Fungal infection and loss of viability
4. Weather forecasts are useful in seed production programs for:
   a) Reducing germination rate
   b) Planning pollination, harvest, and post-harvest operations
   c) Minimizing labor use
   d) Avoiding seed certification
5. The ideal weather for harvesting seeds to maintain quality is:
   a) Rainy and humid b) Foggy and cold
   c) Dry and sunny d) Hot and windy
6. Which of the following parameters directly affects pollen viability during seed production?
   a) Cloud cover and rainfall b) Soil pH
   c) Temperature and humidity d) Wind direction

7. Weather-based advisories are useful in seed technology to:
   a) Boost seed coloring
   b) Ensure proper timing of operations to avoid weather damage
   c) Increase seed dormancy
   d) Change seed size
8. Seed drying is most efficient under conditions of:
   a) High humidity and no wind
   b) High temperature and low relative humidity
   c) Cloudy skies and drizzle
   d) Calm, moist conditions
9. Seed vigor and viability in open fields are highly influenced by:
   a) Solar activity
   b) Weather extremes during seed development and maturity
   c) Pest infestation only
   d) Manual harvesting
10. Which agrometeorological element is most important for planning isolation distance in seed production plots?
   a) Rainfall
   b) Wind direction and speed
   c) Soil moisture
   d) Solar radiation

Answer Key

1	b	2	b	3	d	4	b	5	c	6	c	7	b
8	b	9	b	10	b								

34

Soil Science

1. Agricultural meteorology contributes to soil science by:
   a) Developing synthetic fertilizers
   b) Managing soil-climate interactions for better crop production
   c) Altering soil texture
   d) Determining soil taxonomy
2. Which weather parameter most directly influences soil moisture availability?
   a) Atmospheric pressure
   b) Wind speed
   c) Rainfall and evaporation
   d) UV index
3. Evapotranspiration data is important in soil science for:
   a) Fertilizer application
   b) Estimating water loss from soil and plant
   c) Monitoring pesticide residues
   d) Soil classification
4. Which meteorological factor affects the rate of organic matter decomposition in soil?
   a) Solar radiation
   b) Air temperature and soil moisture
   c) Wind direction
   d) Cloud cover
5. Soil erosion risk increases under which meteorological conditions?
   a) High temperatures and low humidity
   b) Heavy rainfall and strong winds
   c) Low rainfall and cool weather
   d) Fog and dew formation

6. Weather-based soil moisture forecasting is essential for:
   a) Increasing salinity
   b) Scheduling irrigation and managing drought risk
   c) Determining soil depth
   d) Reducing clay content
7. Which meteorological parameter is crucial for calculating soil water balance?
   a) Sunshine hours
   b) Temperature
   c) Rainfall
   d) Rainfall and evapotranspiration
8. Prolonged dry spells affect soil by:
   a) Increasing microbial activity
   b) Enhancing soil compaction and reducing fertility
   c) Decreasing wind erosion
   d) Improving drainage
9. Agrometeorological inputs are used in soil nutrient management to:
   a) Alter soil structure
   b) Time fertilizer application based on rainfall forecasts
   c) Increase leaching losses
   d) Remove micronutrients
10. The risk of salinization increases in irrigated soils under:
   a) Well-distributed rainfall
   b) High rainfall and deep drainage
   c) High evaporation and low rainfall conditions
   d) Low temperatures

Answer Key

1	b	2	c	3	b	4	b	5	b	6	b	7	d
8	b	9	b	10	c								

35

Social Sciences

1. Agricultural meteorology contributes to social sciences by:
   a) Promoting chemical-based agriculture
   b) Studying how weather and climate impact rural livelihoods and behavior
   c) Developing biotechnology products
   d) Enhancing seed packaging
2. Which of the following is a key social science outcome influenced by agrometeorological events like droughts?
   a) DNA mutation
   b) Community displacement and migration
   c) Increase in soil fertility
   d) Higher rainfall
3. Agrometeorological advisories support rural societies by:
   a) Promoting monoculture
   b) Reducing vulnerability through timely decision-making
   c) Replacing traditional knowledge
   d) Limiting access to resources
4. Weather-based crop failures can lead to which social issue?
   a) Higher literacy
   b) Rural unemployment and food insecurity
   c) Urban beautification
   d) Increase in biodiversity
5. Social scientists use agrometeorological data to:
   a) Determine chemical residues
   b) Understand adaptation strategies in farming communities
   c) Identify soil pH
   d) Analyze pesticide efficiency

6. Participatory climate risk management in villages is based on:
   a) Market price tracking
   b) Local weather data and community knowledge
   c) Internet usage
   d) Livestock export trends
7. Climate literacy at the grassroots level improves through:
   a) Mobile-based agromet advisories and local extension outreach
   b) Centralized irrigation
   c) Urban planning models
   d) GMO trials
8. Social science studies in agrometeorology often focus on:
   a) Atmospheric chemistry
   b) Human behavior and societal response to weather extremes
   c) DNA sequencing
   d) Seed multiplication
9. Agrometeorology helps in disaster preparedness by:
   a) Measuring seed moisture
   b) Enabling early warning systems and response planning
   c) Managing forest cover
   d) Forecasting election outcomes
10. A key role of agricultural meteorology in social policy is:
    a) Designing soil maps
    b) Informing drought relief, crop insurance, and food security programs
    c) Regulating fertilizer subsidies
    d) Enhancing tractor efficiency

Answer Key

1	b	2	b	3	b	4	b	5	b	6	b	7	a
8	b	9	b	10	b								

36

Spices Cultivation

1. Agricultural meteorology supports spices cultivation by:
   a) Forecasting market demand
   b) Providing climate data essential for optimizing sowing, growth, and harvesting of spice crops
   c) Improving packaging materials
   d) Enhancing seed coloring
2. Which weather parameter is most crucial for black pepper cultivation?
   a) Cloud type
   b) Rainfall and humidity
   c) Wind speed alone
   d) Soil bulk density
3. High relative humidity in spice crops often leads to:
   a) Faster seed germination
   b) Increased risk of fungal diseases like leaf spot and root rot
   c) Better aroma
   d) Improved yield only
4. Temperature data is important in spices cultivation because:
   a) It determines packaging needs
   b) It affects flowering and essential oil synthesis in crops like coriander and fennel
   c) It enhances stem thickness
   d) It controls weed growth
5. Agrometeorological advisories are particularly useful in spices for:
   a) Predicting branding strategies
   b) Timely planting and pest/disease control operations
   c) Processing of spices
   d) Export documentation

6. In cardamom plantations, prolonged dry spells may result in:
   a) Better flavor
   b) Flower and fruit drop, leading to reduced yields
   c) Enhanced oil concentration
   d) Faster ripening
7. Which spice crop is highly sensitive to frost and sudden temperature drops?
   a) Saffron b) Turmeric
   c) Black pepper d) Ginger
8. Wind direction and speed are considered in spice cultivation for:
   a) Aesthetic layout
   b) Planning windbreaks and managing cross-pollination in crops like cumin
   c) Coloring spice pods
   d) Seed extraction
9. Rainfall variability in spices like turmeric and ginger can:
   a) Improve oil yield
   b) Cause rhizome rot and reduced stand establishment
   c) Increase shelf life
   d) Delay flowering
10. Climate-smart practices in spices cultivation promoted by agrometeorology include:
   a) Monoculture
   b) Mulching, staggered sowing, and weather-based irrigation
   c) Delayed harvesting
   d) Increased pesticide usage

Answer Key

1	b	2	b	3	b	4	b	5	b	6	b	7	a
8	b	9	b	10	b								

37

Science of Agricultural Stresses Agrometeorology

1. What is the primary goal of agrometeorology in the context of agricultural stress?
   a) To study the structure of the atmosphere
   b) To predict earthquakes
   c) To manage and reduce weather-induced crop stress
   d) To increase atmospheric CO_2 concentration
2. Which of the following types of stress is most directly addressed by agrometeorological services?
   a) Pesticide resistance
   b) Heat and drought stress
   c) Soil nutrient deficiency
   d) Genetic mutation in crops
3. Agrometeorological advisory services help farmers primarily by:
   a) Offering subsidies
   b) Providing insurance schemes
   c) Delivering weather-based crop management tips
   d) Conducting field inspections
4. Which weather phenomenon can lead to terminal heat stress in wheat?
   a) Prolonged rainfall during germination
   b) Sudden temperature fall in early growth
   c) High temperatures during grain filling stage
   d) Early frost in spring

5. A meteorological drought is defined by:
   a) Reduced nutrient levels in soil
   b) Prolonged period of below-average rainfall
   c) Increase in pest infestations
   d) Sudden floods in low-lying fields
6. Which of the following tools helps simulate crop responses under stress due to weather variability?
   a) SPSS b) GIS
   c) DSSAT d) PCR
7. Heat stress in plants is generally caused when temperatures exceed:
   a) 10°C b) 25°C
   c) 30–35°C (depending on crop) d) 5°C
8. What is the effect of prolonged cloudy weather on crop growth?
   a) Increased photosynthesis
   b) Enhanced transpiration
   c) Reduced solar radiation and photosynthesis
   d) No effect at all
9. Which of the following stress events can be forecasted using agrometeorological models?
   a) Soil salinity
   b) Insect pest outbreaks due to temperature and humidity patterns
   c) Genetic mutations
   d) Market price crashes
10. The integration of remote sensing and agrometeorology helps in:
   a) Conducting lab experiments
   b) Monitoring real-time crop stress and variability
   c) Writing weather reports
   d) Soil taxonomy classification

Answer Key

1	c	2	b	3	c	4	c	5	b	6	c	7	c
8	c	9	b	10	b								

38

Vegetable Science

1. Agricultural meteorology supports vegetable science by:
   a) Providing data for crop insurance only
   b) Enhancing post-harvest handling
   c) Offering weather-based insights for crop planning and management
   d) Reducing seed cost
2. Which meteorological parameter most influences bolting in onion and radish?
   a) Humidity
   b) Day length and temperature
   c) Soil pH
   d) Wind speed
3. Weather-based forecasting in vegetable crops helps in:
   a) Estimating soil texture
   b) Determining packaging cost
   c) Timing of sowing, harvesting, and disease control
   d) Controlling rodents
4. Excessive rainfall during the flowering stage of tomato can lead to:
   a) Higher vitamin C content
   b) Improved fruit size
   c) Poor fruit set and fungal disease incidence
   d) Increased sweetness
5. Heat units (Growing Degree Days) are useful in vegetable crops to:
   a) Estimate seed dormancy
   b) Forecast pest migration
   c) Predict maturity and harvest time
   d) Measure chlorophyll content

6. Which vegetable crop is highly sensitive to frost?
   a) Tomato
   b) Spinach
   c) Pea
   d) Okra
7. Prolonged cloudy weather reduces yield in leafy vegetables by:
   a) Increasing transpiration
   b) Reducing photosynthesis due to low solar radiation
   c) Enhancing pollination
   d) Stimulating chlorophyll breakdown
8. Agricultural meteorology helps in managing irrigation in vegetables by:
   a) Monitoring fertilizer use
   b) Estimating crop evapotranspiration
   c) Testing leaf turgor
   d) Assessing pesticide residue
9. High relative humidity in vegetable fields often leads to:
   a) Early flowering
   b) Improved shelf life
   c) Disease outbreaks like downy mildew
   d) Increased seed viability
10. Use of weather advisories in vegetable cultivation can help farmers:
   a) Reduce reliance on certified seeds
   b) Schedule farm operations and reduce losses due to weather extremes
   c) Avoid mechanized tools
   d) Replace chemical fertilizers

Answer Key

1	c	2	b	3	c	4	c	5	c	6	a	7	b
8	b	9	c	10	b								

39

Veterinary Sciences

1. Agricultural meteorology supports veterinary sciences by:
   a) Developing feed additives
   b) Providing climate data to predict, manage, and prevent weather-related animal diseases
   c) Producing vaccines
   d) Enhancing animal breed identification
2. Which meteorological factor is most associated with the outbreak of vector-borne diseases in animals?
   a) Cloud type
   b) Temperature and humidity
   c) Soil moisture only
   d) Wind direction alone
3. Prolonged high temperatures can cause which of the following in animals?
   a) Increased milk fat
   b) Heat stress and immune suppression
   c) Better weight gain
   d) Reduced reproduction issues
4. Seasonal weather forecasting in veterinary sciences helps in:
   a) Identifying animal species
   b) Planning vaccination and disease prevention programs
   c) Changing pasture shape
   d) Monitoring water pH
5. Livestock disease surveillance benefits from meteorological inputs by:
   a) Measuring feed prices
   b) Correlating disease patterns with weather variables like rainfall and temperature
   c) Calculating animal taxes
   d) Designing pens

6. Humid and wet conditions are favorable for which veterinary concern?
   a) Hoof hardening
   b) Spread of bacterial and fungal infections in livestock
   c) Increased fertility
   d) Cleaner barns
7. Agrometeorological advisories assist veterinarians by:
   a) Offering breed registration services
   b) Warning against stress-related illnesses during weather extremes
   c) Printing vaccination cards
   d) Selling supplements
8. Cold stress in animals due to low temperature and high wind speeds can lead to:
   a) Heat tolerance
   b) Hypothermia and reduced immunity
   c) Enhanced digestion
   d) Disease resistance
9. Which tool is used to assess the combined effect of temperature and humidity on animal health?
   a) Thermometer only
   b) Temperature-Humidity Index (THI)
   c) Altimeter
   d) Rain gauge
10. Climate-smart veterinary practices include:
   a) Ignoring weather changes
   b) Modifying shelter, nutrition, and vaccination schedules based on agromet data
   c) Removing shade from animal shelters
   d) Avoiding disease surveillance

Answer Key

1	b	2	b	3	b	4	b	5	b	6	b	7	b
8	b	9	b	10	b								

40

Watershed/Drought Management

1. Which meteorological parameter is most crucial in determining watershed runoff potential?
   a) Relative humidity
   b) Wind speed
   c) Rainfall intensity and duration
   d) Solar radiation
2. Drought monitoring primarily involves the analysis of:
   a) Cloud types
   b) Soil temperature
   c) Rainfall deviation and evapotranspiration
   d) Atmospheric pressure
3. Agro-meteorological data helps in watershed management by:
   a) Increasing irrigation demand
   b) Predicting pest outbreaks
   c) Estimating runoff and infiltration rates
   d) Enhancing fertilizer use
4. The Standardized Precipitation Index (SPI) is used for:
   a) Measuring soil fertility
   b) Classifying drought severity
   c) Calculating heat index
   d) Estimating wind erosion
5. Which agro-meteorological technique helps in planning check dam placement in a watershed?
   a) Soil temperature forecasting
   b) Solar radiation analysis
   c) Rainfall-runoff modeling
   d) Wind direction tracking
6. Drought early warning systems use agrometeorological inputs such as:
   a) Soil salinity levels
   b) Evapotranspiration and rainfall anomalies
   c) Pest infestation patterns
   d) Crop sowing dates

7. Water harvesting structures in watershed areas are better planned using:
   a) Monthly wind data
   b) Long-term rainfall records
   c) Humidity observations
   d) Night-time temperatures
8. Which meteorological factor has the greatest influence on drought onset?
   a) Increase in wind velocity
   b) Decrease in sunshine hours
   c) Deficit and poorly distributed rainfall
   d) Drop in atmospheric pressure
9. The Palmer Drought Severity Index (PDSI) integrates:
   a) Solar radiation and humidity
   b) Wind speed and temperature
   c) Precipitation and temperature
   d) Cloud cover and dew point
10. Integration of weather forecasts in watershed management helps in:
    a) Minimizing seed cost
    b) Enhancing soil nutrient uptake
    c) Scheduling soil conservation practices
    d) Promoting weed growth

Answer Key

1	c	2	c	3	c	4	b	5	c	6	b	7	b
8	c	9	c	10	c								

C. Agricultural Meteorology
ICAR-ASRB Syllabus

1

General Meteorology

1. Which gas is most abundant in the Earth's atmosphere by volume?
   a) Oxygen
   b) Nitrogen
   c) Carbon dioxide
   d) Argon
2. The lowest layer of the atmosphere is called:
   a) Mesosphere
   b) Thermosphere
   c) Stratosphere
   d) Troposphere
3. The height of the troposphere is greatest over:
   a) Poles
   b) Oceans
   c) Equator
   d) Deserts
4. Temperature decreases with height in the:
   a) Troposphere
   b) Stratosphere
   c) Thermosphere
   d) Exosphere
5. The instrument used to measure atmospheric pressure is:
   a) Thermometer
   b) Anemometer
   c) Hygrometer
   d) Barometer
6. The unit of measurement of atmospheric pressure is:
   a) mm
   b) Newton
   c) hPa
   d) Lux
7. The radiation balance between incoming and outgoing radiation is known as:
   a) Radiation flux
   b) Heat budget
   c) Solar constant
   d) Temperature lapse
8. The primary source of energy for the Earth's atmosphere is:
   a) Earth's core
   b) Moonlight
   c) Sun
   d) Radioactive decay

9. Which process is responsible for heating the Earth's surface?
   a) Convection b) Radiation
   c) Conduction d) Reflection

10. The solar constant is approximately:
   a) 1.36 W/m^2 b) 136 W/m^2
   c) 1360 W/m^2 d) 13.6 W/m^2

11. Wind blows due to:
   a) Magnetic force b) Coriolis force
   c) Pressure gradient force d) Frictional force

12. Coriolis force is maximum at the:
   a) Equator b) Tropic of Cancer
   c) Poles d) 30° latitude

13. A line joining points of equal pressure on a weather map is called:
   a) Isobar b) Isotherm
   c) Isohyet d) Isohel

14. Clouds are formed mainly due to:
   a) Condensation b) Radiation
   c) Sublimation d) Evaporation

15. Which layer of the atmosphere contains ozone layer?
   a) Mesosphere b) Stratosphere
   c) Troposphere d) Thermosphere

16. The instrument used to measure wind speed is called:
   a) Hygrometer b) Anemometer
   c) Barograph d) Thermograph

17. The earth's atmosphere extends up to approximately:
   a) 10 km b) 50 km
   c) 1000 km d) 1600 km

18. The boundary between troposphere and stratosphere is known as:
   a) Tropopause b) Stratopause
   c) Mesopause d) Ionosphere

19. Which component of radiation is responsible for heating the lower atmosphere?
    a) UV rays
    b) Reflected solar radiation
    c) Terrestrial radiation
    d) Cosmic rays
20. The angle between sun rays and Earth's surface is called:
    a) Zenith angle
    b) Solar angle
    c) Declination angle
    d) Latitude
21. The primary gas responsible for the greenhouse effect is:
    a) Oxygen
    b) Nitrogen
    c) Water vapor
    d) Argon
22. What causes the change in seasons on Earth?
    a) Earth's rotation
    b) Moon's gravity
    c) Earth's axial tilt
    d) Sunspots
23. The annual variation of temperature due to Earth's revolution is called:
    a) Diurnal variation
    b) Seasonal variation
    c) Latitudinal variation
    d) Annual anomaly
24. The maximum heating of the day usually occurs at:
    a) Solar noon
    b) 8 AM
    c) 3 PM
    d) Sunset
25. Which of the following is not a permanent gas of the atmosphere?
    a) Oxygen
    b) Nitrogen
    c) Water vapor
    d) Argon

Answer Key

1	b	2	d	3	c	4	a	5	d	6	c	7	b
8	c	9	b	10	c	11	c	12	c	13	a	14	a
15	b	16	b	17	c	18	a	19	c	20	a	21	c
22	c	23	b	24	c	25	c						

2

General Climatology

1. Climatology is the scientific study of:
   a) Earthquakes b) Atmosphere
   c) Climate and its variations d) Agriculture
2. Who is known as the father of modern climatology?
   a) Alfred Wegener b) Koppen
   c) Aristotle d) Thornthwaite
3. The primary basis of Köppen's climate classification is:
   a) Wind speed b) Soil type
   c) Temperature and precipitation d) Cloud type
4. India's climate is predominantly classified as:
   a) Tropical wet b) Tropical monsoon
   c) Semi-arid d) Subtropical humid
5. The term "microclimate" refers to:
   a) Global climate b) National average climate
   c) Localized climate of a small area d) Climate of oceans
6. The Inter-Tropical Convergence Zone (ITCZ) is associated with:
   a) Polar high pressure b) Westerlies
   c) Trade winds convergence d) Jet streams
7. Jet streams are located in which part of the atmosphere?
   a) Troposphere b) Stratosphere
   c) Mesosphere d) Thermosphere
8. ENSO stands for:
   a) Earth's Northern Storm Oscillation
   b) El Niño Southern Oscillation
   c) Equatorial Neutral Sea Oscillation
   d) Environmental Seasonal Oscillation

9. Which ocean current is associated with El Niño?
   a) Canary b) Kuroshio
   c) Humboldt d) Gulf Stream
10. During La Niña conditions, the Indian monsoon becomes:
   a) Weak b) Normal
   c) Stronger than normal d) Unpredictable
11. Tropical cyclones generally form between:
   a) 0°–5° latitude b) 5°–30° latitude
   c) 30°–45° latitude d) 45°–60° latitude
12. Which phenomenon explains the deflection of wind due to Earth's rotation?
   a) Advection b) Radiation
   c) Coriolis effect d) Albedo
13. Climate of a region is typically averaged over a period of:
   a) 5 years b) 10 years
   c) 15 years d) 30 years
14. Monsoon in India is primarily caused by:
   a) Westerlies
   b) Temperature gradient
   c) ITCZ migration and pressure difference
   d) Ocean currents
15. Which of the following is not a factor influencing climate?
   a) Latitude b) Altitude
   c) Longitude d) Ocean currents
16. Desert climates are generally classified under which Köppen type?
   a) A b) B
   c) C d) D
17. Thornthwaite's classification is based on:
   a) Rainfall only b) Temperature only
   c) Moisture index d) Latitude
18. The Polar Front Theory is related to the origin of:
   a) Tropical cyclones b) Cold waves
   c) Temperate cyclones d) Dust storms

19. Rain shadow regions are mostly found on:
   a) Windward side b) Leeward side
   c) Ocean coasts d) Equatorial zones
20. Which of the following regions has an equable climate?
   a) Continental interiors b) Deserts
   c) Coastal regions d) Mountainous regions
21. Which of the following best explains "continentality" effect?
   a) Proximity to equator
   b) Oceanic influence
   c) Temperature extremes in inland areas
   d) Rainfall pattern
22. Climate variability refers to:
   a) Permanent shift in climate
   b) Short-term fluctuations in climate elements
   c) Yearly fixed climate data
   d) Uniform weather over decades
23. Which region is most affected by ENSO events?
   a) East Africa b) Pacific Ocean
   c) Arctic Ocean d) Indian Ocean
24. The humidity which affects climate is mostly in the form of:
   a) Water vapor b) Clouds
   c) Ice d) Dew
25. Which climatic factor influences the growing period of crops most significantly?
   a) Wind speed b) Solar radiation
   c) Temperature and rainfall d) Soil type

Answer Key

1	c	2	b	3	c	4	b	5	c	6	c	7	a
8	b	9	c	10	c	11	b	12	c	13	d	14	c
15	c	16	b	17	c	18	c	19	b	20	c	21	c
22	b	23	b	24	a	25	c						

3

Agricultural Climatology

1. Agricultural climatology primarily deals with:
   a) Climate of cities
   b) Impact of crops on weather
   c) Interaction between climate and agriculture
   d) Study of forests and rivers
2. The length of growing period (LGP) is influenced by:
   a) Soil pH only
   b) Rainfall and temperature
   c) Cloud cover
   d) Wind direction
3. The minimum temperature required for wheat germination is:
   a) 5°C
   b) 8°C
   c) 10°C
   d) 15°C
4. The term "heat unit" or "growing degree day" (GDD) was introduced to estimate:
   a) Soil erosion
   b) Temperature range
   c) Crop phenology
   d) Evaporation rate
5. The formula for Growing Degree Days (GDD) is:
   a) Tmax + Tmin
   b) (Tmax + Tmin)/2 − Tbase
   c) Tmax − Tmin
   d) Tmin × Tmax
6. Thermal time is used to estimate:
   a) Crop production
   b) Crop growth stages
   c) Rainfall probability
   d) Soil nutrient status
7. Cardinal temperatures are defined as:
   a) Extreme temperatures
   b) Average seasonal temperatures
   c) Minimum, optimum, and maximum for crop growth
   d) Night temperatures

8. Optimum temperature for rice growth is around:
   a) 18°C
   b) 22°C
   c) 25°C–30°C
   d) 35°C–40°C
9. The base temperature for calculating GDD for maize is generally considered as:
   a) 0°C
   b) 5°C
   c) 10°C
   d) 15°C
10. Which factor is not considered in agroclimatic zoning?
   a) Rainfall
   b) Temperature
   c) Political boundaries
   d) Soil type
11. Which agroclimatic zone of India has the highest cropping intensity?
   a) Arid zone
   b) Coastal zone
   c) Trans-Gangetic plain
   d) Eastern Himalayan region
12. Water requirement of a crop is least influenced by:
   a) Wind velocity
   b) Sunshine duration
   c) Leaf colour
   d) Crop duration
13. Which climate is best suited for wheat cultivation in India?
   a) Arid and semi-arid
   b) Tropical wet
   c) Temperate with dry winter
   d) Equatorial
14. Agrometeorological indices include all except:
   a) GDD
   b) Heliothermal units
   c) Psychrometry
   d) Photothermal units
15. The effective rainfall is the portion of rainfall that:
   a) Is lost as runoff
   b) Percolates deep into aquifer
   c) Is available for crop use
   d) Evaporates from soil
16. Agroclimatic classification helps in:
   a) Deciding soil type
   b) Designing irrigation equipment
   c) Crop planning and land use
   d) Classifying pests
17. Heat-use efficiency is defined as:
   a) Yield per rainfall
   b) Yield per unit GDD
   c) Biomass per evapotranspiration
   d) Water use per crop

18. Which is not an application of agricultural climatology?
    a) Crop-weather modeling
    b) Climate resilience planning
    c) Seismic forecasting
    d) Agro-advisory services
19. Evapotranspiration is highest during:
    a) Humid and cloudy days
    b) Cold and dry days
    c) Hot, dry, and windy days
    d) Rainy and windy day
20. Crop microclimate can be modified using:
    a) Fertilizers
    b) Windbreaks or shelterbelts
    c) Pesticides
    d) Irrigation pumps
21. The crop-weather calendar is mainly prepared for:
    a) Agroforestry systems
    b) Crop planning and weather-based operations
    c) Monsoon withdrawal
    d) Livestock breeding
22. Which of the following crops is most sensitive to frost?
    a) Mustard
    b) Wheat
    c) Gram
    d) Potato
23. Radiation frost occurs on:
    a) Cloudy nights
    b) Windy days
    c) Clear, calm nights
    d) Humid days
24. Photothermal unit is calculated as:
    a) GDD × rainfall
    b) GDD × sunshine hours
    c) GDD × day length
    d) Tmax × Tmin
25. Which crop requires the highest cumulative GDD from sowing to maturity?
    a) Rice
    b) Sorghum
    c) Wheat
    d) Cotton

Answer Key

1	c	2	b	3	a	4	c	5	b	6	b	7	c
8	c	9	c	10	c	11	c	12	c	13	c	14	c
15	c	16	c	17	b	18	c	19	c	20	b	21	b
22	d	23	c	24	c	25	d						

4

Micrometeorology

1. Micrometeorology is the study of atmospheric processes within a height of:
   a) 1–10 km b) 100–1000 m
   c) 1–2 m above ground d) 0–100 m
2. The lowest layer of the atmosphere directly influenced by the earth's surface is called:
   a) Mesosphere b) Stratosphere
   c) Boundary layer d) Tropopause
3. Which layer of the atmosphere is most relevant to micrometeorology?
   a) Stratosphere b) Troposphere
   c) Mesosphere d) Thermosphere
4. The sub-layer of the atmosphere that is in immediate contact with the surface is:
   a) Surface layer b) Free atmosphere
   c) Stratosphere d) Inversion layer
5. The diurnal variaton is most prominent in which meteorological element?
   a) Rainfall b) Wind direction
   c) Solar radiation d) Temperature
6. The energy balance at the crop canopy includes:
   a) Only radiation
   b) Radiation and precipitation
   c) Radiation, latent heat, sensible heat, soil heat flux
   d) Wind and soil temperature
7. Aerodynamic resistance is influenced most by:
   a) Leaf shape b) Soil type
   c) Wind speed and surface roughness d) Soil temperature

8. Roughness length is a parameter used to characterize:
   a) Soil erosion
   b) Canopy albedo
   c) Momentum transfer in turbulent flows
   d) Soil temperature fluctuation
9. Which instrument is used to measure turbulent fluxes directly?
   a) Thermohygrometer b) Barometer
   c) Eddy covariance system d) Stevenson screen
10. Turbulent transfer of momentum, heat, and moisture is mainly caused by:
   a) Radiation b) Diffusion
   c) Convection d) Wind-induced eddies
11. Monin-Obukhov length is used to describe:
   a) Atmospheric pressure variation
   b) Solar radiation absorption
   c) Atmospheric stability near surface
   d) Soil heat capacity
12. Stable atmospheric conditions near the surface usually occur during:
   a) Cloudy days b) Clear nights
   c) Rainy periods d) Windy afternoons
13. Unstable atmosphere promotes:
   a) Inhibition of vertical motion b) Fog formation
   c) Strong vertical mixing d) Calm wind conditions
14. In neutral atmospheric conditions:
   a) Buoyancy suppresses turbulence
   b) Buoyancy enhances turbulence
   c) Turbulence is driven by mechanical forces only
   d) Temperature decreases rapidly with height
15. Leaf Area Index (LAI) is defined as:
   a) Leaf biomass per unit volume b) Leaf length per square meter
   c) Leaf area per unit ground area d) Height of canopy per leaf

16. Which method is commonly used to study vertical profiles of micrometeorological parameters?
   a) Stevenson screen b) Balloon sounding
   c) Gradient method d) Cup anemometer
17. Latent heat flux represents the energy used for:
   a) Heating the soil b) Heating the air
   c) Evaporation and transpiration d) Groundwater recharge
18. Sensible heat flux refers to:
   a) Heat lost by radiation
   b) Heat transferred by air temperature differences
   c) Heat used in transpiration
   d) Soil heat conduction
19. The Penman-Monteith equation is used to estimate:
   a) Net radiation b) Rainfall
   c) Evapotranspiration d) Solar declination
20. Which factor does not directly affect evapotranspiration rate?
   a) Wind speed b) Solar radiation
   c) Soil color d) Humidity
21. Bulk transfer method is used for calculating:
   a) Cloud cover b) Radiation balance
   c) Heat and moisture fluxesd) Soil salinity
22. The aerodynamic method of evapotranspiration requires:
   a) Wind speed and humidity gradient
   b) Solar radiation and net radiation
   c) Soil temperature
   d) Crop coefficient
23. In a crop canopy, temperature is usually highest at:
   a) Soil surface b) 1 m above ground
   c) Mid-canopy d) Just below soil surface
24. Zero-plane displacement height (d) refers to:
   a) Height where wind is maximum
   b) Height above canopy where pressure is constant

c) Height above the ground where wind speed theoretically becomes zero

d) Height where temperature equals air temperature

25. Which parameter is not measured in micrometeorology?

a) Canopy temperature
b) Soil salinity
c) Soil heat flux
d) Leaf wetness

Answer Key

1	d	2	c	3	b	4	a	5	d	6	c	7	c
8	c	9	c	10	d	11	c	12	b	13	c	14	c
15	c	16	c	17	c	18	b	19	c	20	c	21	c
22	a	23	a	24	c	25	b						

5

Biometeorology

1. Biometeorology is the study of:
   a) Climate classification
   b) Effects of atmosphere on biological systems
   c) Soil weathering
   d) Wind patterns
2. The branch of meteorology that studies the interaction between living organisms and atmospheric conditions is:
   a) Synoptic meteorology
   b) Agricultural climatology
   c) Biometeorology
   d) Physical meteorology
3. Heat stress in animals is typically indicated by:
   a) Reduced water intake
   b) Increased feed conversion
   c) Elevated body temperature and respiration rate
   d) Decreased sweating
4. The Temperature Humidity Index (THI) is used to evaluate:
   a) Rainfall probability
   b) Drought severity
   c) Heat stress in animals
   d) Crop growth stage
5. Which combination is most stressful for dairy animals?
   a) Low temperature, high humidity
   b) High temperature, low humidity
   c) High temperature, high humidity
   d) Low temperature, low humidity
6. THI values above ___ indicate heat stress in dairy cattle.
   a) 65
   b) 70
   c) 72
   d) 80

7. Which livestock species is most sensitive to heat stress?
   a) Sheep b) Poultry
   c) Goats d) Buffalo
8. Cold stress in newborn calves can be critical below:
   a) 20°C b) 15°C
   c) 10°C d) 5°C
9. Frost injury in plants occurs due to:
   a) Excess radiation b) Freezing of cell water
   c) Oxygen deficiency d) Soil compaction
10. The microclimate affecting livestock is termed as:
   a) Canopy climate b) Agroclimate
   c) Bioclimate d) Shelterbelt climate
11. Which parameter is not used to assess livestock environment?
   a) Wind speed b) Soil pH
   c) Humidity d) Ambient temperature
12. To alleviate heat stress in poultry, the common measure is:
   a) Red light
   b) Decrease air circulation
   c) Increase ventilation and sprinklers
   d) Feed extra protein
13. Radiation fog is most hazardous for:
   a) Rice b) Poultry
   c) Bees and pollinators d) Fish
14. Which of the following is a direct biometeorological hazard?
   a) High soil salinity b) Hailstorm
   c) Excess irrigation d) Delayed sowing
15. Livestock housing should ideally be oriented:
   a) East-West b) North-South
   c) Circular d) Underground
16. Which indicator best reflects plant stress due to weather extremes?
   a) Chlorophyll content b) Biomass
   c) Leaf temperature d) Canopy height

17. Which of the following is a biotic stressor influenced by weather?
   a) Solar radiation b) Drought
   c) Temperature extremes d) Pest outbreak
18. Sunscald in fruits is primarily caused by:
   a) Cold weather b) Cloudy weather
   c) High radiation and temperature d) High humidity
19. Photosynthesis is most sensitive to:
   a) Soil salinity b) Leaf wetness
   c) Light intensity and temperature d) Soil pH
20. The Wet Bulb Globe Temperature (WBGT) index is used to assess:
   a) Cold stress b) Risk of frost
   c) Heat load on humans or animals d) Soil moisture deficit
21. In plants, heat stress accelerates:
   a) Photosynthesis b) Leaf expansion
   c) Leaf senescence and flower drop d) Cell division
22. Temperature inversion during winter can lead to:
   a) High humidity b) Crop lodging
   c) Frost damage d) Photosynthetic increase
23. Air pollution stress is monitored in plants using:
   a) Nitrogen index
   b) Bioindicator plants like lichens
   c) Heat stress index
   d) Water use efficiency
24. Anthropogenic climate factors affecting biometeorology include:
   a) Soil pH and moisture
   b) Crop selection
   c) Greenhouse gas emissions and land-use change
   d) Irrigation frequency

25. **Which index combines solar radiation, temperature, wind and humidity to assess human discomfort?**

a) Leaf Area Index

b) Wind Chill Index

c) Discomfort Index

d) Vegetation Health IndexAnswer Key

Answer Key

1	b	2	c	3	c	4	c	5	c	6	c	7	b
8	d	9	b	10	c	11	b	12	c	13	c	14	b
15	b	16	c	17	d	18	c	19	c	20	c	21	c
22	c	23	b	24	c	25	c						

6

Evapotranspiration

1. Evapotranspiration is the combined process of:
   a) Radiation and precipitation
   b) Soil evaporation and plant transpiration
   c) Condensation and infiltration
   d) Percolation and runoff
2. The unit of evapotranspiration is typically expressed in:
   a) mm/hour b) m^3/sec
   c) mm/day or mm/month d) cm^2/day
3. Which of the following methods is considered standard for estimating reference evapotranspiration?
   a) Thornthwaite method b) Hargreaves method
   c) Penman-Monteith method d) Pan evaporation method
4. Which factor does not influence evapotranspiration?
   a) Wind speed b) Atmospheric pressure
   c) Solar radiation d) Air temperature
5. Crop evapotranspiration (ETc) is calculated as:
   a) ETc = ETo × Kc b) ETc = ETo / Kc
   c) ETc = Kc / ETo d) ETc = ETo + Kc
6. The crop coefficient (Kc) accounts for:
   a) Soil moisture variation b) Type and stage of crop
   c) Weather condition d) Irrigation interval
7. Pan coefficient (Kp) in pan evaporation is used to:
   a) Estimate soil water holding capacity
   b) Convert pan evaporation to reference evapotranspiration
   c) Measure rainfall
   d) Correct transpiration values

8. The main driver of evapotranspiration is:
   a) Soil fertility b) Soil texture
   c) Solar radiation d) Soil salinity
9. In arid regions, evapotranspiration is typically:
   a) Less than rainfall b) Equal to infiltration
   c) Greater than precipitation d) Zero
10. Which instrument is used to measure pan evaporation?
   a) Lysimeter b) Anemometer
   c) Class A evaporation pan d) Thermograph
11. Which instrument gives the most accurate measurement of actual evapotranspiration?
   a) Rain gauge b) Pan evaporimeter
   c) Lysimeter d) Thermometer
12. In the Penman-Monteith equation, stomatal resistance is considered through:
   a) Wind function b) Net radiation
   c) Surface resistance d) Humidity term
13. The Bowen ratio method estimates evapotranspiration using:
   a) Radiation and temperature gradients
   b) Wind and humidity
   c) Solar angle
   d) Soil moisture content
14. Thornthwaite method for ET estimation is primarily based on:
   a) Wind speed b) Humidity
   c) Temperature d) Net radiation
15. Which stage of crop growth usually has the highest crop coefficient (Kc)?
   a) Initial stage b) Mid-season (full canopy)
   c) Late-season d) Germination
16. When soil moisture is limiting, actual ET will be:
   a) Equal to potential ET b) Greater than rainfall
   c) Less than potential ET d) Independent of plant type

17. Under water stress conditions, transpiration rate:
    a) Increases sharply b) Becomes constant
    c) Reduces due to stomatal closure d) Is unaffected
18. Crop coefficient (Kc) is generally highest for which crop type?
    a) Rice b) Wheat
    c) Sorghum d) Chickpea
19. Which of the following is not a component of evapotranspiration estimation?
    a) Net radiation b) Soil temperature
    c) Wind speed d) Vapor pressure deficit
20. The difference between potential ET and actual ET is mainly due to:
    a) Soil fertility b) Soil water availability
    c) Plant age d) Wind direction
21. The latent heat of vaporization of water is approximately:
    a) 250 J/g b) 540 cal/g
    c) 100 J/g d) 1 cal/g
22. In humid regions, actual ET is usually:
    a) Lower than precipitation b) Higher than rainfall
    c) Zero d) More than potential ET
23. Pan evaporation method tends to overestimate ETo because:
    a) Pan is shallow
    b) Pan is made of metal
    c) Pan water is directly exposed and lacks vegetation
    d) Pan temperature is low
24. The latent heat flux in an energy balance equation represents:
    a) Soil heat conduction b) Evapotranspiration
    c) Air heating d) Canopy temperature
25. In lysimeter studies, actual ET is calculated based on:
    a) Water table depth b) Soil temperature change
    c) Water input and weight loss d) Leaf water potential

Answer Key

1	b	2	c	3	c	4	b	5	b	6	b	7	b
8	c	9	c	10	c	11	c	12	c	13	a	14	c
15	b	16	c	17	c	18	a	19	b	20	b	21	b
22	a	23	c	24	b	25	c						

7

Crop Weather Modeling

1. Crop weather models are used to:
   a) Predict market prices
   b) Forecast crop diseases
   c) Simulate crop growth and yield based on weather
   d) Measure soil salinity
2. The full form of DSSAT is:
   a) Data Simulation System for Agricultural Technology
   b) Decision Support System for Agrotechnology Transfer
   c) Daily Simulation Support for Agriculture and Technology
   d) Direct Soil Sampling and Testing
3. Which of the following is a dynamic crop growth model?
   a) Thornthwaite model
   b) Penman model
   c) CERES-Maize
   d) Water balance model
4. The WOFOST model was developed in:
   a) USA
   b) Netherlands
   c) India
   d) Australia
5. Which is not a component of crop simulation models?
   a) Soil module
   b) Weather module
   c) Economic policy module
   d) Crop growth module
6. Crop models simulate yield mainly based on:
   a) Crop insurance data
   b) Genotype, environment, and management (GxExM)
   c) Market demand
   d) Government policies
7. The APSIM model is widely used for:

a) Remote sensing
b) Forest ecosystem analysis
c) Agricultural systems simulation
d) Carbon dating

8. In crop models, the rate of photosynthesis is mainly influenced by:
a) Wind speed
b) Soil color
c) Solar radiation and temperature
d) Soil pH

9. One of the major uses of crop weather models is to:
a) Replace farmers
b) Predict harvest labor requirements
c) Assess impact of climate change on crop production
d) Monitor rainfall only

10. The SUCROS model is based on:
a) Water balance
b) Light use efficiency
c) Nutrient uptake
d) Pest population dynamics

11. Which input is not essential for crop weather models?
a) Soil properties
b) Daily weather data
c) Crop growth parameters
d) Seed market price

12. The phenological development in crop models is mainly a function of:
a) Water salinity
b) Thermal time or growing degree days
c) Soil color
d) Humus content

13. The InfoCrop model was developed in:
a) IARI, New Delhi
b) NASA, USA
c) FAO, Rome
d) IRRI, Philippines

14. Simulation models help in:
a) Increasing land area
b) Reducing pesticide cost only
c) Improving crop management under varying climate conditions
d) Fixing Minimum Support Prices

15. CERES model is part of which crop modeling framework?
a) APSIM
b) WOFOST
c) DSSAT
d) InfoCrop

16. Which model is best suited for rice-wheat cropping systems in India?
    a) AquaCrop b) InfoCrop
    c) CropSyst d) CROPGRO
17. CropSyst model is mainly used for:
    a) Animal feed rationing
    b) Simulating soil water balance and cropping systems
    c) Weed infestation analysis
    d) Aquaculture
18. Calibration of a crop model involves:
    a) Changing soil type
    b) Running the model with historical climate
    c) Adjusting model parameters to match observed data
    d) Using only satellite images
19. Validation of a crop model means:
    a) Releasing the model for public use
    b) Checking simulation results with independent field data
    c) Formatting model output
    d) Ignoring minor errors
20. Which weather parameter is most important for predicting flowering time in crops?
    a) Rainfall b) Maximum temperature
    c) Photoperiod and temperature d) Humidity
21. Which modeling approach simulates crop growth over time using physiological processes?
    a) Empirical modeling b) Deterministic modeling
    c) Process-based modeling d) Statistical modeling
22. Which is a limitation of crop weather models?
    a) High accuracy
    b) Dependence on quality input data
    c) Ease of use in all languages
    d) Elimination of field trials

23. Which model is designed for simulating crop yield under different irrigation levels?
   a) AquaCrop b) DSSAT
   c) InfoCrop d) WOFOST
24. Which of the following models was developed by FAO?
   a) InfoCrop b) AquaCrop
   c) CERES d) WOFOST
25. GDD (Growing Degree Days) is calculated as:
   a) Maximum temp – Minimum temp
   b) (Tmax + Tmin) / 2 – Base temperature
   c) Solar radiation × Base temperature
   d) Humidity / Temperature

Answer Key

1	c	2	b	3	c	4	b	5	c	6	b	7	c
8	c	9	c	10	d	11	b	12	a	13	c	14	c
15	b	16	b	17	c	18	b	19	b	20	c	21	c
22	b	23	a	24	b	25	b						

8

Weather Forecasting for Agriculture

1. Short-range weather forecast refers to a forecast valid for:
   a) Less than 12 hours b) 1–2 days
   c) 3–10 days d) More than 10 days
2. IMD issues medium-range weather forecasts for a period of:
   a) Up to 12 hours b) 1–2 days
   c) 3–10 days d) 15–30 days
3. The National Centre for Medium Range Weather Forecasting (NCMRWF) is located at:
   a) Pune b) New Delhi
   c) Bengaluru d) Hyderabad
4. Agromet Advisory Services (AAS) in India are coordinated by:
   a) IARI
   b) CRIDA
   c) IMD and ICAR
   d) State Agriculture Universities
5. The forecast that helps in crop planning and field operations is called:
   a) Economic forecast b) Strategic forecast
   c) Agricultural weather forecast d) Synoptic forecast
6. Which of the following types of forecasts is most useful for day-to-day agricultural operations?
   a) Long-range forecast b) Medium-range forecast
   c) Seasonal forecast d) Monthly forecast
7. Which satellite series provides real-time meteorological data for weather forecasting in India?
   a) INSAT b) IRS
   c) CARTOSAT d) SPOT

8. Which organization prepares seasonal monsoon forecasts in India?
   a) ICAR b) NCMRWF
   c) IMD d) ISRO
9. Numerical Weather Prediction (NWP) models primarily use:
   a) Mathematical equations of atmospheric physics
   b) Satellite images only
   c) Radar images
   d) Soil moisture data
10. The ensemble forecasting method improves forecast reliability by:
   a) Using a single deterministic model
   b) Combining multiple weather observations
   c) Using multiple runs with varied initial conditions
   d) Avoiding numerical models
11. Which of the following is not an element of weather forecasting?
   a) Temperature b) Soil salinity
   c) Rainfall d) Humidity
12. Remote sensing is useful in weather forecasting because it:
   a) Uses underground sensors
   b) Captures soil profiles
   c) Provides synoptic scale weather data
   d) Detects irrigation frequency
13. Doppler Weather Radar (DWR) is useful for detecting:
   a) Temperature inversion b) Wind erosion
   c) Precipitation and thunderstorms d) Soil pH
14. Which parameter is most crucial for issuing cyclone warnings?
   a) Wind direction
   b) Soil temperature
   c) Sea surface temperature and pressure
   d) Sunshine hours

15. Long-range forecast in India is primarily used for:
    a) Daily field operations
    b) Disaster recovery
    c) Seasonal planning and crop selection
    d) Pesticide application
16. IMD issues Agromet Advisories under the scheme called:
    a) Pradhan Mantri Fasal Yojana
    b) GKMS (Gramin Krishi Mausam Sewa)
    c) Atma Nirbhar Krishi Yojana
    d) AgroForecast Bharat
17. Which of the following is an output of weather forecasting models?
    a) Soil type b) Rainfall prediction
    c) Crop sowing time d) Fertilizer dose
18. The acronym IMD stands for:
    a) Indian Meteorological Development
    b) Indian Monsoon Division
    c) India Meteorological Department
    d) Indian Mesoscale Data
19. Forecast issued up to 7 days is referred to as:
    a) Short-range b) Medium-range
    c) Long-range d) Strategic
20. Which of the following components is not required in weather forecasting models?
    a) Temperature b) Cloud cover
    c) Soil fertility index d) Wind speed
21. Which of the following tools is used for visualizing weather forecast maps?
    a) Google Maps b) AgrometDash
    c) GIS software d) GPS device
22. One of the main limitations of weather forecasts is:
    a) Accuracy decreases with time range
    b) Always underestimates rainfall
    c) Not applicable in dryland farming
    d) Cannot be used in crop planning

23. Agromet Field Units (AMFUs) in India are operated by:
    a) IMD only
    b) ICAR institutes and SAUs
    c) Private companies
    d) NGOs
24. Which of the following forecasts would be most helpful during pest outbreaks?
    a) Long-range forecast
    b) Nowcast
    c) Seasonal forecast
    d) Economic forecast
25. Which of the following is not a use of weather forecasting in agriculture?
    a) Planning irrigation
    b) Market price estimation
    c) Scheduling pesticide application
    d) Choosing planting dates

Answer Key

1	b	2	c	3	b	4	c	5	c	6	b	7	a
8	c	9	a	10	c	11	b	12	c	13	c	14	c
15	c	16	b	17	b	18	c	19	b	20	c	21	c
22	a	23	b	24	b	25	b						

9

Remote Sensing for Agricultural Meteorology

1. Remote sensing refers to:
   a) Physical measurement by contact
   b) Data collection from a distance without physical contact
   c) Internet-based sensing
   d) Ground station analysis
2. Which of the following platforms is used in remote sensing?
   a) Tractor b) Rain gauge
   c) Satellite d) Tensiometer
3. The most commonly used remote sensing satellite in India is:
   a) SPOT b) NOAA
   c) IRS d) GOES
4. The reflectance in the near-infrared region is highest for:
   a) Water b) Healthy vegetation
   c) Soil d) Dry leaves
5. Which sensor provides thermal imagery from satellites?
   a) Panchromatic sensor b) Thermal infrared sensor
   c) Radar sensor d) Microwave sensor
6. NDVI is used to measure:
   a) Wind speed b) Vegetation health
   c) Soil pH d) Atmospheric pressure
7. NDVI stands for:
   a) National Data for Vegetation Index
   b) Normalized Difference Vegetation Index
   c) Nominal Dynamic Visual Indicator
   d) Normal Diurnal Vegetation Intensity

8. Which wavelength range is used for thermal remote sensing?
 a) 0.4–0.7 μm b) 1.55–1.75 μm
 c) 8–14 μm d) 0.2–0.4 μm
9. Landsat satellites are launched and maintained by:
 a) ISRO b) NASA
 c) ESA d) JAXA
10. In agricultural meteorology, remote sensing helps monitor:
 a) Rainfall only b) Soil nutrients
 c) Crop condition and drought d) Livestock movement
11. Which of the following sensors works in all weather conditions?
 a) Optical sensor
 b) Passive microwave sensor
 c) Thermal sensor
 d) Active microwave (Radar) sensor
12. Which of the following is a passive remote sensing system?
 a) Radar b) LIDAR
 c) Thermal scanner d) SONAR
13. Which ISRO satellite series is designed for meteorological observations?
 a) IRS b) INSAT
 c) SPOT d) Oceansat
14. Which satellite sensor can measure land surface temperature?
 a) OLI b) TIRS
 c) PAN d) MSI
15. Remote sensing contributes to drought assessment through:
 a) Evapotranspiration estimation
 b) Groundwater level monitoring
 c) Reflectance pattern of crops and soil
 d) Rainfall measurement
16. Spatial resolution of a satellite image refers to:
 a) Time taken to capture image
 b) Area represented by each pixel
 c) Spectral wavelength
 d) Radiometric sensitivity

17. The primary advantage of remote sensing in agriculture is:
    a) Improved rainfall measurement
    b) Localized pesticide application
    c) Large-area monitoring in real-time
    d) Seed certification
18. Which index is used to assess vegetation moisture stress?
    a) VCI (Vegetation Condition Index) b) SPI
    c) LST d) TSI
19. Hyperspectral sensors capture:
    a) Single band images
    b) Only visible bands
    c) Narrow and continuous spectral bands
    d) Thermal bands only
20. What type of resolution affects how frequently a satellite can image the same area?
    a) Spectral resolution b) Spatial resolution
    c) Radiometric resolution d) Temporal resolution
21. Which remote sensing technique is useful for monitoring soil moisture?
    a) Optical sensing b) Radar remote sensing
    c) NDVI imaging d) Panchromatic scanning
22. The wavelength region of microwave remote sensing is:
    a) 0.4–0.7 μm b) 1–100 mm
    c) 10–14 μm d) 200–400 nm
23. Which sensor is suitable for night-time data collection in remote sensing?
    a) Optical sensor b) Panchromatic sensor
    c) Thermal infrared sensor d) RGB sensor
24. Which of the following is not a common application of remote sensing in agrometeorology?
    a) Estimating rainfall b) Mapping crop type
    c) Monitoring crop stress d) Testing fertilizer quality
25. Which software is widely used for remote sensing image analysis?
    a) MS Excel b) AutoCAD
    c) ERDAS Imagine d) SAS

Answer Key

1	b	2	c	3	c	4	b	5	b	6	b	7	b
8	c	9	b	10	c	11	d	12	c	13	b	14	b
15	c	16	b	17	c	18	a	19	c	20	d	21	b
22	c	23	c	24	d	25	c						

10

GIS for Agricultural Meteorology

1. GIS stands for:
   a) Geographical Image System
   b) Global Imaging System
   c) Geographical Information System
   d) Geographic Integrated Software
2. The key components of GIS include:
   a) Hardware, Software, Data, People, Methods
   b) GPS, Sensors, Maps
   c) Hardware, Maps, Satellites
   d) Maps, Photos, Videos
3. In GIS, data represented by points, lines, and polygons is called:
   a) Raster data b) Vector data
   c) Grid data d) Matrix data
4. Raster data in GIS is stored as:
   a) Tables b) Coordinates
   c) Pixels or cells d) Vectors
5. Which GIS data format is commonly used for weather raster maps?
   a) CSV b) Shapefile
   c) TIFF d) DOCX
6. Which GIS software is open source?
   a) ArcGIS b) AutoCAD
   c) QGIS d) ERDAS
7. The spatial resolution of a raster defines:
   a) Number of spectral bands b) Area covered by each pixel
   c) Color of the map d) Type of soil

8. A common coordinate system used in GIS for India is:
   a) UTM b) MSL
   c) GMT d) ISO

9. Which function in GIS overlays two or more thematic maps?
   a) Buffer b) Interpolation
   c) Map Algebra d) Overlay analysis

10. Which GIS operation estimates values for locations not sampled?
   a) Buffering b) Interpolation
   c) Reprojection d) Digitization

11. In agricultural meteorology, GIS is used to:
   a) Monitor soil erosion b) Track animal movement
   c) Analyze spatial weather patterns d) Identify fertilizers

12. Which GIS tool helps delineate areas prone to drought?
   a) Buffer b) Interpolation
   c) Zonal statistics d) Thematic layering

13. GIS helps in crop yield forecasting by integrating:
   a) Satellite and rainfall data b) Only weather stations
   c) Fertilizer consumption data d) Market data

14. In GIS, shapefiles store:
   a) Raster satellite data
   b) GPS trajectories
   c) Vector data (points, lines, polygons)
   d) Audio-visual information

15. The process of converting paper maps into GIS-compatible digital format is called:
   a) Reprojection b) Buffering
   c) Digitization d) Mosaicking

16. Zonal statistics in GIS helps to:
   a) Compare statistics between countries
   b) Analyze attribute data within zones
   c) Convert raster to vector
   d) Map economic zones

17. In GIS, DEM stands for:
    a) Daily Environmental Monitoring b) Digital Elevation Model
    c) Data Editing Module d) Dynamic Earth Map
18. Which GIS data model is suitable for land use and land cover classification?
    a) Vector model b) Attribute model
    c) Raster model d) CAD model
19. Which function helps in locating all fields within 1 km of a weather station?
    a) Clip b) Intersect
    c) Buffer d) Union
20. GIS-based drought monitoring uses:
    a) Market data
    b) Insurance records
    c) Satellite-derived rainfall and NDVI
    d) Manual reports
21. Which organization in India uses GIS for agrometeorological applications?
    a) CSIR b) ISRO
    c) NABARD d) FSSAI
22. Time-series analysis in GIS is useful for:
    a) Forecasting cyclone movement
    b) Monitoring vegetation over time
    c) Soil mapping
    d) Drawing contours
23. In GIS, a layer refers to:
    a) Set of weather balloons
    b) Individual map theme (e.g., rainfall, temperature)
    c) Meteorological model
    d) Forecast simulation
24. Which of the following is not a GIS data type?
    a) Point b) Line
    c) Polygon d) Volume

25. A typical GIS application in crop-weather studies is:
   a) Crop modeling only
   b) Market price analysis
   c) Spatial mapping of rainfall variability
   d) Tractor routing

Answer Key

1	c	2	a	3	b	4	c	5	c	6	c	7	b
8	a	9	d	10	b	11	c	12	d	13	a	14	c
15	c	16	b	17	b	18	c	19	c	20	c	21	b
22	b	23	b	24	d	25	c						

Bibliography

1. Reference Books

- Mahi, G.S. & Kingra, P.K. 2018. Fundamentals of Agrometeorology and Climate Change. Kalyani Publishers. ISBN: 978-9327288995. Pages 383.
- Mavi, H.S. & Tupper, G.J. 2004. Agrometeorology: Principles and Applications of Climate Studies in Agriculture. CRC Press. ISBN: 978-1032768052. Pages 376.
- Mavi, HS. 1986. Introduction to Agrometeorology. Oxford & IBH Publishing Co Pvt. Ltd. ISBN: 978-8120409101. Pp 296.
- Murthy, V.R.K. 2015. Basic Principles of Agricultural Meteorology. BSP Books Private Limited. ISBN: 978-9352300747. Pages 288.
- Prasada Rao, G.S.L.H.V. 2008. Agricultural Meteorology. ISBN: 978-8120333383. PHI Learning Pvt Ltd. Pages 384.
- Ramana Rao, B.V. & V. Uma Maheswara Rao. 2024. Agricultural Meteorology. Jain Brothers. ISBN: 978-9390576975. Pages 154.
- Ramana Rao, B.V., Surender Singh, V. Uma Maheswara Rao. 2025. System Simulation and Agromet Advisory Services. Publisher: New India Publishing Agency, New Delhi. ISBN: 978-9372196191. Pages 510.
- Ramana Rao B.V., Surender Singh, V. Uma Maheswara Rao, Anu Bulusu. 2025. Farming Weather: Harnessing Citizen Science for Smart Agriculture. Publisher: Professional Prints. New York USA. ISBN: 978-1966695561. Pp 154.
- Ramana Rao B.V., Surender Singh, V. Uma Maheswara Rao. 2025. Conceptual Meteorology. Publisher: New India Publishing Agency, New Delhi. ISBN 978-9358874501 Pp 152.
- Ramana Rao B.V., Surender Singh, V. Uma Maheswara Rao. 2025. Forecasting the Future: Effective Climate Guidance on Monsoons for Farm Prosperity. Publisher: Professional Prints. New York USA. ISBN: 978-1966695912. Pp 246.
- Ramana Rao B.V., Surender Singh, V. Uma Maheswara Rao. 2025. Preparatory Microclimatology. Publisher: Professional Prints. New York USA. ISBN: 9781966695189 Pp 167.
- Ramana Rao B.V., Surender Singh, V. Uma Maheswara Rao. 2025. Primer on Agrohydrometeorology. Publisher: Professional Prints. New York USA. ISBN: 978-1966695301 Pp 144.
- Seemann, J.; Chirkov, Y.I.; Lomas, J. & Primault, B. 1979. Agrometeorology. Springer Berlin, Heidelberg. ISBN: 978-3642672903. Pages 326.
- Surender S., V. Uma Maheswara Rao, B.V. Ramana Rao. 2025. Introductory Agricultural Meteorology. Publisher: New India Publishing Agency, New Delhi. ISBN: 9789358871487. Pages 392.
- Surender S., V. Uma Maheswara Rao, B.V. Ramana Rao. 2025. Weather Forecasting. Publisher: New India Publishing Agency, New Delhi. ISBN: 9789358875492. Pages 392.

- Varshneya, M.C. & Pillai, B.P. 2004. Textbook of Agricultural Meteorology. ICAR Publication. ISBN: 978-8171640195. Pages 242.

2. Journals

- Agricultural and Forest Meteorology. https://www.sciencedirect.com/journal/agricultural-and-forest-meteorology
- Chinese Journal of Agrometeorology. https://zgnyqx.ieda.org.cn/EN/1000-6362/home.shtml
- Italian Journal of Agrometeorology. https://riviste.fupress.net/index.php/IJAm/issue/view/15
- Journal of Agril Meteorology. :https://journals.indexcopernicus.com/search/details?id=46231
- Journal of Agrometeorology. https://journal.agrimetassociation.org/index.php/jam/issue/view/73
- MAUSAM. https://mausamjournal.imd.gov.in/index.php/MAUSAM

3. Web Resources

- https://mausam.imd.gov.in/
- https://imdagrimet.gov.in/
- https://www.tropmet.res.in/
- https://nwp.ncmrwf.gov.in/
- https://www.skymetweather.com/
- https://icar.org.in/
- https://www.icar-crida.res.in/
- https://niasm.icar.gov.in/
- https://www.sac.gov.in/Vyom/
- https://www.isro.gov.in/
- https://www.icrisat.org/
- https://www.ecmwf.int/
- https://wmo.int/
- https://www.fao.org/climate-smart-agriculture/en/
- https://www.agrimetassociation.org/
- https://safoam.org.in/
- https://www.insam.org.in/